Christian Ethics
and the
Community

Christian Ethics and the Community

James M. Gustafson

A Pilgrim Press Book
Philadelphia

For two friends
Raymond P. Morris
Julian N. Hartt

Contents

Introduction

One may view the writings of Prof. James M. Gustafson of Yale University as being marked by a concern to ask and answer an elemental question. What are the sources for theological ethics, and how are they related? Obviously the question is a multifaceted one that admits to a variety of responses. Indeed, the question is so rich and germinal that it is probably best viewed as an inexhaustible one. Still, men continue to ask and answer it, and one may discern various patterns, both in the ways the question has been put and in the ways it has been answered. Each of the ten essays by Gustafson in this book is a witness to his own developing convictions concerning how the question about the sources for theological ethics might be asked and answered. I shall focus attention in this introduction primarily on religion and morality as two distinct but related sources for theological ethics. I do not suggest that this introduction is an accurate reproduction of Gustafson's mind, and it is also clear, of course, that these essays are marked by a variety of interests that cannot be reduced to this one concern. Nonetheless, I feel that this concern provides a perspective for viewing the essays which is not out of accord with what Gustafson has written. Moreover, it is my opinion that these articles, while not fully developed into a systematic ethics, constitute a point of departure for theological ethics which deserves the attention not only of specialists in the field, but also of that larger public which for various reasons has become fascinated by or disenchanted with theological ethics in the past decade. I shall consider the first five essays primarily from the point of view of asking, What are the sources for theological ethics? I shall consider the last five essays primarily in terms of Gustafson's constructive proposals in answering that question.

The first essay, "Christian Ethics in America," consists largely of a historical-thematic analysis of American theological ethics from 1930-65. This essay, of course, has intrinsic value as a purely historical account, but it also demonstrates that history is a formative source for theological ethics whether its shaping tendencies are acknowledged or not. Gustafson points out that theological ethics in America has been largely dominated by practical moral concerns, and that the theoretical issues for inquiry that have emerged have been largely a result of these practical interests. Gustafson also asserts that in response to the social crisis of the 1930's a new academic seriousness emerged in the discipline. Thus the history of American theological ethics from 1930-65 also demonstrates that the way in which theoretical issues are conceived is influential in shaping how one perceives or responds to those issues which are deemed to be practical and moral.[1] In particular, Gustafson isolates three themes in theological ethics which illustrate that the early 1930's were a crucial turning point in Protestant Christian ethics. Gustafson's treatment of these three themes—the interpretation of man, the changing use of the Bible, and the procedures of ethical reflection[2]—indicates that discourse in theological ethics from 1930-65 was primarily a matter of "internal conversations between ethics and theology." The next section of this essay, however, demonstrates that the discipline of theological ethics may also be in conversation with a variety of cognate disciplines, e.g., biblical, philosophical, and historical studies, which are thus viewed as additional sources for theological ethics. The essay is concluded by a succinct bibliographical survey that serves to document the practical interests of American Christian ethics.[3]

The second essay, "Theology and Ethics," sets forth three categories or loci for reflection which are seen as being intrinsic to ethical inquiry: the nature of the good or the locus of value, the nature of man as a moral agent, and the criteria of moral action. This particular article, along with its assumptions and implications, is so pivotal to Gustafson's thought that comment on it in some detail is justified. The essay may be viewed as the analytical basis of Gustafson's book, *Christ and the Moral Life*, which was concerned to explicate the claims that theologians have made for the significance of the work of Christ for the moral life, and which was organized around the three substantive issues designated here as being intrinsic to moral inquiry. In the first chapter of his book Gustafson stated:

> I am using an understanding of moral experience that is not itself derived from "revelation" or even from theological writings. . . . [This book]

assumes that questions of ethics, Christian or any other, can be established on the basis of both general human experience and reflection on literature in the field [of ethics].[4]

"Theology and Ethics" makes clear the basis for these statements. If one acknowledges, for example, that all ethical reflection, Christian or any other, has a substantive concern to designate the nature of man as a moral agent, then he is alerted to the fact that there are a variety of sources for claims about the nature of man, and that these claims are made on a variety of different grounds. The differing worlds of science provide familiar examples. A sociologist may suggest that one understands the nature of man as he participates in a social structure; a psychoanalyst may suggest that the nature of man may be specified in terms of the strength of his ego; a biologist may claim that the nature of man is accurately portrayed in terms of the interaction between one's hereditary endowment and his environment. The ethicist, then, must adjudicate the varying claims in accord with his own ethical interests. What is the significance of these different claims for the moral life? How may these claims be given proper valence in terms of moral experience? The ethicist is thus forced to ask how other frames of reference may be viewed as constituting sources for ethical reflection, or how they may inform, complement, or negate his own moral concerns. Thus, it is assumed that the discipline of ethics has some autonomy as a discipline, and that it is not simply a derivative discipline that is dependent on sociology, psychiatry, or biology.

If the ethicist does theological ethics he is acutely aware that theologians have made and will continue to make normative claims about the nature of man. Indeed, the theological ethicist is aware that there are differing disciplines within theology. It is not unusual, for example, for the historical theologian to make claims about the nature of man that are not out of accord with his own interests as a historian; likewise, the biblical theologian may make claims about the nature of man that in part are a product of the procedures he uses in exegesis, and the systematic theologian may make claims about the nature of man that are informed by the assumptions of his own discipline. Indeed, it may be observed that some theologians have been wont to make theological ethics a derivative of their own discipline although that day seems to be passing quickly.

I do not think that Gustafson wishes to deny the normative claims of the varying theologians. Certainly he does not wish to say that theology has no normative role to play in theological ethics. Indeed, this particular article makes clear that in virtue of the nature of one's theological convictions, there is a "distinctive approach" of Christian ethics in each of the three loci for reflection. But even here it would be mistaken to make judgments about what is distinctive or normative in terms of quantity.[5] The question might best be put not in terms of *what* but *how*. How is the theological ethicist to take into account the various theological claims and convictions about the nature of man? This essay makes clear some of Gustafson's own proclivities. Moreover, the structure of the essay makes clear that the sources for theological ethics are multiple, that they include the normative claims of theology, and that entrée into the multiple sources for ethics may be structured in terms of the three central loci for reflection that are outlined in this essay.

The third essay, "Context Versus Principles: A Misplaced Debate in Christian Ethics," concerns the structure or the logic of moral decisions and moral action. The point of departure for the essay is a twofold polemic against two tendencies. On the one hand, there is the tendency to stress the role of principles in the moral life by assuming that there are moral principles which are embedded or grounded in theology and which provide a sufficient basis for making moral decisions because they can be more or less directly applied to particular historical situations. Those who have taken this position run the risk of making theology an exclusive source for ethical inquiry and moral guidance and thereby collapse theological knowledge with moral principles; or they may run the risk of assuming that the correct application of moral principles will more or less assure one that his actions are absolutely right or are congruent with God's will. On the other hand, there is a tendency to stress that the moral agent must immerse himself in the historical contingencies of the world in the belief that it is only in the context of particular "situations" that one can accurately perceive what is right or what God is doing or what is God's will. Those who have taken this position run the risk of assuming that theology, or moral principles which might be congruent with or derived from theology, cannot provide a normative direction for making moral decisions; or, those who take this position might be charged with having such a fluid theological base that just about any moral position could be authorized as being right or congruent with God's will. In rejecting both these tendencies as simplifications or distortions of the problems presented to moral reflection, Gustafson asserts that a closer analysis of the morphology of moral action reveals that there are four major points of reference for theological ethics. Each may be viewed as a source for theological-ethical reflection. The four sources include social or situational analysis, fundamental theological affirmations, moral principles, and a conception of Christian existence which might be called a moral anthropology. The essays in the second part of this book make clear that Gustafson himself prefers to begin reflecting about theological ethics at the latter point. But the way in which each of these four base points or sources may be used in analyzing the structure or logic of moral decisions and moral actions is clearly evident in this essay.

Chapter 4, "Two Approaches to Theological Ethics," delineates two typical modes in which theological ethics has proceeded. The first approach may be said to begin at the point of claiming to perceive what God is doing in the world, while the second approach begins at the point of claiming that one's acts are more or less congruent with one's beliefs about God. Distinctions between the two positions are drawn primarily in terms of the interaction between the answers given to two epistemological questions. How does one know what God is doing? How does one know what is morally right? Each question, then, focuses attention on two related but distinct sources of knowledge for theological ethics. It is argued that the second position enlarges the extent to which moral discourse may take place in the public domain.[6]

In chapter 5, "God's Transcendence and the Value of Human Life," Gustafson states that he wishes to avoid two major pitfalls in relating theology to ethics. On the one hand, he wishes to avoid collapsing theology into ethics in such a way that one's ethics are simply deductions from prior assumptions of theology. On the other hand, he wishes to avoid a radical distinction between ethical and theological discourse which would confine the significance of theology to soteriology. Various dimensions of this problematic are explored in this essay by examining three distinct but related affirmations: that human life is not of absolute value, that human life has many values, and that human values concern several kinds of relations and several aspects of individual experience. On what basis does one make such affirmations or argue for them? Gustafson asserts that they can be viewed as a mutual product of theological beliefs about the transcendence of God, on the one hand, and of the human experience of values and valuing, on the other hand. The subtlety of this essay is found in tracing the interaction between these two sources of human understanding.

How might we summarize the convictions of Gustafson about the sources for theological ethics that are present in these first five essays? I think Gustafson's general point of departure can be fairly delineated as the third of three major and typical alternatives for viewing the relation of religion and morality as sources for theological ethics.[7] These three alternatives are delineated here in terms of the question, What would count to justify a theological-ethical argument?

In the first place, it could be argued that religion and morality constitute autonomous or self-governing realms, each of which is independent of the other. With a logic resembling Gertrude Stein's comment about roses, for example, it has been argued that the so-called "naturalistic fallacy" is committed whenever religious reasons are given to justify a moral act. If we were to assume, for instance, that to give money to the poor was a moral act, then it could be argued that our judgment is intrinsically a moral judgment which must be judged to be moral or immoral independent of any religious valuation that we might place on it; i.e., we approve it, we say it is good, we say it is right, on purely moral grounds.[8] Other examples could be given, but the point, we think, is clear. It is possible to affirm that the realms of religion and morality are distinct and autonomous. It is obvious, of course, that different reasons can be given for this kind of judgment, but the result is that the distinction between religion and morality remains a distinction and not a dialectic.

In the second place, it could be argued that religion and morality are categories which are so integrally related that one must be collapsed into the other. This collapsing of categories, of course, could proceed in either of two directions. On the one hand, it has been maintained that the significance of morality is to be comprehended in terms of religion. It could be argued, for example, that no act can be judged to be moral unless it is done for the right religious reason. It could thus be argued that if one gave money to the poor, the decisive criterion for judging whether the act was truly moral or not would concern whether the money was given as a spontaneous, free gift of gratitude in response to God's prior love. More generally, it might be argued that religion is the exclusive source for moral norms. The extreme position would be that only a religious person can be moral.

On the other hand, it has been maintained that the significance of religion is to be understood in terms of morality. It could be argued, for example, that religion becomes meaningful as it is translated into moral categories. It might be argued, for instance, that giving money to the poor through a welfare program is the meaning of the theological doctrine of reconciliation. More generally, all religious categories and concepts could be translated into moral terms and could then be judged to be relevant and significant. The extreme position would be that there is no meaning to a religious category unless it receives a moral translation. Again, other examples of both tendencies could be given, but we feel that the point is clear. One alternative to the dialectic between religion and morality as sources for theological ethics is to resolve the dialectic in favor of either religion or morality.

In the third place, it could be argued that religion and morality are distinct but related categories, a position that embodies portions of both of the above positions. This third position agrees and disagrees with the first position. It agrees by assuming that religion and morality may be viewed as being distinct sources for theological ethics. Unlike some adherents of the first position, however, this third position assumes that the justifications given for a moral act are important and on occasion may very well be influential. Unlike other adherents of the first position, this third position is willing to commit at least one form of the "naturalistic fallacy" by giving theological reasons for a moral act. This third position also agrees and disagrees with the second position. It agrees that there is a dialectical relation between religion and morality, but it does not wish to resolve this dialectic in favor of either religion or morality. Unlike the adherents of the first tendency in the second position, this third position does not wish to undercut the relative autonomy of moral reasoning. It might be the case, for example, that one would give money to the poor both because he adopted the moral maxim to be kind to his neighbor in need and *also* because he believed that God commands one to be charitable to his neighbor. This third position also recognizes that moral justifications and religious justifications are not of one piece. It recognizes the possibility, for example, that particular religious justifications might encourage a particular act that purely moral justifications might not, and that the act itself might be judged to be moral on purely religious grounds. Unlike the adherents of the second tendency of the second position, this third position recognizes that religious language can be justified on other than moral grounds. In brief, this third position wishes to affirm that religion and morality are distinct but related sources for theological ethics.

I think that this third position is an accurate reflection of Gustafson's view, as seen in these chapters, about the relation of religion and morality as two distinct but related sources for theological ethics. The last five chapters of this book suggest a constructive point of departure for theological ethics that is consistent with this view. It is increasingly clear that Gustafson wishes to begin doing theological ethics at the point of reflecting on the nature of Christian moral existence. If one chooses to begin doing theological ethics at the point of a moral anthropology, several pertinent questions are in order. What are the salient elements of moral existence? In what sense or in what ways are they judged to be salient? How are these salient elements of moral existence related to theological views? These and other questions can be pressed in a number of directions. They can be posed, for example, in terms of the person as a moral agent. Or they may be pressed in the direction of notions about community and social structure. It is clear, however, that Gustafson wishes to emphasize the continuities between personhood and community, an emphasis which in large part is due to his conviction that a description of "moral existence" should be amenable for analyzing both the self and his communities.

The Gustafson corpus is plentiful in various enumerations of the factors or elements that could be entered in an accounting of the morally relevant aspects of human existence. In a recent essay, for example, Gustafson has drawn distinctions between beliefs or convictions, character traits or habits or dispositions, the affective or emotive aspects of selfhood, motives or intentions, and discernment or the capacity to make decisions.[9] Gustafson has also reflected on such factors as one's biological endowment or one's psychological unconscious as being of potential relevance in reflecting on the nature of moral existence and its limitations. This list, of course, is a sample and not a summary of Gustafson's thoughts on the matter. Indeed, we must await from his pen a systematic ordering of these (or other) elements in what would be his portrayal of moral existence.

In the meantime, it is clear that Gustafson has focused attention on the role that the virtues might play in a moral anthropology. His use of the term virtue [10] is akin to Thomas Aquinas' use of the word "habit." Moral virtues may be called habits which "are in accord with human nature." They designate those "persisting tendencies" which lead one to act in such a way that human action may be said in part to be directed by dispositions. It is clear that Gustafson does not wish to assert that a portrait of the moral virtues is equivalent to a delineation of "man's true nature and end." But he does wish to suggest that the moral agent does have lasting dispositions, that these habits are one feature of moral existence, and that they may be correlated with theological loyalties, convictions, and beliefs. Again, Gustafson does not wish to claim that all Christians have or should have the same dispositions or that every aspect of every moral habit should be equally present in every action.[11] The point is Gustafson's conviction that it is possible to delineate or portray the virtues as part of a description of moral existence, and that this portrait may be correlated with one's theological loyalties. In these essays Gustafson emphasizes the dispositional character of the moral virtues although it is clear that he is willing to use the term virtue in a broader context. We must remember, moreover, that the virtues are only one part of a description of moral existence, although they refer to other features as well. Finally, it must be observed that a portrait of moral existence of which the virtues are one part, consists of only one of the four major base points of theological ethics that Gustafson outlined in the third chapter of this book. It remains for us to briefly indicate how Gustafson has used his developing understanding of the role of the moral virtues in a variety of contexts. The last five essays in this book illustrate that Gustafson has utilized his understanding of the moral virtues in a variety of ways, and that his point of departure embodies the relationship between morality and religion as outlined previously.

"The Moral Conditions Necessary for Human Community" asks "What are the necessary moral conditions for a human community to exist, to enrich itself, to flourish?" The moral conditions are delineated in terms of the virtues of faith, hope, and love, each of which is used to specify various kinds of relationships that exist between persons and groups. For example, faith as confidence points to the fact that the existence of human communities depends on relationships of trust, faith as fidelity points to the fact that the existence of human communities depends on relationships that are worthy of trust, and the absence of faith as trust and trustworthiness in human relationships demonstrates that human communities depend on a capacity for forgiveness. We have, then, a depiction of certain features of moral existence. It is argued that certain "persisting tendencies" must be present if a human community is to exist, and these "conditions" may be called moral because they point to qualities of life which are valued and esteemed. Finally, it is obvious that these qualities of life are consistent with and can be correlated with a number of normative theological concerns, although these qualities of life are not simple deductions from prior theological assumptions.

"The Personalist Factor" is a polemic against "personalism" as an adequate basis upon which to build a portrait of moral existence. In drawing a distinction, but not a dichotomy, between the "is" of descriptive analysis and the "ought" of normative judgments, Gustafson is led to make two assertions. The first is that adherents of personalism frequently overlook the fact that personal existence displays features of consistency which are relevant for a picture of moral existence. These persistencies, of course, may be called moral virtues, and Gustafson makes several observations that would enable one to account for the fact that persons display character. A major point, obviously, is that theological ethics must take into account the process of character formation if it is to give an adequate portrayal of moral existence. The second assertion is that adherents of personalism are frequently deficient in their portrait of moral existence because they accept too easily a strict dichotomy between the personal and impersonal as referring to two different kinds of community. Gustafson argues that "a necessary common moral basis" may be discerned "beneath both the impersonal and personal" aspects of community. Several theological implications are then drawn.

"Christian Humanism and the Human Mind" may be viewed from the perspective of how Gustafson's portrayal of moral existence provides a basis for making moral judgments about the research of molecular biologists on the brain. The essay contains an analysis of the distinctions and relationships between "fact" and "value." One can assume, for example, that the knowledge gained by research on the brain is a positive value, but the question remains about the ways in which that knowledge might be used. Gustafson asks the question, What makes life *worth* living? The answer is a brief portrait of moral requisites for existence which indicate, in part, what values ought to be preserved, sustained, and developed in the uses of neurobiological research. A brief exposition of the moral requisite of trust, for example, indicates that men live in reliance on the trustworthiness of others. Thus we are inclined to condemn those applications of knowledge which would depreciate the place of trust in human existence, while we are inclined to laud those applications of knowledge which would enhance those values which are compatible with trust. This chapter also includes sections on the attitudes one might adopt toward research on the brain and an outline of some "moral and social directives" that are appropriate in regard to our new knowledge about the brain. The point is that Gustafson's portrait of human existence in terms of the moral virtues is a basis for making judgments about the research of molecular biologists on the brain; these moral judgments, moreover, can be judged to be consistent with certain theological convictions about God.

"Christian Style of Life: Problematics of a Good Idea" also concerns a portrait of moral existence, this time in terms of style of life. Two questions are salient, one concerning the descriptive sense of the term style and the other concerning the normative sense of the term. Gustafson explores the distinctions and the relationships between these two uses of the term. He makes clear that descriptively the term style may be used to refer to the visible behavior of collectivities or individuals, that it may be used to refer to characteristic dispositions and attitudes such as hope and love, and that it may also be used to refer to intentions. Each of these latter descriptions of moral existence, however, border on a normative use which leads Gustafson to reflect on the thorny problems that are related to any description of moral experience which gains a normative status. Our sources for such normative descriptions, he suggests, are multiple, and are the product of imagination and faith as well as historical research. The problems of legalism are alluded to, and Gustafson is sensitive to them. In my opinion it is ironic that many contemporary theologians have condemned all portraits of moral existence in terms of the moral virtues because they are "legalistic," yet they have been quite willing to encourage a particular "style" of Christian existence. Gustafson pleads for pluralism. Finally, Gustafson comments again on the familiar problem of how a particular normative style of life might be embodied in visible behavior; the point, again, is that the processes of character formation require the attention of theological ethicists.

"The Conditions for Hope: Reflections of Human Experience" is tersely written, but it merits close attention because it embodies the type of questions that Gustafson thinks must be asked and answered if an adequate portrayal of moral experience is to be given; the essay illustrates, as well, Gustafson's proclivities in answering these questions. It is suggested that our common experiences of hope point toward the fact that it is an attitude or disposition that is qualified both by its bases and by its objects. Certain questions can thus be asked. What are the sources of these bases and objects of hope and how might they be related? Gustafson suggests that there are both religious and experiential sources and that somehow they inform each other while remaining independent. How is a general attitude of hopefulness related to particular instances of hope? Gustafson's answer again stresses the interrelationships between religious and experiential categories. Since the objects of hope may be distinguished from the bases of hope, it can be asked, How are they related? Gustafson's answer distinguishes between more immediate and more ultimate bases and objects of hope and how they might be related. Finally, how do the bases and objects of hope affect action? Gustafson suggests that hope as an attitude is morally neutral, i.e., it is morally commendable only insofar as it is modified by its bases and objects; we are again reminded that both the objects and the sources of hope may be distinguished in terms of particularity and generality or ultimacy. An obvious but general point, then, is that if a portrait of moral existence is to be adequate for the task of theological ethics it must take into account the types of problems that are addressed by the questions raised in this essay. The essay ends in a plea that theological affirmations can be related to moral action and related in such a way that they may play a normative function; still, the moral life is not simply a deduction from prior theological categories.

In concluding this introduction, it may be observed that there is a remarkable consistency in much of Gustafson's written material. As early as 1961 Gustafson had formulated as one of the most disquieting puzzlements for theological ethics the following problematic.

> In seeking to know how Christian action ought to be governed by the divine action and the divine order, we are in what is to me the most difficult problem in Christian action. We are in the perilous position of having to say something, but knowing that almost anything we say is either claiming too much, or is saying not enough. It is either claiming too much for our particular actions to say that they follow the pattern of

God's objective action, or it is saying that we know so little about what God's ordering activity is that no moral knowledge comes from our knowledge of God.[12]

On the one hand, he is opposed to the notion that our knowledge of God is so great that we can be sure that our conduct is congruent with God's will. Such a claim, he thinks, overestimates our capacity to discern the will of God and frequently results in the supposition that theology in itself provides an exclusive basis for making moral decisions. On the other hand, he is opposed to the notion that our knowledge of God is so limited that little if any moral knowledge can be derived from theology. Such a claim, he thinks, underestimates our capacity to discern the will of God and frequently results either in the supposition that theology in itself cannot provide any basis for making moral decisions or provides such a fluid basis that just about any moral decision may be authorized on theological grounds. It is the middle road that proves so difficult to work out, i.e., to assume that theology is related to ethics, indeed, to suppose that theology has a normative function to play in theological ethics, yet not to reduce moral decisions to deductions from prior theological premises. We have seen that much of Gustafson's work has been directed toward working out the way in which a theological ethics might begin at the base point of a moral anthropology. We may await with anticipation his further reflections on the character of moral agency, on the nature of moral existence, and on the role of the virtues in the Christian life.

I wish to express my gratitude to Professor Gustafson for his confidence in allowing me to select from his written materials as I have deemed appropriate and for his trust in allowing me to introduce them in my own way.

Charles M. Swezey
Nashville, Tennessee

Mr. Swezey is an ordained minister of the Presbyterian Church, U.S., and a doctoral candidate in the department of religion at Vanderbilt University.

part one

Theology
and
Ethics

chapter 1

Christian Ethics in America

Background of the Contemporary Period

Scholarship in Christian ethics in the United States has developed in a particularly American way. Writers have clearly been motivated by concern for the actual state of public and private morality. The dominant intention has been to have some practical effect upon the moral behavior of persons and the public policy of institutions. Thus it is far more characteristic to find theoretical work developed out of practical moral concern than it is to find extensive treatises seeking to resolve theological and philosophical ethical questions in the abstract. This can be contrasted with Protestant scholarship in Europe, where until recently the conversation partners for ethics have been dogmatic theology, biblical exegesis, and philosophy almost exclusively. Few major American writings do not move in the direction of offering counsel on one or a number of actual life problems: sex, foreign policy, war, economic justice, etc. Americans have done little work in the history of Christian ethics; they have done less on the relation of ethical thought to biblical scholarship; only a few scholars have moved with ease between systematic theology and ethics, and too little work has been done on the relation of theological ethics to philosophical ethics. American writers in Christian ethics are fundamentally interested in morals, in moral action and activity. This is not only a Protestant mood, but also a Roman Catholic one.

James M. Gustafson, "Christian Ethics," from Paul Ramsey, Editor, *Religion* © 1965. Reprinted by permission of Prentice-Hall, Inc., Englewood Cliffs, New Jersey.

This tradition precedes the contemporary period; indeed, there are those who argue that the concern for practical morality that found fruition in the social gospel movement and its heirs is rooted in the Puritanism that shaped New England and that in revised forms spread across the land in the westward expansion. Willem A. Visser 't Hooft, in *The Background of the Social Gospel in America* (1928), indicates that some of the roots of the practical moral and social concern of later Christian ethics in America can be found in the Puritan concern for social discipline and for the ideal of a thoroughly Christianized society. H. Richard Niebuhr, in *The Kingdom of God in America* (1936), traces the transformations in the Puritan notion of the sovereignty of God through the history of American Protestant ethics, making clear that throughout there was a concern for social and personal conformation to the current interpretation of God's sovereignty and God's kingdom.

During the nineteenth century several identifiable movements emerged that continued this practical interest. One was the extensive teaching of "moral philosophy" in American colleges, usually under the direction of churchman-scholars who were also deeply involved in the public life of the time. Wilson Smith, in *Professors and Public Ethics* (1956), delineates some of the major strands of this movement: moral philosophers were really professors and executors of social ethics in America, having in their purview not only analysis of political and economic problems, but also the right to make moral judgments about them. Another nineteenth-century phenomenon, the great revivals, had a profound effect not only in the explication of moral discipline in personal conduct, but in motivating and directing important social concerns as well. Timothy Smith, in *Revivalism and Social Reform* (1957), makes the strongest case for the positive impact of American evangelicalism on matters of public morality. Later in the century, and decisive for the shaping of the concerns and procedures of Christian ethics in Protestantism even into the present, was the social gospel movement. In response to urbanization, industrialization, immigration, and their consequent problems on the one hand, and to biblical and theological "liberalism" on the other, a host of writers and reformers emerged on the American scene. Two accounts of this movement are C. Howard Hopkins' *The Rise of the Social Gospel in American Protestantism, 1865-1915* (1940) and Henry F. May's *Protestant Churches and Industrial America* (1949). The movement not only issued in institutional reform in church life, but also evoked a body of systematic literature. Two of the most scholarly books were Newman Smyth's *Christian Ethics* (1892) and

Walter Rauschenbusch's *A Theology for the Social Gospel* (1917). Smyth's book draws heavily upon the theology of Schleiermacher and his successors in German Protestantism, and upon English philosophical idealism. Ethics has to do with ideals and their actualization; in Christian ethics the moral ideal has been revealed in Jesus Christ and in his teachings. The task of the Christian community, then, is progressively to realize the Christian ideals in the actual conduct and affairs of the human community. Rauschenbusch's title, *A Theology for* . . . , is itself symbolic of much of Protestant ethics: given in the society and the Christian community is a moral concern that has a high degree of autonomy; what is required is the formation of a theology that supports, sustains, and directs that concern. Indeed, it was at the end of a lifetime as a powerful writer of quite practical moral treatises, such as *Christianizing the Social Order* (1912), that the German-American Baptist Professor of Church History defined the basic principles for his life work.

Parallel to the social gospel movement in Protestantism was the growth of Roman Catholic social theology. In 1891 Pope Leo XIII issued the famous encyclical *Rerum novarum,* which dealt with the fundamental rights of workers to just wages, to organize themselves in "workmen's associations," and so forth, for the sake of the health of the whole social body. This nourished a Catholic social movement in the United States that culminated in the important career of Father John A. Ryan, who became the principal interpreter for American public life of the theological and moral principles of the developing Roman Catholic tradition. The most recent history of this development is Franz Mueller's essay "The Church and the Social Question" (in J. N. Moody and J. G. Lawler, eds., *The Challenge of Mater et Magistra,* 1963). The essential point is that Roman Catholic Christian ethics in the United States also turned some of its most creative intelligence to questions of social ethics and social policy. Aaron Abell, in *American Catholicism and Social Action, 1865-1950* (1960), tells the story of Catholic involvement in public morality.

In the 1920's, the seeds of dissolution of the intellectual foundations of Protestant ethics were sown. The American sower and reaper was Reinhold Niebuhr, who is without doubt the towering figure during the period since 1930. Idealism grounded in theology such as that delineated by Newman Smyth and in the appropriation of the Old Testament prophets and of Jesus that was made by Rauschenbusch and others seemed impossible of realization in economic and social life. What was actually occurring is symbolized by the titles of two excellent studies that deal with the period between the World Wars, and appropriately Reinhold Niebuhr is the pivotal figure in both. Paul A. Carter's *The Decline and Revival of the Social Gospel* (1954) narrates how the social criticism characteristic of the early 1920's did not have the capacity to grapple with more than highly particularized and oversimplified issues, such as the prohibition of liquor, nor was it rooted in an intellectual tradition that could bear the toppling of optimism by crisis events in history. Under the impact of Niebuhr and of the thought of the ecumenical movement, new theological foundations were established that permitted a greater degree of social realism and thus a revitalization of a social gospel that could face the brutal realities of totalitarianism and war. The title of Donald B. Meyer's *The Protestant Search for Political Realism, 1919-1941* (1960) suggests the main thrust of both the reflective and the active side of Protestant ethics. How could Protestantism avoid mere verbalization of social criticism and social goals, and become a shaping force in the critical historical events of depression, totalitarianism, and war? What fundamental theological affirmations were in such error that they fostered illusions about man and society? What reappropriations from traditional Christian doctrine would release Protestants from their optimistic illusions and enable them to penetrate historical experience, to govern the realities of injustice, social evil, and power?

Thus, the earlier 1930's were crucial as a turning point in Protestant Christian ethics. Since the discipline was more practical than academic, it had to face the existence of a depression, the emergence of the powerful Soviet experiment with its radically alternative way to deal with social ills, and the rise of Hitler as grave crises in practical morality. The aspiration to preserve the peace by preaching pacifism, to change the social structure by changing personalities either through conversion or through education, to establish justice by making proclamations or organizing Christian campaigns, was critically called into question. With this, the intellectual foundations of "Applied Christianity" or "Practical Philanthropy," as seminary chairs were named, were also called into question. Had the biblical view of man, a creature of rebellion and sin, been lost in a preoccupation with the possibility of moral progress led on by a high religious moral ideal—Jesus and the kingdom of God? The discipline of Christian ethics took on a new academic seriousness in response to the social crisis. Inadequate perceptions of what was occurring, inadequate prescriptions for what ought to occur, and inadequate ways to effect what might occur all called for more serious intellectual and academic effort.

The ferment engendered by historical events coincided with the theological ferment that had begun to occur in European Protestantism in the Twenties. "Crisis theology" returned to Paul as well as the teachings of Jesus, viewed the Old Testament prophets as more than religiously motivated social reformers, returned to the Reformation interpretation of man as sinner even while justified, saw the vast distance between God and man, and fed on a newly discovered Kierkegaard. This crisis theology was seeping into the thought of the young American theologians: Christianity was faith before it was morality; it spoke of the divine-human relation that is perennially in a critical state rather than of a continuous cultural tradition based on the pervasive influence of Jesus, or of the power of the human spirit to transcend and in turn control nature. Jesus Christ was not the revelation of a moral idea; he was the God-man—a paradox. God's grace was not an efficacious infusion of a power moving toward the perfection of man; it was the forgiveness of sins, needed newly in each moment. The kingdom of God was not a historical possibility in which cooperation would rule out conflict, peace would rule out war; it was rather God's perfect reign, which would come not by the building of men, but by the act of God when he saw fit to bring it. Thus in 1931, the young German-American theologian Wilhelm Pauck could publish a book, *Karl Barth, Prophet of a New Christianity?* The intellectual ferment in Protestant ethics engendered by historical crises was fed by the far-reaching theological ferment created by European pastors and young theologians. The writings of Barth, Brunner, and others found minds ready to take them seriously.

Roman Catholic ethics, more deeply embedded in a stable intellectual tradition, faced the recent decades with greater equanimity. The English manuals of moral theology, such as *Moral and Pastoral Theology* (4 vols.) by Henry Davis, S.J., could be published in 1935 in the United States without a sense of intellectual revolution. Indeed, new developments in some areas of moral life, for example in medical care, required new refinements of casuistry, but the fundamental principles of natural law in its Thomistic form remained unaltered. In matters of social policy, the historical events had to be faced, and were. But this was more by development and application of a continuing intellectual tradition than by agonizing reappraisal of theological foundations. Thus, following World War I, the bishops' Program of Social Reconstruction could bring to bear the principles of *Rerum novarum* on the social needs of America. When Pius XI issued his social encyclical *Quadragesimo anno* in 1931, the American Catholic intellectuals and practitioners had a new basic document from which to launch their fundamental support for such social reforms as were proposed and enacted by the New Deal. New questions had to be faced, primarily with reference to a democratic society founded upon civil liberties in which the Roman Catholic population was a minority. The creative work was to come in that regard. But development, rather than crisis, was the appropriate response.

The fundamental interest in practical morality remains in more recent Christian ethics in America. But it has taken a new academic seriousness. Professorships in the field exist in theological schools and in universities and colleges. New vitality in biblical and theological studies abroad and in the United States contributed to the clarification of both the procedures and the content of the fundamental principles of Christian ethics. The ecumenical movement, earlier within the Protestant community, more recently including Orthodox and Roman Catholic participants, has enlarged the scope of the discourse and argumentation in the field. New philosophical movements have entered the conversation: Christian ethics is related by various scholars not only to natural law, pragmatism, and value theory, but also to existentialism and in a lesser measure to empiricism and linguistic analysis. With the translation of major works of contemporary Roman Catholic moral theologians from Europe, new language begins to appear in Roman Catholic ethics as well—the language of existential phenomenology. (An interpretation of what is occurring in Catholicism can be found in John C. Ford and Gerald Kelly's *Contemporary Moral Theology,* 1958.) The interpretation of the discipline's developments since about 1930, then, requires careful analysis.

Issues in Theological Ethics in the Contemporary Period

The bulk of this essay is a thematic interpretation of developments in the discipline of Christian ethics since 1930. In this section I have selected three themes of theological ethics: the changing interpretation of man, the changing use of the Bible in Christian ethics, and the controversy over the proper procedures of Christian ethical reasoning. These themes draw attention to issues that extend beyond the headings, and thus enable one to describe fairly inclusively what is occurring on the "theoretical" side of the discipline. Basically, these three themes deal with internal conversations between ethics and theology, though subordinately between Christian ethics and philosophy. The third section is a critical evaluation of contemporary work in Christian ethics in relation to some of its adjacent fields in their own right: biblical studies, philosophical ethics, and historical studies. In section 4, a critical overview of literature on Christian ethics and moral problems is made, indicating again the way in which Christian ethics in America has continued to be dominantly interested in actual moral problems, and thus is in conversation with various fields of the social sciences. I have throughout sought to do justice to Catholic as well as Protestant developments, though it will be obvious to the reader that Protestant material is more familiar to me. It is also the case, however, that until very recent years Roman Catholic ethics has been done in a traditional Thomistic manner, and consequently there is not as much change to report.

The Interpretation of Man

For ethics, whether Christian or non-Christian, the fundamental convictions about man are crucial for understanding the nature of moral achievement. If man is viewed as utterly free, creating himself and his moral world out of his actions, the interpretation of ethics is bound to be different from that that occurs if he is viewed as having within his being an inherent purposiveness or law, an inclination toward the good, that is related to the whole order of being. If man is viewed primarily as curved in upon himself even when he knows God's mercy, there will be a tentativeness about his moral judgment that will not exist if he is viewed primarily as basically restored in his personal moral being by God's redemption. American Christian ethics has moved in several directions during the past decades in its view of man.

Roman Catholic ethics has maintained its fundamentally Thomistic view of man as a creature of appetite, will, and reason, participating in the natural law that gives him a basic inclination toward the good. The signs of a revised pattern of interpretation of man's nature are only currently beginning to appear in Catholic ethics with the growing study of European Catholics who have begun to take the language of existential phenomonology—the language of I and thou, of being for the other, of historicity and temporality—and overlay it upon traditional Thomistic views. American conservative Protestantism, which has not contributed much to academic discussions of Christian ethics, continues to operate with a more individualistic view of man, in which the religious experience of redeeming grace is the principal way for moral reform. In the mainstream of American Protestantism, several trends are discernible. The most obvious is what was popularly called "the recovery of sin" and is identified with the writings of Reinhold Niebuhr. Alongside this has existed a self-conscious effort to resist the impact of Reinhold Niebuhr—this is visible in the writings of D. C. Macintosh and Albert Knudsen, who represent a continuation of an older liberal theology. Two other developments, however, are also noteworthy: one is the appropriation of a social theory of the self, informed not only by such American philosophers as G. H. Mead and John Dewey, but also by the social existentialism of a man like Martin Buber. This development is most cogently demonstrated in the work of H. Richard Niebuhr. Another development might be noted as "the recovery of grace," in which a radical affirmation of God's goodness and freedom issues in a participation in the events of the moral world without much self-consciousness or scrupulosity about man's sin. Such a view is implied in Paul Lehmann's work.

Reinhold Niebuhr: man as nature, spirit, and sinner.

The most notable and culturally influential reinterpretation of man, that of Reinhold Niebuhr of Union Theological Seminary in New York, is the obvious point at which to begin. Niebuhr protested vehemently against the excessive expectation of change in moral character that was assumed by religious pietism and by liberal rationalism. The former relied too heavily upon a moral renewal that was assumed to be the consequence of the work of grace and the life of piety, and had unwarranted assurance about its definitions of what the crucial moral issues were and how they could be rather simply solved. Religious and nonreligious liberalism (e.g., John Dewey) relied too heavily upon the re-education of man, on his ability to develop new methods of moral nurture and to shape moral ideals and sentiments. It led also to illusions about the pliability of persons and institutions, assuming, for example, that peace could be achieved by declarations against war and by the growth of the pacifist movement. The biblical myth of the fall, taken seriously as a basis for the interpretation of human existence, enabled Niebuhr to criticize the oversimplifications and pitfalls of pietism and liberal rationalism by stressing the limits of human capacities to know and achieve the temporal good, and the necessity to use coercive power to resist evil.

Niebuhr's interpretation of sin and its consequences for morality has continuity with the moral idealism of American Protestantism, however, at one crucial point: it is delineated in relation to the problem of how *ideal possibilities* of human existence particularly in society, can and cannot be actualized in history. It assumes a distinction between spirit and nature, between freedom and necessity, between finite and infinite that has roots in the idealistic tradition.

> Sin lies at the juncture of spirit and nature, in the sense that the peculiar and unique characteristics of human spirituality, in both its good and evil

tendencies, can be understood only by analyzing the paradoxical relation of freedom and necessity, of finiteness and the yearning for the eternal in human life [*An Interpretation of Christian Ethics,* Harper & Bros., 1935, p. 76].

By virtue of being spirit as well as nature, man knows of higher possibilities in his freedom that cannot be realized in the natural, finite world; he knows therefore the imperfections of the actions that he is forced to take. Indeed, he is constantly under the judgment of these higher possibilities, and out of this contrast between ideal and actual comes his moral guilt. The problem does not rest merely with human finiteness, with the limitations that are set upon us by the fact that we are bodies within historical processes and contingencies. There is also the religious dimension of the problem of the will. In man's perversity of will he does not even achieve that measure of the ideal that is a possibility.

A question necessarily arises, then, about the significance of religious moral ideals (for example, love) that cannot be realized in human experience. Are they useless? Or how are they to be taken? Niebuhr, in *An Interpretation of Christian Ethics,* argues for the "relevance of an impossible ethical ideal" on several grounds. Against those forms of "liberalism, rationalism, and radicalism" that insist upon the possibility of the perfect realization of love in human life, Niebuhr stresses the impossibility of the ideal. Against morally and socially passive forms of orthodox Christianity, he insists upon its relevance, that is, upon the necessity to achieve a closer approximation to the law of love, which is possible through the establishment of social equity and other moral values "in an ascending scale of moral possibilities." With the acknowledgment of sin, and under the judgment and direction of the law of love, men can participate in the realities of social power, political strife, and economic conflict with both determination and contrition.

This basic view of man is refined with great theological sophistication in *The Nature and Destiny of Man* [2 vols., Charles Scribner's Sons, 1941, 1943], the most important American contribution to Protestant theological ethics in the first half of this century. Under the influence of serious grappling with the Bible, the Reformers, Augustine, and Kierkegaard, particularly the latter's *Sickness unto Death,* Niebuhr brings into his view of man as sinner not merely a moral interpretation of the inability to actualize ideals because of perversion of will, but also a religious interpretation of sin arising out of lack of faith. He suggests that the Christian view of man relates three aspects of human existence to each other: (1) "the height of self-transcendence in man's spiritual stature," coming from the doctrine of the image of God; (2) man's "weakness, dependence, and finiteness," his involvement in the contingencies of the natural world, coming from the doctrine that man is creature and always remains creature; and (3) the evil of man as "a consequence of his inevitable though not necessary unwillingness to acknowledge his dependence, to accept his finiteness and to admit his insecurity, an unwillingness which involves him in the vicious circle of accentuating the insecurity from which he seeks to escape" (vol. I, p. 150). Sin is inevitable though not necessary, because man could trust in God but does not, and in turn he seeks to avoid by various escapes his anxiety over being a creature and not God. The forms of escape are the forms of sin: pride, which is basically man's tendency to have more confidence in his power, his knowledge, his virtue, and his religiosity than these things deserve; and sensuality, which is basically man's flight from his responsibility of being spirit as well as nature into sexuality and other forms of loss of "transcendence."

The consequences of such a view of man for morality are evident. Consciousness of human limitation and sin rules out all utopian expectations of the perfect achievement of the social and personal good in history. But two other Christian affirmations qualify the sheer pessimism that might ensue if this were all that could be said. They are the assurance of God's mercy, and love as the law of life. Both refer to the significance of God's revelation in Jesus Christ, and particularly of his crucifixion. The crucifixion reveals the unlimited self-giving sacrificial love of God, his willingness to choose even the death of Jesus as the way to disclose his unfathomable agape. The first affirmation derived from this theory is that even though man continues in creatureliness and sin, he can trust in God's merciful forgiveness and in the final victory of God's kingdom of love. This is an appropriation of a particularly Lutheran emphasis in theology and ethics. Thus while man remains conscious of his sin, the assurance of God's love gives him an inner freedom, an equanimity that removes some of the anxiety and particularly the temptation to pride that corrupt his activities. But he remains a sinner. For Niebuhr, the classical Reformation formula *simul justus, simil peccator* (at once both justified and sinner) is true, but his emphasis is: "To be sure man is justified, but he remains a *sinner*." Niebuhr's stress can be contrasted with Barth's, for whom the same formula testifies to sin rather than love as the "impossible possibility": "To be sure man is sinner, but he is *justified*." For Niebuhr, then, the moral life calls for a sharp awareness of the continuation of human sin even while one pursues the relative good that is achievable in history, though this is done within confidence in the forgiving mercy of God and his final victory.

The second affirmation derived from God's disclosure of his love on the cross is that this very self-sacrificial love is the norm, the fundamental law of life. In the earlier *Interpretation* Niebuhr's view of love was largely based upon the teachings of Jesus, in continuity with the social gospel tradition. In *Nature and Destiny* he avers that Jesus' death disclosed love (agape) even more powerfully than did his teachings. Sinful man is under this law, this norm. Thus a form of moral idealism remains: man is called to achieve the impossible. The impossible remains the light in which all his possible actions are judged, that by which they are informed and qualified. Sinful man is called to approximate self-sacrificial love, and this he does in his pursuit of justice, of equity, and of mutuality, which is the highest form of love that appears to be possible in human experience. His politically realistic actions in the pursuit of justice are to be tempered by mercy and to be conscious of a higher possibility; this is what might distinguish the Christian moral pursuits from those of others. He is to approximate God's agape insofar as it is historically achievable in faithful trust in God's mercy and God's victory, but his sin and creatureliness limit the fulfillment of love.

The attractiveness and influence of Niebuhr's Christian ethics, grounded in this doctrine of man, have been widespread. He has been widely received, it must be noted, for quite American reasons; that is, his intellectual reflection makes sense of human moral experience and enables men to be morally realistic and responsible in very practical matters. To be sure, he resuscitates a doctrine that had been somewhat suppressed, that of sin; he reappropriates biblical, Augustinian, and Reformation motifs; he brings Kierkegaard's existential view of man to bear. He learned from the early writings of Barth, and from Brunner's *Man in Revolt*. But these achievements would not authenticate an American theologian of ethics. His persuasiveness lay in his use of these insights for the interpretation and direction of human moral experience. The validation of ethics rests neither in abstract intellectual finesse, nor in scholarly authority that comes from reference to traditional sources, but in the illumination of human, historical experience. To this Niebuhr brought a virtuosity unsurpassed in this century.

D. C. Macintosh: moral hope in conversion plus science.

Niebuhr's view of man did not, however, sweep away the opinions against which he reacted. Liberal Christian views persisted, and to these one must attend. D. C. Macintosh, a Yale theologian who was once Niebuhr's teacher, had confidence in the converting power of grace, the exercise of will, and the information of science to bring in a better moral order. He represents the continuation of the liberal tradition in both its theological and ethical aspects. He believed in the possibility of "empirical theology"—knowledge of God built upon the experiences of men. In ethics, he refused to be shaken by the eschatological interpretations of the New Testament that believed Jesus' teachings referred to the life of perfection that was possible in the present only because the kingdom of God was expected to come shortly. In piety, he believed that "personal religion" was the foundation of "social religion." "If society is to be saved it must be through saved individuals," he wrote in *Social Religion* [Charles Scribner's Sons, 1939, p. 86]. Saved individuals are not merely well-taught persons; they must recognize their sin, repent of it, and receive the grace of God. But with this religious experience, Macintosh also affirmed the necessity and ability to pattern life after the spirit of the teachings of Jesus. Whereas Niebuhr had come to believe that men must strive for the historical approximation of love, but not expect its fulfillment in the social world, Macintosh believed that Christians should and could fulfill a faithful loyalty to Jesus, though it would be costly. Man, Macintosh said, must accept the absolute sovereignty of God for his own life, and recognize it as the ideal for everyone else and for the whole world. He must learn to love his enemies—and this he can do when he accepts God's will absolutely and begins to work for the salvation of his enemies. He must avoid doing violence to any man, but live peaceably with all.

Evangelism would bring about the root change in individuals, who in turn would express this new life in society. But there is another human "pre-condition" that makes possible a real achievement of social salvation. Niebuhr did not trust it; Macintosh did.

> The one other pre-condition of a steadily progressive realization of the social ideal is an adequate social science and the education of individuals to accept and abide by the findings of genuine experimental science, social as well as material. We may congratulate ourselves that this condition can be more readily fulfilled than in Jesus' day; but even so, it must be admitted that we are still very far from even this nearer goal (*Social Religion,* pp. 113-14).

The mood and temper of this issued in a suggested program for the peace of the world in 1939, which ironically and pathetically was the year that demonstrated how much closer to the realities of human society was Niebuhr than his former teacher. Macintosh's *Social Religion* was fated to be the last great blossom of the pre-1930 tradition, but because of the learning, the intelligence, the piety, and the moral conviction of its author it remains a masterful example of a failing ethos.

Albert Knudsen: good will and high ideals. Another liberal American Protestant tradition that has never been swept away by Niebuhr and other recent currents in theology and ethics is "Boston personalism," identified through three-quarters of a century with the names of Bowne, Brightman, Knudsen, and others. This tradition has made adjustments but has not gone through the revolutions of some others. Its view of man is grounded in a particular understanding of natural law: E. S. Brightman published an influential book called *Moral Laws* in 1933 that has remained something of a landmark for further developments among these Methodist theologians.

Albert Knudsen's *The Principles of Christian Ethics* [Abingdon Press, 1943] represents one systematization of the general point of view. Man has a moral nature, with elements that give content to the moral law: "These are the principle of good will, the conception of a more or less binding human ideal, and the recognition of the sacredness of personality" (p. 76). This native principle of good will is "a manifest basis for the Christian law of love," and the natural human ideal of moral perfection finds content in Jesus. "Natural morality comes first; Christian morality is a later and higher development. But there is no radical difference of kind between them. Christian morality is rooted in the moral nature of man and presupposes both it and the lower expression of it in what has been called natural morality" (p. 83).

How seriously is this moral nature corrupted? For Knudsen most of the traditional interpretation of sin is a "theological fiction." He defined sin essentially in moral rather than religious terms; that is, it is a violation of the moral law (which is also God's law). Conversion, however, makes moral achievement possible. It brings liberation in its release from a sense of guilt; it endows the moral life with a new dynamic, an inspiration; it brings the conviction that man is not left alone in the moral struggle; it brings "new moral insight" through the teaching of Jesus, and even gives "new moral intuitions." Thus the natural moral man, under the power of conversion, moves toward the ideals of love and moral perfection. The Christian moves in life toward the moral perfection of perfect love. Because God is perfect, Christians ought to be perfect. For the Christian, the movement toward perfection involves the "quest after sinlessness," which is the wholehearted devotion to the fundamental principles of love and holiness. Violations of these principles "may now and then occur, but where they are few and not of a serious nature, the moral quality of the life is determined by its obedience rather than by its lapses, and in such a case we may speak of a relative sinlessness" (p. 153). The perfection of man is a moral ideal toward which we move through self-renunciation and through the aid of the divine spirit. Man can move toward the achievement of this in his embodiment of the Christian virtues.

The contrast of Knudsen's view of man with Niebuhr's requires no elaboration. Knudsen represents one of the latter-day forms of Wesleyanism, infused with moral idealism, that Niebuhr found susceptible to excessive self-assurance and pride. For most contemporary students of Christian ethics, Knudsen is easily dismissed as passé. Yet he expressed a Christian idealism that is part of the American intellectual and moral tradition, and is grounded in one strand of the history of Christian ethics.

H. Richard Niebuhr: man as responsible. In the decades of the influence of Reinhold Niebuhr, a less practical interpretation of man's moral nature was being developed by his brother, H. Richard Niebuhr of Yale. His posthumous book, *The Responsible Self* (1963), gives the most concise statement of the position. H. Richard Niebuhr was informed by the social theory of the self that found expression in the writings of the Michigan sociologists Charles Horton Cooley and the philosophers G. H. Mead and Josiah Royce. Mead's *Mind, Self, and Society* (1934) suggested a view of selfhood in which identity was shaped by particular responses to groups and persons, and yet was constantly being reshaped in new responses. But the social determinism imbedded in this genetic view of the self did not permit the kind of freedom for responsibility that Niebuhr's moral interests required. Kant and the existentialists understood the self in terms of radical freedom, but could not account for the socially conditioned self. Martin Buber's thought furnished a notion of the self as both free and significantly related to others, and thus was a contribution to the idea of "social existentialism" that Niebuhr used in *Christ and Culture* (1951). The self is always in relationship to others, and is governed in part by these relations. Yet the relationship is one of responsibility for others and responsibility to God, and thus each being is a center of moral action in relationships.

The distinctiveness of this view for ethics is delineated by H. Richard Niebuhr in *The Responsible Self* [Harper & Row, 1963]. He suggests that three types of ethics emerge out of three types of theory of the self. Deontological ethics, the ethics of obedience to rules of right conduct, emerges from an interpretation of man as citizen. "We come to self-awareness if not to self-existence in the midst of *mores,* of commandments and rules, *Thou shalts* and *Thou shalt nots,* of directions and permissions" (p. 52). In

Christian ethics, this takes the form of Christian legalism, but there is also a more existential Christian deontology, such as one finds in Karl Barth's ethics of obedience to the immediate command of God. Teleological ethics, the ethics of conformation of self and world to an image, emerges from an interpretation of man as maker, fashioner, and artificer. "The image of man-the-maker, who, acting for an end, gives shape to things is, of course, refined and criticized in the course of its long use [beginning with Aristotle's *Ethics*], by idealists and utilitarians, hedonists and self-realizationists" (p. 49). In Christian ethics, this has its greatest tradition in Roman Catholic Thomism, where personal life and the order of society are to be shaped in conformation to what "really is," the pattern of their nature.

In contrast to these, Niebuhr offers the notion of responsibility. "What is implicit in the idea of responsibility is the image of man-the-answerer, man engaged in dialogue, man acting in response to action upon him" (p. 56). The pattern of thought becomes interactional; men are seen as "responsive beings, who in all our actions answer to action upon us in accordance with our interpretation of such action" (p. 57). Using this fundamental model, derived from philosophical reflection on moral experience more than from exclusively Christian sources, Niebuhr interprets the Christian moral life. In order to respond to actions taking place, men have to have some pattern of interpretation to bring to bear upon themselves and events. What theology provides is an interpretation of the one who is finally acting upon us in all human and historical actions, and to whom men are finally accountable and responsible in their personal and communal existences. Men are responding to God's actions; they are responsible to God in all their interactions. God is known in his revelation in the history of Israel, in Jesus Christ, and in the life of the Christian community to be our creator, governor, and redeemer. Thus our responsible action in the particularities of what is going on is to be fitting to the creative, ordering, judging, and redeeming action of God.

The effect of this view of man is to multiply the number of places at which the Christian feels moral responsibility, for every relationship is one in which he is to seek the good of the neighbor in his response to him. It is also to expand the sources of moral insight and reflection, for no one or two principles become the exclusive governing ones in conduct. Christians are to respond in love, to be sure, but love is not defined in terms of a moral rule of conduct. They are to respond also in faith and hope; they are to respond in the way that is morally fitting in the particular network of interaction. A new stress is brought to bear by the ethics of responsibility; namely, the necessity to know what is going on in the world, for moral life is no longer defined by a single end to be achieved, or by particular propositions to be obeyed or applied. Less rationalistic and more personalistic factors begin to play a part: the importance of loyalty, of repentance, of fidelity to God and to man are stressed in the relationships. But if the range of considerations and the sources of moral insight are complicated, yet the full force of a sense of responsibility is maintained. To be sure, man responds to what is being done by God through other men, but he is *responsible to God* and to men for his participation in the moral and social interaction.

In H. Richard Niebuhr's view of moral man, a fundamental pattern of thought is introduced to American Christian ethics that is distinguishable from those of his contemporaries. The language of moral idealism is gone: man is no longer trying to realize transcendent norms or moral ideals either in himself or in society. Nor is he seen as a center isolable from the content of his relationships to others. His sin is not his moral failure to fulfill impossible possibilities or to obey the moral law and achieve a model of perfection; it is unfaithfulness and irresponsibility to God and man in his historical existence. He is not redeemed or converted in moral character, but responds to the redemptive activity of God. He is not plagued with the problem of absolute expectations in the relativities of the world; rather he is created in relationships from which he never escapes; he is in time, in history, and in society, and must be responsible within this context. But he is not simply to realize himself within this history; he is obligated to be a restrainer of evil and an evoker of good in the persons he meets and in the ordered relationships of life.

Tillich and Lehmann: the ethics of the antilegalistic conscience.

H. Richard Niebuhr's interpretation of man leads to an ethic that is against the legalism that often comes from the stress on norms and rules. But it stresses the obligations that are inherent in the structures of human experience. Contemporary theological currents have given rise to other forms of antilegalistic ethics as well. Paul Tillich, for example, very consciously states that "morality is the self-affirmation of our essential being" (*Theology of Culture*, 1959, p. 136). This means for him that moral law is not a strange law, imposed from outside ourselves, but "it is the law of our own being." All moral rules and laws are conditioned; the true moral imperative is our "essential being" seeking affirmation; it drives us not toward commands, but toward "reality." The best interpretation of conscience is not one that makes judgments according to rules of behavior, but one that judges "according to the participation in a reality which transcends the sphere of moral commands" (*The Protestant Era,* 1948, p. 145). Thus, as man participates in the reality of being, as he overcomes the estrangement between himself and being that is in part caused by the existence of human codes of morality, he will be able to express a true and creative moral life. Legalisms are false idols upon which people rest; they are finally obstructions to the relationships between being and man, between man and man, and prevent true self-affirmation.

Tillich's ethics is one expression of his philosophical theology, but as ethics it has had little impact in American Christian ethical discussion. More important is the view of the self that one can discern in the writings of Paul Lehmann. In a reflection of Karl Barth's procedure for theological ethics—namely, finding what is to be said about man not by looking at him but by looking first of all at Jesus Christ—Lehmann criticizes ethics that have an independent doctrine of man. In relation to Jesus Christ, however, one can make certain affirmations about the moral life of the Christian. Christians belong to the community of faith, the *koinonia,* "where prophetic-apostolic *witness* to revelation and *response* of the fellowship in the Spirit coincide" [*Ethics in a Christian Context,* Harper & Row, 1963, p. 51]. In this community, Christians come to "mature manhood," which, rather than morality, is what Christian ethics must talk about. This maturity is "the integrity in and through interrelatedness which makes it possible for each individual member of an organic whole to be himself in togetherness, and in togetherness each to be himself" (p. 55). As Christians come to this maturity in faith, they can discern through the gifts of transformed motivation and of clear understanding the direction of God's activity in the world. They can begin to see what God is doing "to make human life truly human," and thus respond in such a way that their action *coincides* with God's action. The point in the self that registers this coincidence is the conscience.

The conscience for Lehmann is not developed by a persistent scrupulosity in the pursuit of moral perfection, nor is it shaped by the casuistry of the church as it seeks to relate abstract moral principles to concrete human behavior. It is "neither libertarian nor legalistic, neither antinomian nor nomian, but whole, i.e., unified and sensitized in the freedom wherewith Christ has set us free" (p. 350). The Christian conscience is not the pursuit of alien norms of behavior (heteronomy), nor does it assume that man has within himself the ability to create the conditions for making and keeping human life human (autonomy). Rather, conscience is to be "theonomous." "The *theonomous* conscience is the conscience immediately sensitive to the freedom of God to do in the always changing human situation what his humanizing aims and purposes require. The *theonomous* conscience is governed and directed by the freedom of God alone" (pp. 358-59). Thus man in Christ, in the community of faith, has the eyes to see what God, in his freedom, is doing in the world, and to be governed and directed by God's activity. The effect is anything but legalism; it is openness to participation in the changes that are going on in the world, with some assurance that in faith one discerns what God himself is doing there.

Paul Lehmann gives a very different view of man from those of his contemporaries: the first thing to be said about man is not that he is a sinner, and continues to be a sinner, nor that he is one who actualizes moral ideals. It is not that he has a moral law within him. Rather the first thing to be said is that he lives in reliance upon what God is doing, and he is enabled in the Christian *koinonia* to perceive with some reliability what he ought to do. He does not need norms of love to guide him or ideals to lead him on. Rather, he involves himself in God's work of humanization. He is free in Christ to respond to what God is doing in his freedom. He is not defined in terms of responsibility to God and to others, but in terms of freedom before God and others. Theology informs man not about his sinful condition, but his radical freedom in faith; not about a pattern for the interpretation of what might be going on in the world, but a knowledge of God who can, for example, freely require strict sexual behavior in one era and permit less strict behavior in another. Human freedom in faith is the coincidence of sensitized imaginations and consciences of Christians with God's freedom.

Roman Catholic views: from a natural law to a "responsibility" model? Lehmann's view of man must appear to be appalling anarchy to the Roman Catholic moral theologian and philosopher. It minimizes, if it does not abolish, what might be said about the fundamental continuities and requirements of human behavior. It eschews the task of elaborating what really does make human beings human. It seems to deny a stable order of creation and society. And not only to Roman Catholics—a Protestant writer such as Paul Ramsey seeks for the relatively stable principles that can be stated about moral conduct in the human community so that moral counsel can be given with some rational reflection, and with some certainty that it reflects the fundamental characteristics of the created order of life. Roman Catholic ethicists are aware of the danger signals that come from such a situational and contextual view of man,* and have basically kept within the traditional Thomistic assumptions of an order of being, a natural tendency toward the good, and reliable knowledge of what the natural law is upon which to make prescriptions and counsels of moral behavior. Man is to actualize what he really is; he is a creature whose actions are directed toward the end of both his natural and supernatural good.

Traditional Protestant criticisms of Catholic interpretations of man have hardly changed the pattern. Even the more liberal views of Jacques Maritain, widely read in America, are basically Thomistic. Protestants have said over and over that the Catholic view assumes too much competence in knowing what the fundamental order of man and his relatedness to other men is, it does not take seriously enough the persistence and depths of corruption in man, and it too easily identifies what it believes man "really" to be with the history of Catholic morality and the society of the medieval period. In the pre-John XXIII period, in America, these criticisms were answered with defense of the tradition.

There are, however, European trends in Catholic philosophy and ethics that have been sowing the seeds of revision in the Catholic interpretation of man. These are being studied in the United States, and what will finally issue from them is yet to be seen. European Catholics have had their own situationalists in ethics; in 1952 Pope Pius XII condemned the trend, and both Americans and Europeans have written about its potential dangers. But apart from the extreme existentialists in Catholicism there is also the work of Albert Dondeyne and others who describe man in terms of historicity, temporality, being for others, and responsibility. (See, for example, Dondeyne's *Faith and the World*, 1963, and Bernard Häring's *The Law of Christ*, 1961.) The scope of human freedom is stressed, and reliance upon the virtue of prudence to respond creatively to new situations is affirmed. (See Josef Pieper's "Prudence," 1959.) In these works, there is explicit criticism of the rigidity with which the traditional natural law interpretation of man has been carried out, and there is often use of modern psychological and existential language. There is also, however, a marked effort to relate the newer language to the older, which looks to Protestant eyes like a somewhat compromising and inconsistent way of working.

The principal journal that has brought much of the new European Cath-

---

* For a rather sympathetic critical account, see Robert Gleason, S.J., "Situational Morality," *Thought*, XXXII (1957), 533-58.

olic thinking into the general conversation in America is *Cross Currents,* edited by laymen, though important articles have been written by American scholars who are priests. There are clear marks of the influence of the new patterns on the writings of such a theologian as Robert Gleason, S.J., and in conversation one finds its penetration into the thought of philosophers and theologians. Behind it lies the work of an earlier generation of philosophers such as Max Scheler, and more contemporary figures such as Maurice Merleau-Ponty. Albert Dondeyne's *Contemporary European Thought and Christian Faith* (1958) is a major bridge-document that critically assesses and selectively absorbs existential phenomenological language into the Catholic tradition. Duquesne University in Pittsburgh seems to be the American center for this mode of thought.

Summary assessment. American Protestants continue to find Reinhold Niebuhr's view of man to be most useful in the interpretation and direction of moral problems in the political, economic, and international spheres of morality. But it is less satisfactory in illuminating the situation of personal responsibility and the responses required in the interpersonal sphere. It is too early to assess the fate of H. Richard Niebuhr's views on the world that knows him only through the printed page; but upon generations of his students teaching Christian ethics in colleges, universities, and seminaries, it has already had a wide effect. Lehmann's view is attractive to a generation of persons also influenced by a popular version of the thought of the German theologian-martyr Dietrich Bonhoeffer, for it counsels deep identification with what is going on in the "secular" world. Whether the virtually intuitive elements in it will finally be able to bear the traffic of moral experience is open to question. Perhaps the most creative avenue opening to future discussions about moral man in Christian ethics is the language of responsibility, historicity, and temporality now shared by many Catholics and Protestants, chastened in its existentialist extremities by a reassessment of the *nature* of moral experience that is grounded in the creation. The kind of moral idealism that was carried into the recent period by Macintosh and Knudsen seems fated to decline in influence in a generation that has undergone a theological revolution and is hardly optimistic about the resolution of moral tensions, though this idealism continues to be a force in American morals through such a distinguished leader as Martin Luther King.

The Changing Use of the Bible

For Christian ethics, the Bible remains the charter document. But what it charters depends upon a number of other things that the Christian ethical thinker brings to it. For some it continues to be a book of morality; that is, its prescriptive statements and patterns of life have morally authoritative character that requires literal obedience. For many more, such a view is no longer possible, for historical-critical scholarship has indicated the relation of much that is said to the time and history in which it was written, and theological scholarship has questioned whether the morality of the Bible can be properly understood apart from such theological themes as eschatology, divine judgment, God's grace, Christian freedom, and human sin. Indeed, for a large part of Protestant ethics, the Bible is now less a book of morality than it is a book giving knowledge of God, his presence and his activity. Among Roman Catholics it has traditionally been relegated to dealing with questions of man's supernatural end, and questions of historical morality have been settled in terms of the natural law, often reinforced by biblical quotations. But this is also changing, for European books dealing with the "law of Christ" are making the biblical witness more central to the whole work of Roman Catholic ethics.

By examining what has happened to the use of the Bible in Christian ethics, we are forced to view other themes as well. Most particularly, we must examine different views of the importance of the work of God, Jesus Christ, and the Spirit that have profound effects upon the content and procedures of Christian ethics. Broader theological use of the Bible is particularly necessary where the Christian community desires to interpret theologically and ethically the importance of Christian faith for the extensive and complex issues of human morality in politics, economics, and other areas, and where the community accepts some responsibility for the temporal good of the whole society. A stricter *moral* use of scripture tends to lead to the development of an exemplary morality of a committed few who witness in their distinct patterns of life to a "higher" way. To use distinctions made by Ernst Troeltsch and Max Weber, where the community takes the high demands of biblical morality with literal seriousness, it tends to become sectarian (clearly defined over against the world) and sees its effect upon the world in terms of "exemplary" prophecy and conduct that might have indirect consequences for the temporal good. Where the community takes the Bible to refer primarily to more universal themes of God's governing and redeeming work, it tends to become "churchly" (blurring lines between the religious community and the world) and accepts broad social responsibility as an "emissary" people whose duty it is to make compromises and accept responsibility for cultural values.

There are no recent American writings of academic repute that assume in a simple way that the Bible provides the rules for the governing of the whole human community as if it were the rational norm and ideal of morality applicable to all regardless of their status in Christian faith. This kind of rationalistic moral idealism, characteristic of Tolstoy's use of the Christian teaching, forgets that the Bible is much more than a moral textbook; it is for writers of various persuasions a source for knowledge of God and a source for God's word of judgment and redemption to man. Thus, the moral teachings are seen within the wider framework of theological affirmations and of the Christian experience of sin and forgiveness through Jesus Christ. The Bible, to put it simply, has a different moral authority for Christians than it has for others. But the variations within this statement are in effect the story of Christian ethics throughout history.

Radical Reformation groups.
On the American scene there are Christian groups for whom a literal compliance with the gospel ethic—particularly its commands to love, to meekness, to service—is both an aspiration and a pattern of life. The historic peace churches in the Anabaptist and Quaker traditions, for example, have taken part of the moral teaching to require nonviolence, pacifism, and deeply sacrificial service as the proper expression of Christian life. But there are as yet no American academic treatises that give powerful theological defenses of the Anabaptist view, though in occasional writings such a person as John Howard Yoder promises to be a formidable and theologically informed interpreter and defender of this tradition. Among liberal Quakers, Rufus Jones and Douglas Steere have been more or less faithful to the tradition of a pacifist interpretation of both "inner light" and a Sermon on the Mount ethic. There is no expectation of great worldly success in such ethical teaching; these Christians expect to be a minority representation of faithfulness, and are prepared to suffer at the hands of a more expedient and prudential world.

Evangelical conservative Protestants: revealed morality.
A larger segment of American Protestantism is represented by the conservative evangelical position, sometimes the fundamentalist one, in which the "propositional revelation" of the Bible has an authority in matters of both faith and conduct. The words of the Bible are quite literally the word of God, whether they tell us about God and his glory, about man and his rebellion, about the new life that conversion creates, or about the moral conduct that is required of the children of God. This tradition has begun to find new expressions in scholarly work in ethics. The major recent contributor is Carl F. H. Henry, whose *The Uneasy Conscience of Modern Fundamentalism* (1947) opened the way for discussions of social ethics among those groups that had formerly identified that interest with degener-

ate Christian liberalism. In a very large and ambitious work, *Christian Personal Ethics* [Eerdmans, 1957], Henry gives more specific expression to his view of biblical authority for ethics. It is framed by his larger conservative use of the Bible in matters of theology. His preference for the moral use of the Bible seems to combine elements of the Anabaptist tradition, which he honors in part because it does not make Christian ethics subjective and humanistic, and the Reformed tradition, which sought within the scripture a design and order for the lives of the members of the Christian church. The reality of Christian ethics comes from the "unique Divine inbreaking" that is recorded in the Bible. "The Christian ethic is a specially revealed morality—not merely religious ethics. It gains its reality in and through supernatural disclosure" (*Christian Personal Ethics,* p. 193). Since Christian ethics is a special and not a universal revelation, it is not accessible to all men; it is the ethics of the believing church. "The ethics of revealed religion therefore divides mankind into two radically opposed groups: the followers of the broad way and those of the narrow way" (p. 203). The divine will is clear: "What God has revealed in the inspired Scriptures defines the content of his will" (p. 264). The historic conviction is "that God has been pleased to reveal his will, and that he has done so in express commands, given to chosen men through the medium of human language, and available to us as the *Word* of God in written form" (p. 265). This will is particularized in the Old and New Testaments, though in a "progressive" way. "A later age is always called upon to 'fulfill' the continuing moral claim, although God may supersede certain positive laws in the newer era" (p. 269). Henry reminds his readers that they are not to take the moral teaching in isolation from the rest of biblical revelation; this is true of the details both of Old and New Testaments. Thus in studying the Sermon on the Mount, Jesus' larger teaching and the whole of the New Testament must be kept in view. But

> the Sermon remains an "ethical directory" for Christians. It contains the character and conduct which Jesus commends to his followers, the demand which the nature and will of God make upon men, the fundamental law of the Kingdom, and the ideal and perfect standard. It is the ultimate formula of ethics for which ideal human nature was fashioned by creation and is destined in eternity. Fallen nature is justified in Christ in conformity to it, and redeemed nature approximates it by the power of the indwelling Spirit of God (pp. 325-26).

The seriousness with which the moral teachings of the Bible are taken by Henry can best be seen in contrast with Paul Lehmann's view of the Christian life. The way in which the authority of the Bible is understood by these men is, of course, radically different. Whereas Lehmann develops a biblical theology that describes the human maturity in faith in which man in his freedom is sensitive to the freedom of God, Henry is saying that God has declared himself on matters of morals as well as faith in highly particularized ways in the words of the Bible. Henry acknowledges that it is not always easy to move from moral propositions in the Bible to the particular situations in which men must act, but in contrast to Lehmann, he has substantive, authoritative moral propositions from which to begin the process. The Bible is law as well as gospel.

Liberal Protestantism: revealed morality in a different form.

One of the characteristics of the ethics of liberal Christianity was its focus on the "spirit" of Jesus and on the authority of his teachings, as these are depicted in the gospel narratives. No intelligent theologians were so simple-minded as to assume that the teachings of Jesus could be immediately applied to the contemporary world, but they did seek the possibility of "translating" them into current needs. Macintosh is typical of this when he wrote, "What we may have to do . . . is to translate into the terms of our best twentieth-century empirical knowledge and world-view the principles of social action normatively present in the spirit and ideal of the Jesus of history and expressed by him, quite naturally, in terms of the concepts available in his day" (*Social Religion,* p. 5). Various aspects of the teachings and deeds of Jesus were used by various interpreters to serve as the basic framework for the fundamental pattern for moving from the authority of the "Jesus of history" to the contemporary world. Some used the notion of the kingdom of God; some took the command to love the neighbor. Macintosh chose the beatitudes to give the framework to his interpretation of the social content of the gospel. His use of the saying "Blessed are the poor, for theirs is the kingdom of God" not only illustrates his work, but also suggests the kinds of uses of the Bible that others made.

The kingdom of God is to be "the rule of God's will in human life, individually, and socially." Thus when Jesus spoke the saying,

> he must have meant that when, through the divine initiative and man's response, God's rule was established on earth and God's will was being done fully enough in a sufficient number of human lives for them to revolutionize social relations and make society a genuine brotherhood under the divine Fatherhood, poverty would soon be abolished (p. 42).

A related narrative is Jesus' story of the workers in the vineyard (Matt. 20:1-16). From this narrative Macintosh draws the moral: "From everyone according to his ability; to every one according to his need." "A job for every one, and 'a living wage for every one willing to work.' " In summary, Macintosh is able by the alchemy of his religious thought and feeling to move from these accounts in the Bible to a definition of the social order that is coming through both God's work, and man's works.

> In the Kingdom the hungry will be fed, not by mere acts of charity, but by a system of justice under which they will be helped to help themselves. When the Kingdom is established, when God's will is being done, people will be brotherly enough to see to it that none hunger in vain, either for food or for social and economic justice (p. 45).

The use of the Bible typified by Macintosh had important effects upon the work of Christian ethics. It permitted a "translation" of biblical ideas into contemporary language in such a way that a program for "objective ethics"—that is, for the shaping of moral action in the world—could be authorized by the Bible. The kingdom of God could become a kind of co-operative democratic commonwealth, and thus provide the end toward which man's historical activity is to be directed. The beatitude "Blessed are the poor" could become the basis for proposing a genuinely "Christian communism" as both the ideal toward which men should move and the state of life that will exist in the kingdom.

But even before Macintosh wrote, the assumptions upon which this use of the Bible was made in ethics were undercut radically by biblical scholars. Much earlier, Albert Schweitzer had suggested that Jesus' ethic was an "interim" one, to be valid until the soon forthcoming kingdom would arrive. The form critics were questioning the historical authenticity of many of the sayings of Jesus, as well as narratives about him. And historically-minded men were raising questions about the easy translation of first-century language, with its own particular metaphors, into contemporary social life. If the words of the Bible were to be morally authoritative, the writer in Christian ethics had to find some other way to use them. In America as in Europe, he generally chose to depend upon a summary statement of them, such as in the command to love God and thy neighbor. Or biblical words became first of all a revelation of God, and the morality of the Bible more illustrative of a proper life in relation to God and man than a revealed morality. Certainly, what Carl F. H. Henry suggests as revealed morality is generally rejected or radically qualified, and most recent writers would never try to move from biblical statements to contemporary moral statements in the manner of D. C. Macintosh.

Love: the summary of biblical ethics. The "law of love" became the major summary generalization of biblical morality. Reinhold Niebuhr, it will be recalled, suggested the centrality of love as the distinctive

element in Christian ethics. Earlier for Niebuhr the source for this norm was primarily the transcendent morality introduced by the teachings of Jesus; later the crucifixion became the symbol of the highest form of love. In either case, the Bible presents to us an expectation that life is to be governed both inwardly and outwardly by love, both in the intentions of the moral man and in the formation of a state of affairs in the world. Niebuhr's long-time colleague John C. Bennett, whose writings and work in ecclesiastical and ecumenical agencies are of central importance to the story of Christian ethics in recent decades, also fixes upon love as the mark of Christian ethics. "The distinctive element in Christian ethics is the primacy of love, the self-giving love that is known fully to Christian faith in the Cross of Christ" (in A. Dudley Ward, ed., *Goals of Economic Life,* 1953, p. 421). Thus a generalization is made on the basis of the Bible, a generalization that is moral in its language, based upon both moral teachings and example in the New Testament. This view of the Bible builds in a problem of translation, or at least transition, from the general moral propositions given in historically unachievable terms to the realities of the time-bound, historically contingent world. The transition from Bible to contemporary world is then made through the use of less uniquely Christian "values" or terms, such as justice. These terms, and more explicit imperative propositions derived from them, in turn regulate the ends to be sought by moral man and the forms of action he will use to seek those ends. The pure morality of love is always compromised in the movement from the Bible to the world. But there is a sense in which the Bible still contains a revealed morality: it provides distinctive moral norms or values that have authority for the Christian community. These now have a generalized form, rather than the form of the particular propositions given in particular biblical texts. Compromise is required when men who use the Bible in this way wish Christian ethics to inform social and political moral responsibility, and not be merely the "narrow way" for an exemplary Christian community. This use of the Bible is consistent with the preceding generation of liberal theologians, who found in its morality the pattern for contemporary morality; the Bible continued to be in some sense a book of moral teachings with a high level of authority.

The Bible: revealed reality rather than revealed morality.

Concurrently, however, a revolution in biblical theology was taking place in Europe and, to a lesser extent, in America. The shift might be overstated as one from ethics to faith, from religion to God, from man to Jesus

Christ. Under the impact of the crisis theologians, and particularly Karl Barth, men were saying that the Bible is not the revelation of a morality, but the revelation of the living God; it does not cultivate a human cultural phenomenon called religion that has any significance in its own right, but it points to God and to God's call to men for faith in him; it is not centered upon what men are and ought to do, but upon Jesus Christ as the revelation of God, in the light of whom theological knowledge of men comes. This revolution in theology had much more far-reaching consequences for Christian ethics than did the reassessment of the moral potentialities of men, for it changed the prime point of reference for all thinking in ethics and all moral activity on the part of Christians. In the place of moral teachings, particularized or generalized, the new theology put God in his living, free activity. Thus Christian ethics had to think not about morality reduced to propositions, but about God and how life ought to be rightly related to his power and his presence. The Bible then finds a different use in the thinking of ethics, and its moral teachings are set in a different context. For Carl F. H. Henry both knowledge of God and moral knowledge are authoritatively given in "propositional revelation" in the words of the Bible. For Macintosh the Bible did not give propositional revelation, but its moral teachings expressed the spirit of the "Jesus of history" and thus in turn were a basic blueprint for morality. For Reinhold Niebuhr and John C. Bennett the Bible was not propositional revelation, but revealed God's self-sacrificial love, which in turn was conceptualized in images of commands and love. But for Karl Barth, the Bible first of all points toward the living God, known in Jesus Christ, and thus what is required of ethics is obedience to a Person, not a proposition, or, in the language of H. Richard Niebuhr, *response* to a Person, and not a rule.

H. Richard Niebuhr: response to a revealing God. This change in the fundamental way of thinking, and thus in the use of the Bible, can be illustrated by some of the work of H. Richard Niebuhr. He found too much of Christian ethics trying to find "Christian answers" to problems of morality and culture, rather than being open and responsive to the work of the living Lord. In introducing his great work on *Christ and Culture* [Harper & Bros., 1951], Niebuhr says, "The belief which lies back of this effort . . . is the conviction that Christ as Living Lord is answering the question in the totality of history and life in a fashion which transcends the wisdom of all his interpreters yet employs their partial insights and their necessary conflicts" (p. 2). The crucial point is the stress on the

notion that the *"Living Lord is answering"* in the totality of history and life. There are interpretations of what he is doing, but men are not finally to rely upon them, though they give partial insights. This means, it appears, that the Bible itself is of penultimate significance in the work of Christian ethics and that its importance is to enable men to understand and interpret what the "Living Lord" is saying and doing. It points beyond itself; its moral teachings point beyond themselves; the Christian community is to understand its morality in response to God rather than in response to statements about God. The Bible is more important for helping the Christian community to interpret the God whom it knows in its existential faith than it is for giving a revealed morality that is to be translated and applied in the contemporary world. This led Niebuhr to be critical of theologians who use such phrases as "the absolutism and perfectionism of Jesus' love ethic," including his distinguished brother. He retorts, "Jesus nowhere commands love for its own sake"; the virtue of Jesus' character and demand is not "love of love" but "love of God and the neighbor in God." "It was not love but God that filled his soul" (*Christ and Culture,* pp. 15-19). The Christian moral life, then, is not a response to moral imperatives, but to a Person, the living God.

The effect of this transposition in the function of the Bible can be seen in H. Richard Niebuhr's almost lyrical description of the meaning of love in Christian ethics. It is not a norm. Rather, love is an indicative before it is an imperative. "Faith in God's love toward man is perfected in man's love to God and neighbor."

> Through Jesus Christ we receive enough faith in God's love toward us to see at least the need for and the possibility of a responsive love on our part. We know enough of the possibility of love to God on our part to long for its perfection; we see enough of the reality of God's love toward us and neighbor to hope for its full revelation and so for our full response."

Love is not a law, but "rejoicing over the existence of the beloved one"; it is "gratitude" for the existence of the beloved; it is "reverence" that "keeps its distance even as it draws near"; it is "loyalty," the "willingness to let the self be destroyed rather than that the other cease to be" [*The Purpose of the Church and Its Ministry,* Harper & Bros., 1956, pp. 33, 35]. Love is basically defined, then, in terms of attitudes and actions; it comes into being in the close interrelation of "God's love of the self and neighbor, of the neighbor's love of God and self, and of the self's love of God and neighbor." What the Bible makes known, then, is not a morality, but a *reality*, a living presence to whom man responds. For questions of morality, its authority is "educational," giving men knowledge of themselves and knowledge of God in the light of which they interpret their responsibilities and act; its authority is "corroborative," providing a court of validation that aids the Christian community in seeing its perversities and in verifying its true purposes.

Paul Lehmann: ethics of the biblical indicative. The alteration of the imperative mode in Christian ethics that is present in the writings of H. Richard Niebuhr is even stronger in the work of Paul Lehmann. In a widely acclaimed essay of 1953 ("The Foundation and Pattern of Christian Behavior," in *Christian Faith and Social Action,* ed. John A. Hutchison) that influenced the writing of Albert Rasmussen (*Christian Social Ethics,* 1956), Alexander Miller (*The Renewal of Man,* 1955), and others, Lehmann states that "an ethic, based upon the self-revelation of God in Jesus Christ, is more concerned about 'The Divine Indicative' than it is about the 'Divine Imperative.' The primary question is not 'What does God command?' The primary question is 'What does God do?'" (p. 100). Thus, the importance of the Bible for Christian ethics does not lie in its moral imperatives, but in its delineation of what God is doing to "make and keep life human." "Christian ethics . . . is oriented toward revelation and not toward morality"; and "Christian ethics aims, not at morality, but at maturity. The *mature* life is the fruit of Christian faith. Morality is a by-product of maturity" (*Ethics in a Christian Context,* 1963, pp. 45, 54). The importance of the Bible is what it tells about Jesus Christ. Thus in Lehmann's full-length treatise on Christian ethics there is no significant treatment of biblical morality, even as a guide to the mature life. Rather, the mature man discerns through his transformed motivation and his sensitive imagination what God is doing and, therefore, what man should do in correspondence with what God is doing.

Joseph Sittler: the shape of the engendering deed. In a similar mode is the most significant contribution to Christian ethics in America made by a Lutheran theologian, Joseph Sittler's *The Structure of Christian Ethics* [Louisiana State University Press, 1958]. (Lutherans have only within the past decade begun to produce significant literature in Christian ethics: the work of George Forell, William Lazareth, and Franklin Sherman shows the emerging interest.) Sittler wishes to develop biblical ethics. But he does not do this from the distinctly moral statements in the Bible. Rather, there is a more important structure for understanding Christian morality that can be seen in the fact that God is not defined, but simply is what he does; that a vocabulary of relatedness rather than a vocabulary of substance abounds; that its logic is "the inner logic of the living, the organic." Biblical language is primarily descriptive and indicative. Jesus himself is to be seen in this way: the content of his importance is constituted "by a lived-out and heroically obedient God-relationship in the fire of which all things are what they are by virtue of the creator, all decisions are crucial in virtue of their witness to his primacy and glory, all events interpreted in terms of their transparency, recalcitrancy, or service to God's Kingly rule" (p. 12). The prime importance of the Bible for ethics is that it tells the story of "the shape of the engendering deed," that is, the record of what the living God has actually done in creation, redemption, and sanctification. The living God continues to engender man's involvement in what he is doing. Thus Christian ethics gives an account of the Christian life:

> A re-enactment from below on the part of man of the shape of the revelatory drama of God's holy will in Jesus Christ. . . . Suffering, death, burial, resurrection, a new life—these are actualities that plot out the arc of God's self-giving deed in Christ's descent and death and ascension; and precisely *this same shape of grace,* in its recapitulation within the life of the believer and the faithful community, is the nuclear matrix which grounds and unfolds as the Christian life (p. 36).

Christian ethics is the actualization of God's justification of man. It describes life according to a plotted arc; the arc, however, is not the morality given in the Bible, but rather the "shape of the engendering deed."

This indicative mode, with its particular use of the Bible, has not gone unchallenged in American Protestant ethics. It has been criticized in the extreme form for the absence of any procedures of rational reflection about what men are to do. Paul Ramsey, Robert Fitch, Alvin Pitcher, Clinton Gardner, and John C. Bennett have all written critiques on this issue. Indeed, it tends to become what has been called a "contextual" ethics, and against this has been pitted an "ethics of principles," which finds propositional moral imperatives, either directly from the Bible or mediated through the tradition, that are to provide the guidelines of conduct. This issue is reserved for exploration in the next section, "Procedures for Ethical Reflection."

The Bible in Roman Catholic ethics. The use of the Bible has traditionally been the place where the difference between Roman Catholic and Protestant Christian ethics was clearest. Whereas most Protestants have turned to the Bible for the starting point of Christian ethics, whether personal or social, for most questions Roman Catholics have relied upon the natural law that is, in their interpretation, shared by all mankind. The recent American Catholics have shared in that tradition. There is a "science of ethics" independent from revelation. Indeed, the term *Christian ethics* has not been widely used among Roman Catholic writers. For most ethical questions, the distinctively Christian elements have not been of great importance. For example, one of the most widely read recent treatises on matters of American public ethics—*We Hold These Truths* (1960), by John Courtney Murray, S.J.—contains no references to biblical texts that Protestants traditionally grapple with on questions of the state, such as Romans 13:1-7. There is no effort to define what is going on in contemporary society in terms of "what God is doing." Rather, the theoretical foundations are in the Thomistic tradition of natural law. "The doctrine of natural law has no Roman Catholic presuppositions. Its only presupposition is three-fold: that man is intelligent; that reality is intelligible; and that reality, grasped by intelligence, imposes on the will the obligation that it be obeyed in its demands for action or abstention" (p. 109). Most questions of ethics, and particularly public ethics, are dealt with on this natural-law foundation. The more distinctive "Christian" elements of religion deal with the theological virtues and with man's supernatural end, and these relate indirectly back upon the rational moral life. But even here the traditional pattern for interpretation is Thomistic, rather than in the first instance biblical. The morality of saints, with their imitations of Christ, has not been a general expectation for all Christians.

The major American treatise entitled *Christian Ethics* written by a Roman Catholic is remarkably free of biblical references. Dietrich von Hildebrand, in his 1953 publication, makes of Christian ethics a philosophical discipline that is distinct from moral theology.

> It is a pure philosophical exploration introducing no arguments which are not accessible through our *lumen naturale* (light of reason), whereas in moral theology faith is presupposed, and revealed truth which surpasses our reason is included in the argumentation. Christian ethics is a strict *philosophical* analysis, starting from the data accessible to our mind through experience [David McKay Co., p. 455].

All morality presupposes the existence of God, and the philosophical analysis of Christian morality obviously assumes that many human moral responses and virtues are possible only through Christian revelation. But the analysis does not begin with the datum of revelation in the Bible.

To look for the use of the Bible in Roman Catholic morality, then, one turns to *moral theology* and to the discussions of the Christian virtues. Moral theology presupposes divine revelation "and the proved conclusions of dogmatic theology." In moral theology texts long used in America, such as *Moral and Pastoral Theology,* by Henry Davis, S.J., there is a characteristic structure that brings no surprises. The Bible is used to substantiate the existence of a supernatural, ultimate end for man—namely, that he is to enjoy eternal beatitude in the vision of God. But the bulk of moral theology deals with the natural moral acts of man; here the Thomistic structure asserts itself vigorously as the dominant framework, and the Bible is quoted (so it appears to these Protestant eyes) to proof-text a point already established on principles independent of biblical discussion. Or the Bible is quoted as the divine revealed law that, like the natural law, participates in the eternal law in the mind of God. As particular instances of moral problems come into view, the procedures of casuistry are employed with great rational refinement, in contrast with what Sittler called the "organic language" of the scripture.

There are evidences of a changing pattern in Roman Catholic moral theology, however, that ought to be noted. Two currently widely read texts in moral theology—Bernard Häring's *The Law of Christ* [2 vols.; English trans., Paulist-Newman Press, 1961, 1963. Copyright © 1961 by The Newman Press] and Gérard Gilleman's *The Primacy of Charity in Moral Theology* (English trans., 1959)—and other writings appear to soften the distinction between the natural and the supernatural, and to place Christian love at the center of the whole interpretation of ethics. Indeed, the biblical text that gives these books of European origin their titles is from Romans: "For the law of the Spirit of the life in Christ Jesus has delivered me from the law of sin and of death." Whereas traditional Catholic ethics deals with the natural principles of morality first, and later comes to the higher law of love, Häring, Gilleman, and others begin with the more distinctively Christian and biblical principle of love and seek to keep it at the center of the whole enterprise of moral theology. A few quotations from Häring's Foreword demonstrate the new emphasis. "The principle, the norm, the center, and the goal of Christian Moral Theology is Christ. The law of the Christian is Christ Himself in Person. He alone is our Lord, our Saviour. In Him we have life and therefore also the law of our life." The emphasis here is on a *Christian* ethics, expressing the religious relationship with God in moral terms.

In the love of and through the love of Christ for us He invites our love in return, which is a life truly formed in Christ. The Christian life is following Christ, but not through mere external copying, even though it be in love and obedience. Our life must above all be a life in Christ. Christian morality is life flowing from the victory of Christ, the hopeful anticipation of the Second Coming of the Saviour in the glorious manifestation of His final triumph on the great day of judgment (*The Law of Christ*, vol. I, p. vii).

Moral theology is reaffirming the biblical tradition, reaffirming those aspects of the Catholic tradition that set Christian ethics in the context of God's loving action and see the norm for every man to be a life sharing in union with Christ and in imitation of him. Häring affirms his purpose to be to expound the most central truths in the light of the inspired word of the Bible. Younger American clergy are quickly beginning to think in those new modes, and no doubt the Bible will find a different place in indigenous American moral theology as a result.

Discussion of the Christian virtues is a second place to see the use of the Bible. Traditionally, Catholics have tended to follow Thomas Aquinas in his distinction between the cardinal virtues and the theological virtues. The latter—faith, hope, and love—are gifts of grace given by participation in the sacramental life of the church. For them, obviously there is a distinctive Christian referrent, derived through Catholic interpretation from the Bible. This two-level interpretation, however, is also being altered. A notable American book, Dietrich von Hildebrand's *Transformation in Christ,* is one example of a more biblically centered (though obviously Catholic and not Protestant in exposition) interpretation of the Christian life. Perhaps the text that is central to this book is from 1 Peter 2: "That you may declare his virtues, who hath called you out of darkness into his marvelous light." It is a book that seeks to describe how, through baptism and communion, man is allowed to participate in the life of Christ. The shaping of the Christian life is not so much a matter of external heteronomous norms by which men are to be governed and ruled as it is one of finding the appropriate expression in life for what God has done for man in Jesus Christ. The "supernatural life" is not relegated to achievement by those set apart in the orders, nor is it in von Hildebrand's treatment something to be received in the life beyond death; it is both a reality and a task for the Christian believer (the author is himself a layman) in his present existence.

If a study of more recent Roman Catholic ethics leaves a correct impression, it is clear that the Bible is coming to play a far more significant role and have a more central location in Catholic literature. The traditional distinctions between the ethics of natural law and special Christian morality are being blurred. The biblical witness to God's own presence and action as being both matrix and context for Christian life is being stressed. And the central biblical conception of Christian love is becoming the norm under which all action is judged and directed. Yet no important writers have left the traditional philosophical language behind. What the impact of these mostly imported European writings will be on American Catholic ethics is still unclear, but if it continues to make its way on this continent, men like Father Murray who have reputations in Protestant America for being liberals are likely to appear to be highly traditionalistic.

European influences have been very important among both Catholics and Protestants in altering the place of the Bible in the study of Christian ethics. Between the World Wars American Protestant theologians followed the developments and debates of European theology and biblical scholarship with increasing care. The ecumenical movement, particularly the great 1938 Oxford Conference on Life and Work, provided the occasion for personal discussion and for the influence of Europeans on American ethics. The struggle of the confessing Christians in Germany against the Nazi state provided one of the most significant occasions in modern church history for reflections on the relation of biblical faith to moral concerns. Some of the writings of participants in the "theological revival" in Europe were translated into English. Anders Nygren's *Agape and Eros* was particularly influential in raising issues about the meaning of Christian love.

Since World War II, many important volumes of European theological ethics have become available in English and thus are widely read by students and teachers alike: H. Emil Brunner's *The Divine Imperative,* major volumes of Barth's *Church Dogmatics* that deal with ethics, the writings of Dietrich Bonhoeffer, Kierkegaard, Rudolf Bultmann, Helmut Thielicke, Gustaf Aulen, Gustaf Wingren, Jacques Ellul, and others. The points at issue between these writers are important, and the American reception of them has not lacked in discriminating sophistication. They all do, however, work from an understanding of the high theological authority of the Bible and thus, as conversation partners for American theological ethics, keep the Bible quite at the center of discussion.

Among Roman Catholics, biblical studies have had a new status in all spheres of theological research and discourse since World War II. This is bound to have effects not only on dogmatic theology, but also upon traditional Catholic distinctions between the general science of ethics, moral theology, ascetic theology, pastoral theology, and so forth. Very important also is the way in which the renewal of interest in biblical studies in both

Catholicism and Protestantism has coincided with the expansion of the ecumenical discussion. It is clear that one of the directions that scholarship in Christian ethics will take in the next decades is cross-confessional critique and interpretation nourished in part by a common interest in the Bible as the charter document for the Christian movement in history. And one of the questions that will be dealt with is that of the relation between revealed reality (God's presence, his love, his sustaining and redeeming work) and morality (the shape of personal life and social order that is appropriate to faith in God). One aspect of this question is what procedures of ethical reflection are appropriate to the Christian community and to Christian theology.

Procedures of Ethical Reflection

The basic theological convictions of a scholar in Christian ethics deeply affect the manner in which he will delineate the procedures of ethical reflection. If the Bible is a revealed morality, either he will require a literal obedience to its moral teachings or he will design a procedure by which they can be applied to contemporary experience. If moral propositions can be derived from the nature of man's being, these must be brought to bear upon behavior. If man is interpreted as a creature responding to the presence of God and his work in the world, the scholar must describe a way to discern whether one's response is "fitting" or coincides with what God is doing. If the tradition provides viable summary propositions concerning Christian morality, these must be directed to current issues of morality. The scholar's view of the Bible and its importance, of man and his relation to others, and of God and the mode of his involvement in the world will shape the pattern of his ethical thought.

In recent American Protestant literature, advocates of positions sometimes called "contextualism" and an "ethics of principles" have published a series of charges against one another. *Ethics of inspiration* and *ethics of ends* are the terms the English ecumenical leader J. H. Oldham has used to describe the positions. The discussion is grossly oversimplified in its polarized form, but it points to two tendencies present in recent discussion. Paul Lehmann is the contextualist par excellence; H. Richard Niebuhr's thought tends to go toward contextualism, though by a different path. The name is earned by virtue of the stress placed upon doing the right thing in relation to what is occurring. What is occurring has both its empirical aspects (a reading of the events and the times) and its theological aspects (discerning what God is doing). Those who apply the term *contextualism* prejoratively see little place for the use of traditional ethical principles and moral reasoning in this mode of work. They see in it an excessively existentialist posture that relies too heavily upon imagination, intuition, and free response. Paul Ramsey and John C. Bennett have been, in different ways, the defenders of "principles." They have stressed the importance of statements of moral imperatives: in Bennett's case, *goals* derived from the biblical norm of love; in Ramsey's case, *principles of right conduct* shaped by Christian love and natural law. The critics of ethics of principles believe that this view errs in not taking the activity of the living God as the theological starting point for ethics; that it excessively intellectualizes the moral life by reducing it to the logical applications of ethical generalizations; and that consequently it has a hard time closing the gap between principles and actions.

The issues that divide the extremes are hardly theological alone, however, for theologians display in their procedures affinities for certain points of view in philosophy. It is not an accident that Lehmann finds William James to be a congenial philosopher, and that H. Richard Niebuhr is indebted to G. H. Mead, to Martin Buber, and other existentialists. It is clear that Ramsey wants to be identified with the natural law tradition, with its affirmations of man's capacity to appropriate moral truth and to exercise his reason in the direction of his action. Though he is harder to identify with particular philosophers, John C. Bennett shows the marks of the kind of moral idealism (not with reference to the expectation of moral perfection, but to the distinction between ideal and actual) that informed liberal Protestant ethics.

Roman Catholicism has traditionally been on the "principles" side of this particular polarization, finding laws both in nature and in scripture that are to be applied to the actualization of the inherent purposes in man. But with the new stresses on biblical theology in Catholicism, and with the impact of the language from phenomenological existentialism, one finds movement out of the traditional procedures into a more situational approach. American Catholic writers tend to be critical of situational ethics: this can be seen especially in *Contemporary Moral Theology* (1958) by John C. Ford, S.J., and Gerald Kelly, S.J. In his widely read article "Situational Morality" (*Thought*, XXXII [1957], 533-58), Robert Gleason, S.J., states the issue in the following terms:

> The ultimate differences between this new morality and traditional morality come down then to this: in an objective system of ethics the moral judgment is submitted to an extrinsic norm, an ontological norm founded

on the principles of being. In situational ethics the moral judgment is measured only by the subjective, immanent light of the individual in question.

Gleason gives a more sympathetic interpretation of contextualism than do Ford and Kelly, but in the end he is sharply critical. "The subjectivism and relativism that are in some degree implicit in situational ethics make it quite unacceptable to the Christian mind, even though the excellent intentions and partial intuitions of the system may be admired" (pp. 555, 558).

Contextualists earn the appellation for different reasons. Some, such as Kenneth Underwood, who are concerned with social policy, believe that the moralist must have technical knowledge of economics, political science, urban renewal, or other pertinent areas. For them, one cannot be a good ethicist without knowing the "nonethical" materials about which moral judgments are to be made. Sociological, political, economic, and other kinds of research are necessary for the intelligent conduct of ethical discourse. Social action and policy statements require such information. A recent example of literature that stresses this point is Bruce Morgan's *Christians, The Church, and Property* (1963). This affirmation of the importance of technical knowledge, however, is accepted by such people as Ramsey and Bennett.

Others are called contextualists for doctrinal reasons. If one stresses *the freedom of God* to do and to command different things at different times, a sensitivity to the changing conditions under which moral responsibility is exercised is necessary. There are no fixed rules through which God acts; there are no absolutely clear principles that govern the divine ordering of the world. Paul Lehmann, in this instance following closely upon Karl Barth, invokes the freedom of God as the theological principle of prime importance in the determination of thought and action in Christian ethics —it is more important than God's love or God's law, for example. If the Christian ethical thinker stresses in his doctrine of God the present *creating, governing, and redeeming work of God* in the world, he must seek to interpret the events and situations of which he is a part in the light of these theological affirmations. Thus, in the ethics of H. Richard Niebuhr one finds the dictum "Responsibility affirms: 'God is acting in all actions upon you. So respond to all actions upon you as to respond to his action' " (*The Responsible Self*, p. 126). Each occasion of responsibility requires an action that is fitting to the actions that are occurring in which God is himself acting. The ability to interpret situations in the light of theological principles is stressed.

Contextualism is derived not only from certain doctrines of God but from certain Christological emphases as well. Proponents of an ethics of principles tend to stress Christ as a source of moral norms that stem from both his teachings and his deeds, whereas contextualists tend to stress Christ as the living, reigning Lord. Paul Lehmann, for example, builds his Christian ethics upon the idea that in the lordship of Christ a new humanity has been given. The world is to be regarded in the light of the victory of Christ over the powers of sin, death, and law. Both believer and unbeliever are confronted by an environment "being shaped by Christ's royal and redemptive activity." The moral action of Christians has the symbolic significance of pointing to what Christ is doing for men in the fact of their new humanity that he has given. Thus there are no set principles that define what men ought to do; Christians are to have "imaginative and behavioral sensitivity to what God is doing in the world to make and to keep human life human, to achieve the maturity of men, that is, the new humanity" (*Ethics in a Christian Context,* p. 117). For Joseph Sittler, Christian action is defined in terms of the "re-enactment" in every sphere and realm of life of the "shape of grace" that has been given in Christ. The relation of the moral actor to the world is an organic one; he participates in its life in a way analogical to the way Christ has participated in the life of the world. This cannot be reduced to principles or to rules of conduct, but is a matter of living out our justification in Christ, of "faith-facts" in which the action of men will be appropriate to the occasion.

Certain views of the nature of man also lead to a contextualism. This is clearest in H. Richard Niebuhr's notion of the man living in response to actions upon him. As we have seen, he distinguishes his view from teleological and deontological views. In the Christian form of the first, man is reminded that God has a plan for his life and that he is to shape his life according to a plan. This would lead, in its procedures of moral reflection, to the delineation of what God's plan is, and then to a means-ends scheme to bring the actual conditions into accord with that plan. In the Christian form of deontological ethics, man is reminded that he is to obey God's law in his obedience to all finite rules. This would lead to the delineation of how finite rules are related to God's law and to an assessment of which particular rules are most in accord with God's rule. In contrast to these, the idea that man is characterized by responses to particular actions upon him makes the definition of moral responsibility by means of plans, ends, and rules almost invalid. Man is in a pattern of relationships; he is to do what is fitting in response to what is being done to him.

The effect of these various reasons for espousing contextualism on the procedures of reflection and action becomes clear. The ethical thinker does not design ideal schemes and then propose the procedures by which they can be actualized. For one thing, changing historical circumstances make this impossible. One cannot control the shape of events that are subject to so many different sources of determination. God has not provided some grand plan for the world's moral life; he is not the great designer, but the active being who calls for proper action in the face of new occasions and new opportunities. To be sure, the Christian community is to act in accord with what it believes God to be saying and doing, but the mode of discerning this is not the delineation of a set of goals or rules, but the *interpretation* of events as occasions in which God's humanizing work (Lehmann) or God's governing and redeeming work (H. Richard Niebuhr) is occurring. God is not the lawgiver, and man is not principally the being who obeys rules; God is the active being, and man is the responder to his actions.

To those who are schooled in more traditional procedures of ethical reflection, in the natural law tradition, the Kantian deontological tradition, or the tradition of moral idealism, this contextualism appears to be a chaotic wasteland, providing no firm basis for the determination of conduct and no clear rational procedures for prescription of action. It appears to rely too heavily on intuitive responses, upon the illumination of the Spirit in the moral life, on the capacity through imagination and sensitivity to discern what God is doing, and how man's action can be coincident with God's action. Not all contextualists are equally culpable on each charge, but on the whole they appear to underestimate the importance of traditional modes of ethical reflection and are in danger of permitting what actually is occurring to dominate morality, of having the empirical *is* overwhelm the moral *ought*.

The tension between ethics of principles and contextualism is not new in the history of Christian ethics. Father Edward Duff, in *The Social Thought of the World Council of Churches* (1956), indicates that these two emphases represent roughly certain Roman Catholic and Protestant tendencies on the history of ethics. Not all Protestants would agree that Protestantism provides an ethics of inspiration, and in the contemporary American scene there have been counterstatements in the face of the emergence of American contextualism. Two important writers, until now only briefly mentioned, can be interpreted as resisters to contextualism and as affirmers of an important place for principles in Christian ethical discourse. They are John C. Bennett and Paul Ramsey. To Protestant writers can be added the continuing tradition of Roman Catholic natural law ethics, vigorously espoused and widely influential in this country through the writings of the American John Courtney Murray, S.J., and others.

John C. Bennett has had a long career of writing in Christian ethics and of involvement in ecumenical social thought and action. A brief but very influential book that he wrote in mid-career, *Christian Ethics and Social Policy* (1946), illustrates the particular way in which he would use principles in the development of Christian social ethics. Bennett critically expounds four strategies of Christian social ethics—the Catholic, the sectarian, the identification of Christianity with particular social programs (often the error of the social gospel), and the "double standard for personal and public life"—that he finds characteristic of Lutheranism. He proceeds to develop a fifth strategy, which includes a statement of procedure for the formation of social goals. In fairness to Bennett, this goal-forming procedure has to be set in the context of other elements of his fifth strategy: these are the control of the *motives* of Christians by their faith and ethics in making decisions, the self-criticism that is encouraged by Christian humility, the criticism of all proposals in the light of Christian love, and the margin of freedom that is given to Christians in the exercise of any policy or judgment. For purposes of indicating the issues that are drawn between contextualism and principles, however, Bennett's notion of "middle axioms" is of particular significance.

The idea of middle axioms was first expressed in those words by J. H. Oldham in *The Church and Its Function in Society* (1937), a volume written in preparation for the Oxford Conference of 1938 held by the Life and Work Movement. Oldham states that "middle axioms" are "an attempt to define the directions in which, in a particular state of society, Christian faith must express itself. They are not binding for all time, but are provisional definitions of the type of behavior required of Christians at a given period and in given circumstance" (p. 210). Bennett suggests that a middle axiom "is more concrete than a universal ethical principle and less specific than a program that includes legislation and political strategy" [*Christian Ethics and Social Policy*, Charles Scribner's Sons, p. 77]. These axioms are to "give a sense of direction" to the activities of Christians. There is no Christian formula that can be given to the particular issues of foreign policy, or economic life, or strategy for race relations, but there are provisional statements that can be made of goals that represent the purpose of God in a particular time.

An example will show how this procedure works. Christian love is a universal principle that cannot be easily applied to the area of economic life. Yet Christians are involved in the debates between free enterprise and social planning, and between particular policy options on particular levels of legislation and bargaining. Bennett proposes two middle axioms that could be a minimum basis for common action by American Christians: "That the national community acting through government in cooperation with industry, labor, and agriculture has responsibility to maintain full employment" and "That the national community should prevent all private centers of economic power from becoming stronger than the government" (p. 81). These axioms, then, provide a statement of consensus (hopefully) that is formed with reference to universal moral principles, and with reference to the American economy as of 1946. They posit goals (full employment), means to achieve them (government action), and rules for the limitation of conduct (private interests must not become stronger than the national interest). These goals, means, and rules can then inform the discussions of particular policies, and can be applied to particular actions.

What would a contextualist response be to this kind of proposal? Those concerned with disciplined knowledge of the facts of economic life and policy would suggest that one has not yet gotten to the real moral and technical issues, if this is where Christian ethics ends. The crucial issues are in the analysis of what constitutes full employment (what percentage of the labor force can be tolerated as "hardcore" unemployment, what rate of growth of national product is needed to achieve full employment, and so forth). The discussion of ethics must be embedded in the analysis of the information needed to make a decision, and in the very concrete formulations of policy.

From Lehmann's point of view, the critical issue is at another point, and can be stated in his own words.

> For a *koinonia* [contextual] ethic the clarification of ethical principles and their application to concrete situations is ethically unreal because such clarification is a logical enterprise and there is no way in logic of closing the gap between the abstract and the concrete. Ethics is a matter not of logic but of life, a certain kind of reality possessed by the concrete.

The resolution of a problem in economics is not ethical because it has been directed by moral principles. Economic action is ethical insofar "as it bears the marks of God's transformation of the world in accordance with his purposes, of the world's resistance to what God is doing, and of God's ultimate overcoming of the world." An action is ethical "in so far as it is a *sign* of the new humanity" (*Ethics in a Christian Context,* p. 152). The defender of principles asks, "How does one discern what God is doing in the sphere of economic life, if not by the establishment of certain middle axioms or principles?" Lehmann appears to answer, "By the theonomous conscience that is sensitive to what God is doing."

The existence of such contextual ethics has been the occasion for Paul Ramsey to sharpen his polemic against the "wastelands of relativism," and to define a position he has called "Christ transforming natural law" or "faith effective through in-principled love." The crucial stress appears to be on the assertion that whatever transformation of the world Christ enables includes law, and that Christian freedom and love are normally expressed through rules of right conduct, through law. To state it another way, faith is active in love, as Luther and the Lutherans are quick to remind us, but the love through which faith is active is "in-principled." The ethical thinker and actor does not have to rely upon his more or less intuitive response to what is fitting in a particular event; he does not assume that his sensitivity and his theonomous conscience are adequate to discern the coincidence of his own free action and God's free action in the world. For Ramsey, speculation about consequences is hardly adequate to determine what is proper and improper.

Ramsey's view is most systematically worked out in *War and the Christian Conscience* [Reprinted by permission of the Publisher. Copyright 1961, Duke University Press, Durham, North Carolina]. This book has the merit of being a treatise in the methods of Christian ethical thought that at the same time deals substantively with a critical moral question, "How shall modern war be conducted justly?" This question, which forms the subtitle of the book, is itself stated in a way that indicates Ramsey's way of work. He does not first ask "For what ends can a war be fought?" but "*How* shall war be conducted?" With reference to war, as to other questions, the task of the Christian ethicist is to seek to determine what love permits and requires to be done and not to be done. "Thus, love posits or takes form in principles of right conduct which express the difference it discerns between permitted and prohibited action" (p. 4). For Ramsey, Christian ethics is not another form of utilitarianism, seeking to calculate prudentially the consequences of action according to technical political reason. To be sure, there is a place for consideration of the objectives of war. But one does not reason back from some statement of a calculated end to finding the means to achieve it. Ends and means interpenetrate, and this can be stated as follows: "Limited (or unlimited) means or weapons are available and resolved to be used, and *therefore* limited (or unlimited) political objectives may be thought to be proper goals in war" (p. 7). The decision of proper means of conduct is as important as that of objectives; Christian ethics deals with *right conduct* according to in-principled love, and not just with concern for good and evil consequences.

In his statement of this position Ramsey clearly has various contextualists in view, and might even include John C. Bennett's goal-forming and goal-seeking ethics under the banner of things he wishes to criticize.

> Those theologians who most stress the fact that Christian ethics is wholly predicated upon redemption or upon the Divine indicative, and who say that decisive action is made possible by virtue of *justification* in Christ and by God's *forgiveness,* are often precisely the thinkers who strip politics of norms and principles distinguishing between right and wrong action. For them policy decisions are always wholly relative or "contextual," pragmatically relating means to ends (pp. 12-13).

The course then is set for Ramsey's consideration of the problems of modern war, as it is for his consideration of questions of sexual morality or any other issue. There are reliable principles given to govern conduct. In the case of war these are the traditional ones of the just-war doctrine developed in Christian thought from the time of Augustine, and particularly the principle of noncombatant immunity. His argument is executed with a great deal of congeniality with Roman Catholic casuistry.

But Ramsey finds the natural law ethics of the Roman Catholic to be excessively static. The issue between Ramsey's procedure and that of Roman Catholics is not one of whether the principles of casuistry are too refined, but the relation of Christian love as a principle to "nature." He finds in Catholic arguments against abortion, for example, that the moral theologians fail "to allow divine charity any vital role in the matter of morality" (p. 176). Theoretical reflection about wrong and right in concrete cases needs to be "kept open to the impact and guidance of Christian love, rather than smothering the requirements of love under what 'nature itself teaches.' " "Charity enters into a fresh determination of what is right and wrong in the given concrete context, and it is not wholly in bondage to natural law determination of permitted or prohibited means. These rules are opened for review and radical revision in the instant *agape* controls" (pp. 177, 179). Finally, for Ramsey, as for Edward L. Long, principles of action devised in accordance with love are to be employed "not as a reliance but as a service."

Ramsey's position can be seen more sharply against that of Lehmann. For Ramsey, Christian love generally acts within the law and lays down rules or principles for the guidance of action, but it still exerts "a free and sovereign pressure—since Jesus Christ is Lord—toward fresh determination of what should be done in situations not rightly covered by the law, by natural justice, or even by its former articulation in principle" (p. 190). Ramsey works basically with Christian principles, and allows for the possibility that a more spontaneous act of love might be required. For Lehmann, to work with principles at all tends to become absolutistic, and the first fact is man's response in freedom to God's free action. Even in the determination of man's response there is little development of the place of rational moral reflection in Lehmann's book, though perhaps his theory permits more than in fact he has exercised. Lehmann works basically with open ends—man's freedom and God's freedom—and principles find little or no place.

Indeed, the proper method of reflection is just now a very live issue in Protestant Christian ethics, with Niebuhr's posthumous *The Responsible Self* joining works of Ramsey and Lehmann among the recent publications that address it. It is likely that the extreme poles set by Ramsey and Lehmann will both be subject to critical revision, and that a methodological pluralism will be recognized as valid in Christian ethics. Ramsey, as a previous quotation indicates, moves toward the "context" in which some more free spontaneous act is proper under certain circumstances. Lehmann frequently writes about God's "humanizing work," something that is probably capable of more precise explication in terms of moral principles than Lehmann gives. (See my "Context vs. Principles: A Misplaced Debate," *Harvard Theological Review*, April 1965, and below chapter 3.)

Perhaps a comparable dialogue is emerging in Roman Catholic ethics as well. At present, American Catholic moral theologians have in print no *radical* revisions of the traditional natural-law foundations or of the procedures of casuistry that have been exercised with reference to them. But the European trends referred to earlier will probably begin to have more effect at this point as well. Josef Pieper, in a widely read essay on "Prudence" [*The Four Cardinal Virtues,* copyright 1954, © 1955, 1959 by Pantheon Books, Inc., © 1965 Harcourt Brace Jovanovich, Inc.], suggests that the excessive refinements of casuistry are a symptom of the human desire to achieve security.

> It is rather that the striving for certainty and security can gravitate, by virtue of its own direction and its natural inclination, into the degenerate, anti-natural state of non-human rigidity. Indeed, this danger is all the greater the more powerfully the desire for certainty is concerned with the decision-making center of the spiritual person. Casuistry falls into this

trap the very moment it claims to be more than a (probably indispensable) makeshift, an aid for sharpening judgment, a technique for temporary approximation, and more than the manipulation of a lifeless model (p. 26).

The refinements of casuistry have their traditional authority sharply challenged: all casuistry can do is to provide aid, "certainly not . . . an absolute standard for making ethical judgments and performing ethical actions" (p. 27). Pieper maximizes the virtue of prudence, particularly Christian prudence that is molded by charity. This Christian prudence

> means precisely the throwing open of [the realm of determinative factors of our actions] and (in faith informed by love) the inclusion of new and invisible realities within the determinants of our decisions. . . . The highest and most fruitful achievements of Christian life depend upon the felicitous collaboration of prudence and charity (p. 37).

Not only the stress on the virtue of prudence, a possibility that exists within the Thomistic system, but also the introduction of the language of response and responsibility that one finds in Häring and others could radically alter the procedures of ethical reflection in Roman Catholic ethics. The freedom of conscience to determine what is the right action, the responsible action, after being informed by the moral tradition of the church, could lead in the direction of contextualism. The personalistic model in which the relation of the believer to Jesus Christ is now often interpreted could mean a stress on doing what is in accord with the gifts Christ has given, rather than doing what experts in casuistry define as proper conduct on the basis of their reasoning from natural law. The act might be the same, whether derived from one avenue or the other, but the context of meaning out of which it emerges would be different.

Christian Ethics in Relation to Other Fields

Having suggested the way in which Christian ethics is related to biblical, theological, and philosophical work, I shall try here to lift out more clearly some of the relations of Christian ethics to these and other disciplines, and to suggest some of the influences on Christian ethics from other studies.

Ethics and Biblical Studies

In spite of the great interest in ethics in the past thirty years, and in spite of the extensive growth of biblical studies, there is a paucity of material that relates the two areas in a scholarly way. Writers in ethics necessarily

make their forays into the Bible without the technical exegetical and historical acumen and skills to be secure in the way that they use biblical materials. But few biblical scholars have provided studies upon which writers in
ethics can draw.

One would think, for example, with the renewal of interest in biblical
theology and particularly in the Pauline and Johannine parts of the New
Testament, that major monographs would have been written on New Testament ethics or at least on the relation of the faith of the early Christian
community to its moral outlook. But this is not the case. For Pauline ethics, the best American work available is Morton Scott Enslin's *The Ethics
of Paul* (1930), which has recently been reprinted. Amos N. Wilder has
written occasional articles that relate New Testament themes to ethics, no-
tably his essay "Kerygma, Eschatology, and Social Ethics," in W. D. Davies and David Daube's *The Background of the New Testament and Its Eschatology* (1956). Occasional monographs, such as Clinton D. Morrison's
The Powers That Be (1960), bring technical exegetical competence to passages of Pauline materials that are important for ethics, but they are rare.

The ethical teachings of Jesus continue to be of great interest to both
biblical scholarship and Christian ethics. The principal movements of biblical interpretation that have brought a reassessment of their historical validity
and their place in theology and ethics, however, have been European in origin. Earlier it was the work of Albert Schweitzer; in the contemporary period it is the work of Rudolf Bultmann and other form critics. Amos N.
Wilder's *Eschatology and Ethics in the Teaching of Jesus* (1939; rev. ed.,
1950) is the major American interpretation of the questions involved, and
continues to be an important resource for the study of biblical ethics. A
major work by W. D. Davies, *The Setting of the Sermon on the Mount,*
has just been announced. Other American scholars who have written very
brief but useful studies in the contemporary period are John Knox (*The
Ethic of Jesus in the Teaching of the Church,* 1961) and E. C. Colwell
(*An Approach to the Teaching of Jesus,* 1947).

The resources of American Old Testament scholarship that contribute to
the study of ethics are even more meager. G. E. Wright's *God Who Acts*
(1952) provides an overview of a major theological theme that can be appropriated by ethics. James Muilenberg's essays on the prophetic ethics
are of some help—for example, his *Way of Israel* (1961). Various books
on Old Testament theology provide analyses of key terms in Hebrew ethics
(for example, Millar Burrows, *An Outline of Biblical Theology,* 1946) or
interpretations of key events in Israel's history, but no major treatises on
Old Testament ethics, as a whole or in part, have been provided.

Thus, for the biblical background of Christian ethics, one turns primarily to the work of European scholars. For Old Testament, the influence of such writers as Eichrodt and von Rad is beginning to be felt; for New Testament background, the works of Manson, Bultmann, and Cullman are particularly influential.

Work in Christian ethics is dependent upon biblical scholarship to some extent, but obviously moralists can never have the competence in the documentary and historical work that biblical scholars have. Further, the ethicist cannot adjudicate the competing interpretations within the biblical field, and therefore must make choices about the use of that material with reference to his own terms and interests. But it is not unfair to say that biblical scholars have provided a very limited amount of writing in ethics. More exegetical works like Edwin Larsson's *Christus als Vorbild* (1962) are needed.

Ethics and Philosophical Studies

The parallels between the problems dealt with in Christian ethics and in non-Christian philosophical ethics are notable. Questions of the authority of moral claims, of the nature and locus of the good, of the moral self— its motives, intentions, and actions—and of ethical reasoning are pervasive in ethical discourse, whether the language is particularly Christian or not. Some of this has been indicated in section 2. Here I shall limit my comments to designated points of view in philosophy, and the ways in which Christian ethics has or has not been related to them.

Logical positivism and, more particularly, linguistic analysis have swept across American philosophy with great rapidity in the contemporary period. Curiously, they have been largely ignored by writers in Christian ethics. This is easily understandable with reference to the work of A. J. Ayer, but the writings of such persons as Charles Stevenson, R. M. Hare, Patrick Nowell-Smith, Stephen Toulmin, H. D. Aiken, and Stuart Hampshire provide a less dogmatic way of working with the uses of language and with the relations of language, thought, and action. With some revision, the meta-ethics of these philosophers could well be pursued or paralleled in the areas of theological ethics. The effect might be a clarification of the logic of Christian moral discourse, an opening of new ways to pursue problems within systematic theological ethics, and a pedagogically significant approach to students schooled in such philosophy. As yet, however, there are no works written by Christian ethicists that seek critically to appropriate the philosophical procedures of linguistic analysis.

A brief example indicates what could be done. H. D. Aiken, who is more complex than the appellation *linguistic analyst* indicates, has an essay on "Levels of Moral Discourse" in his *Reason and Conduct* (1962). In this he suggests that moral discourse takes place on four levels: the "expressive level," the "level of moral rules," the "level of ethical principles," and the "post-ethical level." The last-named deals with the question "Why be moral?" The level of ethical principles asks whether the rules and convictions that govern conduct are really right, and why they are right. The level of moral rules asks what patterns of conduct and rules of behavior are appropriate under particular circumstances: the question is "What ought I to do?" The expressive level is more emotive in character, giving vent to moral approval or indignation. Surely the literature in Christian ethics works on all of these levels and on the relation of these levels to each other. I would suggest that Aiken's simple pattern could provide a way for clarifying the logical movement within Christian ethical thought, and could provide a framework for "unpacking" many hidden issues in Christian ethics. This is an area in which important work can be done in the future.

The other new movement in philosophy that has not been used significantly in Christian ethics, either by appropriation or in polemics, is existential phenomenology. This is identified with the names of Husserl, Heidegger, Merleau-Ponty, and perhaps Sartre. Since this movement is only currently getting wide introduction in America, particularly in its latter-day European forms, it is not surprising that it has been largely ignored. I have previously suggested the ways in which it is influencing Roman Catholic philosophy and indirectly moral theology. In American Protestantism its transmuted influence can be detected in the phenomenology of moral experience provided by H. Richard Niebuhr in *The Responsible Self*. Some of this work, together with writings such as Stuart Hampshire's *Thought and Action* (1959) and John MacMurray's *The Self as Agent* (1957) and *Persons in Relation* (1961), could provide a pattern for the construction of a phenomenology of Christian moral experience. This could take the shape of an analysis of the patterns of thought and action that are characteristic of Christian moral life. From this, in turn, a constructive interpretation of how the moral life ought to be conducted might be forthcoming.

Value theory seems to be passing from the scene in philosophical ethics, but it has had some importance in theological studies. The works of Hartmann, Urban, Scheler, and Perry come to mind, each with its own point of view. In Catholic ethics, Dietrich von Hildebrand's *Christian Ethics* is obviously indebted to objective value theory in ethics. Indeed, in a crucial point in his argument he suggests that an ethics derived exclusively from the "nature of being" (natural law ethics) has "mere factual and neutral character," whereas moral norms are rooted in values and thus "possess an outspoken importance and relevance." Norms derived from the immanent logic of being have only a hypothetical character, whereas those derived from objective values have a "categorial obligation" (pp. 180 ff). Von Hildebrand takes value theory as his primary philosophical stance, and the traditional philosophy of being is secondary in his development of Christian ethics.

In Protestant thought, H. Richard Niebuhr was most concerned to come to grips with value theory. This he did in several essays, but primarily in "The Center of Value" (reprinted in *Radical Monotheism*, 1960). There he develops a "relational value theory" that asserts that value arises when beings are related to each other. God is the center of values, and finally all values emerge in relation to him. Niebuhr shapes his view in argument against both subjective (Perry) and objective (Hartmann) value theories.

It is doubtful whether discussion between Christian ethics and value theory in the forms that it took during the decades 1920-40 will continue to be a major interest in Christian ethics. Yet, this might well be reopened if phenomenology becomes important, for such a value theorist as Hartmann conceived his task to be the delineation of a phenomenology of moral experience, and thus he was driven to deal with the ultimate status of "value"-experience.

The language and thought of existentialism has been pervasive in a great deal of contemporary theology and ethics, even when it has been metamorphosed so that its effects are not obviously clear. Certainly one of the elements of the contextualism now current is the influence of existentialism, stressing the personal responsibility of the free self to accept accountability for the shaping of the moral world by his individual action. The European theologians who are now influencing American Christian ethics have strongly personalistic models at the heart of their work: this is certainly true of Barth's hearing the command of God and responding to it in obedience; of Brunner's view of the existence of the truly Christian and moral community in the relationship of I to thou; of Bultmann's whole interpretation of the New Testament, and particularly of his view of faith as free obedience; of Bonhoeffer's stress upon obedience and suffering. On the American scene the impact can be seen in Reinhold Niebuhr's appropriation of Kierkegaard's views of finitude, anxiety, and sin, and his concern for the "dramatic" view of selfhood in *The Self and the Dramas of His-*

tory (1955); in H. Richard Niebuhr's "social existentialism" that he describes in *Christ and Culture* and in his notion of the self as "responding"; in Lehmann's stress on imagination, sensitivity, and freedom in the moral life; and in the lesser known works such as George Forell's *Ethics of Decision* (1955) and Gordon Kaufman's *The Context of Decision* (1961).

The American concern for social ethics, however, keeps the existentialist influence at a distance, or at least severely qualifies its appropriation in dealing with questions of public morality. The language of existentialism is more appropriate to the discussion of the individual's decision-making and the realm of interpersonal relations than it is to complex social policy. Americans have been concerned with large moral problems like the conduct of war, full employment, racial integration; they are concerned with policy, strategy, and tactics in these areas, and to these existentialism does not readily relate. Perhaps also, the existentialist posture is not attractive to much of the mood of American Christianity. Roman Catholicism particularly provides a mode and style of ethics that does not readily incorporate motifs from existentialism.

Older and more traditional philosophies have had a wider impact on Christian ethics. This is symbolized in the one contemporary book that seeks to relate theological and philosophical ethics as part of its major contribution, George Thomas's *Christian Ethics and Moral Philosophy* (1955). Thomas suggests that moral philosophy must be "transformed or 'converted'" before Christians make use of it. He goes on to discuss, then, mostly classical and historical writers: Plato, Aristotle, Kant, Paulsen, Sidgwick, Bradley, Nicolai Hartmann, and others. Paul Lehmann expounds various philosophies in his recent publication, including linguistic analysis, but obviously he is more at home with Aristotle, Kant, and particularly William James. Paul Ramsey's first book, *Basic Christian Ethics* (1950), shows his indebtedness at that time to philosophical idealism; his more recent writings show his indebtedness to the natural-law tradition. Surely Kant remains *the* philosopher of greatest impact on European Protestant ethics—Brunner and Barth particularly—just as Thomism is dominant in Catholic ethics. The Boston theologians acknowledge their continuation of a tradition grounded in German idealism. And pragmatism and utilitarianism, if only culturally absorbed, abound in the writings of the contextualists, of Reinhold Niebuhr and John C. Bennett, and almost all the publications that seek to deal with social policy.

This obvious deference to traditional philosophies provokes speculation. One reason for it could be simply that theological ethics is always out of date, because it takes at least thirty years for the Christian thinkers really to absorb what is going on in secular philosophy. Another reason could be that theologians working in ethics have been so preoccupied with actual moral problems and their solution that they have not consciously defined themselves in relation to current fields of philosophical study. A third might be that those philosophies that were more impregnated indirectly by theological modes of thought—Kantianism, Thomism, idealism—are naturally more congenial to theologians. Perhaps there is something correct about each of these reasons. In any case, it is clear that if Christian ethics is to be in conversation with contemporary movements in philosophy, a great deal of work needs to be done by theologians.

Ethics and Historical Studies

In addition to writing Christian ethics in response to biblical work and philosophy, it is quite appropriate to study Christian ethics as history. This can be done in several ways. A systematic Christian ethicist turns to historical figures to find insight on the questions he is dealing with in the present. This is the most common approach to history among Christian ethicists. Or a scholar might relate a particular ongoing tradition to contemporary problems: Roman Catholics interpret new issues out of a Thomistic background; Lutherans bring characteristic distinctions of law and gospel, two realms, and so forth, to bear on the present. Or Christian ethics can be studied as a field with its own history; that is, methods of historical research can be used on materials in ethics.

The most common use of history is turning to historical figures to see how they met certain perennial problems. One sees this in Ramsey's uses of Augustine, Thomas Aquinas, and others in the development of his own position on the just war; in Lehmann's frequent references to Luther and Calvin in the exposition of his theological foundations for ethics; in Reinhold Niebuhr's forays into Augustine, the reformers, and Kierkegaard; in H. Richard Niebuhr's reflections on the problem of Christ and culture in relation to a typology of historical solutions to this question.

Historical research on the development of Christian ethics is a rare thing in American scholarship. Histories of American Christian ethics have been done as often by "secular" historians as by church historians. Books by Meyer, Carter, and Robert Miller on the period from 1918 to 1940 are cases in point. H. Richard Niebuhr, in *Christ and Culture* and in *The Kingdom of God in America,* has provided us with the most competent historical work done by a man whose major concern is ethics. By and large, however, Americans must continue to rely upon European works for the history of

Christian ethics, most of which are written to defend a thesis: K. E. Kirk's *The Vision of God*, Anders Nygren's *Agape and Eros*, Newton Flew's *The Idea of Perfection*, Troeltsch's *The Social Teaching of the Christian Churches*, and Luthardt's *History of Christian Ethics*.

It is understandable that a scholar trained in ethics may not have the historical knowledge and the method to deal with the history of ethics. Roland Bainton, a church historian, has provided the most competent material written by an historian in his *The Travail of Religious Liberty* (1951), *Christian Attitudes Toward War and Peace* (1960), and *What Christianity Says About Sex, Love, and Marriage* (1957). William Cole has done a survey of teachings on sex in a book that has another purpose, *Sex in Christianity and Psychoanalysis* (1955). There are monographs on historical figures hidden in the archives of Ph.D. dissertations, but, in the main, historical research in Christian ethics has been badly neglected in America.

It is important for ethics that more be done. This is the case not merely to fill in lacunae on library shelves, but also to make contemporary writers and students aware of changing patterns of ethical thought and moral action, and some of the reasons why these shifts have occurred. Some of this occurs in general surveys of western morals by Crane Brinton and William E. H. Lecky, but more work of the sort done by Bainton is obviously required in future years.

Comparative Religious Ethics

A totally ignored area is that of comparative religious ethics. There are in a number of volumes both careful and not so careful differentiations between Protestant ethics and Catholic ethics, between Christian ethics and Jewish ethics. But careful comparative studies on particular figures are yet to be done even in these cases. Beyond that, there are in comparative religion texts some general remarks about the differences between Hindu, Islamic, Taoist, Buddhist, and Christian ethics, but nothing of major significance has been published in this regard. Again, the competence of a theologian working in ethics is quickly exceeded when this type of research and writing is engaged in, but certainly for the future more will need to be done. Perhaps the comparative sociologists of religion, building from Max Weber's studies of the religion, ethics, and cultures of Judaism, Protestantism, Chinese and Indian religions will provide the literature needed in this area.

This rapid overview of the literature relating Christian ethics to biblical, philosophical, historical, and other religious fields indicates that there is ample opportunity for further research and publication. It calls for persons trained in more than one discipline in most instances, i.e., in Bible and ethics, or in Hindu and Christian ethics. But because of the nature of the field of Christian ethics, it is important that such persons be trained.

Christian Ethics and Moral Problems

This chapter began with the contention that the dominant characteristic of American Christian ethics is its concern with practical moral issues. That theme has occasionally reappeared, but a full substantiation of the continuing importance of practical morality has now to be made. A survey of the literature indicates that the bulk of writing and thus the preoccupation of the teachers and scholars in Christian ethics continues to deal with Christian ethics in relation to particular moral questions. This is as true of the contemporary period as it was of earlier decades.

This becomes clear when the many general textbooks on Christian ethics are brought before review. The pattern is almost stereotyped: a brief section on biblical ethics, a brief section on historical ethics, particularly the Reformation, and then chapters that deal with politics, economics, international relations and war, sex and marriage, race, church and state, "culture," etc. Indeed, if there is a surplus of one kind of literature in the field it is of survey textbooks that try to treat large and complex subjects in short and simple chapters, and thus do not do justice to the biblical and theological problems involved, nor to the particular moral problems, each of which deserves several monographs rather than a brief synoptic treatment. These chapters often are so generalized that their intention to clarify moral issues in behavior is not achieved; often they are sprinkled with dubious empirical as well as moral generalizations. But the practical concern that is central to the American way of work in ethics seems to require that the bulk of the textbooks be addressed to moral questions that the authors seem to believe the readers face.

This practical intention requires that the energies of many able writers be given to the preparation of books and pamphlets that are more oriented to pedagogy than to research. Not only textbooks, but also a vast number of "study books" are prepared for use in churches and college discussion groups. Some of these are prepared by ministers; but many are prepared by men who might better spend their energy exploring undeveloped areas of the subject matter. The practical books are important in a "moralistic" nation, and in religious communities, Protestant and Catholic, that take moral responsibility seriously. But all too often they are of ephemeral value in the development of an academic discipline.

The practical orientation also dictates that professors of Christian ethics be more conversant with materials from fields such as economics, politics, race relations, and other parts of sociology, sex, etc., than with philosophy, biblical studies, and history. Thus there is a sizable amount of literature that appropriates, necessarily and properly, the theories, information, and insights of the social sciences for the resolution in theory and, hopefully, in action of moral issues that are detailed in the languages of these disciplines. Indeed, interest in social ethics led to significant empirical research in sociology of religion, such as Liston Pope's *Millhands and Preachers* (1942), Kenneth Underwood's *Protestant and Catholic* (1951), and Paul Harrison's *Authority and Power in the Free Church Tradition* (1959). Some of these areas deserve comment.

The concern for economic life goes well back into the social gospel period when Protestantism faced the injustices that accrued from urbanization and industrialization. In that time socialism (loosely defined) became almost a panacea for economic ethics. In the 1930's some ethicists were still socialists, and most supported organized labor and the New Deal. As the problems of economic ethics became more complex and the ethical thinkers more sophisticated about them, a particular literature on economic ethics began to emerge. One example is Walter Muelder's *Religion and Economic Responsibility* (1953), which is still couched largely in big ideological terms rather than in terms of the technical data of national income analysis and economic growth. Indeed, the literature has tended to be rather simply concerned with the problems of equitable distribution of wealth rather than with issues of monetary and fiscal policy. In the 1950's the National Council of Churches gathered scholars in ethics and in economics and other fields to develop an extensive series of books, usually called "The Ethics and Economic Life Series." Persons of technical competence wrote texts: e.g., Kenneth Boulding on *The Organizational Revolution,* Howard Bowen on *The Social Responsibilities of the Businessman,* several economists on the uses of American income. This series was a step in the right direction, but the considerations of ethics and those of technical economics remain rather unconnected in some of the material. American Protestantism has yet to produce a Denis Munby, the English economist and lay theologian who combines both interests in his *Christianity and Economic Problems* and *God and the Rich Society* to develop a kind of Christian and Keynesian commentary.

Part of the Protestant difficulty in approaching economics and other particular areas is the lack of consensus within the tradition as to *how* one goes about this task. Theological foundations and procedures of ethical reflection are in dispute. Roman Catholics at this and other points have more consensus, and thus a more coherent body of literature. They have been able to move from the social encyclicals of the popes, with their concern—grounded in natural law—for working conditions, just wages, and the right of labor to organize, to the issues that face contemporary society. Notable writers in America during the contemporary period are John A. Ryan and A. J. Cronin, plus many more. Catholics have moved with certainty to a position favoring the involvement of the state in welfare and other related questions, while Protestants have been trying to decide whether the Christian interpretation of life supports limited government and laissez faire (there is a strong Protestant right wing, though no scholars of Christian ethics of any reputation belong to it) or some form of welfare state.

Two other broad areas have received much attention in recent decades. One is the general problem of social justice in American life, and the political means for implementing it. The other is the area of international relations. In many respects Reinhold Niebuhr in his voluminous occasional writings and his books on political problems has been at the center of the discussion.

Beginning with his *Moral Man and Immoral Society* (1932), which, in fact, had been preceded by many articles in popular journals, Niebuhr began to interpret the social problem in terms of balances of power, rather than in more "sentimental" terms. Groups must organize and exercise coercive power through various means in order to achieve their due in the human exchange. This was true for Negroes (for whom Niebuhr suggested boycott, etc., at that time), for labor, and for other groups. He applied his fundamental theories with great specificity to particular problems through many decades of writing for the *Christian Century, Radical Religion, Christianity and Society, Christianity and Crisis,* and liberal secular political journals. Many of these occasional writings have been collected in *Love and Justice* (1957) and *Essays in Applied Christianity* (1959), and in them one can recapture some of the force that his polemic had on less realistic Christians and others. In *The Children of Light and the Children of Dark* (1944), an essay on democratic theory, he coined the famous statement that gets at the heart of his political philosophy: "Man's capacity for justice makes democracy possible; but man's inclination to injustice makes democracy necessary" (p. xi).

Niebuhr's thought and activity led many other scholars and teachers of Christian ethics into active participation in political parties and in voluntary associations that sought to establish "rough justice" in American life through the use of political means. Thus most Christian ethicists consider themselves to be "political realists," and though there are disputes about the methods and assumptions of Niebuhr's position, almost no one writing in Protestant social ethics could deny the heavy influence of his thought.

Prior to World War II, and of course since, war and international relations have received a great deal of attention, both from Protestants and Catholics. For Protestants the intellectual process of the late 1930's was one of being weaned away from a pacifist tendency that aspired to see war abolished. The rise of Hitler and the articulation of a theology and ethics that saw the need for coercive power to restrain evil brought most American Protestants into the war with a sense of being involved in a "just and mournful war." There continued to be the traditional dissenters: the historic peace churches, and others, including a few important theologians. The literature about the war took more the form of articles in journals and reports by ecclesiastical commissions than it did major books. For Catholics, whose ecclesiastical consensus on the just war tradition remained, the agony of the decision to participate in the war did not exist. Both, however, had theologians who were concerned enough with the problems of the right conduct of war to express regret at the breakdown of certain just war principles, particularly the bombing of noncombatants. Yet even some Christians were overcome with the crusade mentality, and justified the use of the atomic bomb in 1945.

Since the war, the ethics of international relations has drawn more attention of talented Christian ethicists than any other problem. In this discussion there has been more Catholic-Protestant dialogue than in any other area or in any other time in the United States. Fathers John C. Ford and John Courtney Murray have been among the leading participants on the Catholic side; among Protestants Reinhold Niebuhr (whose *The Structure of Nations and Empires,* 1959, is his most recent major book), John C. Bennett, and Paul Ramsey have done important writing. There are hundreds of pages in books, pamphlets, and journals by other authors as well. Nontheological writers who are informed by Christian ethics, such as Kenneth Thompson, Paul Nitze, and Thomas Murray, have participated. The consensus of this main line of thinking in recent years can be expressed in terms of a movement toward a view of limited war for limited purposes.

The knowledgeability of the theological moralists in the materials produced by military strategists, political scientists, and others is remarkable. Hans Morganthau, Herman Kahn, Henry Kissinger, Oskar Morgenstern,

Robert Osgood, William T. R. Fox, and many others have written books and essays on problems of international relations and military strategy that have been carefully studied by the writers in ethics. Writings by Christian ethicists, Catholic and Protestant, take into account the arguments produced by these men in a serious and learned way.

There continue to be those for whom the consensus to support limited war as a means of foreign policy is a dubious one from a Christian perspective. Among these are "nuclear pacifists" as well as traditional pacifists.

More has been written in the area of international relations about war than about some other facets, such as economic assistance programs and the revolutions among the younger nations. There are theologians of note, however, who tend to identify themselves with the aspirations of anticolonialist powers. The World Council of Churches studied issues in this nest of problems, and the report volume, *The Churches and Rapid Social Change* (1961), was written by an American staff member, Paul Abrecht. While the major figures in American Christian ethics have tended to be anti-anti-Communists in their critiques of the crusading mentality that informs the American right wing, they have also been "realists" about Russian expansionism, and at the same time sympathetic to the emerging new nations. One of the most important interpretations of Protestant Christian ethics to appear in recent years deals with the problems of Christianity and communism and has the new nations sympathetically in view; it is Charles West's *Communism and the Theologians* (1958).

The issues of civil liberties were much in the minds of the Protestant writers during the period of McCarthyism, when many earlier and current leaders were under the attack of the right wing. A major research study that digs into the facts of the matter is Ralph Roy's *Communism and the Churches* (1960). We have, however, no major theological treatises that are focused upon the area of civil liberties—either their theological ground or the rationale for them within law and custom—except John Courtney Murray's *We Hold These Truths* (1960). Symptomatically, one finds almost no distinguished Christian ethics professors on lists of leaders in the American Civil Liberties Union, and those who are there tend to be regarded as liberals in theology, whereas Americans for Democratic Action is well supplied with distinguished Protestant names.

The question of church and state emerges larger and larger as Americans come to grips with religious and cultural pluralism. This is at present a major concern. Symbolic is the fact that a recent review article in the *Christian Century* dealt with five books pertaining to the question that had been published within a few months. Among Roman Catholics, the major theoretician has been John Courtney Murray, whose "Contemporary Orientations of Catholic Thought on Church and State in the Light of History," published in *Theological Studies* in 1949, is a landmark of American Catholic thought. Murray's view can be called dyarchical, in that it seeks to avoid the dominance of either over the other. He states that "in the native structure of the American system the citizen-of-religious-conscience is placed in the mediating position between Church and state. The Church is free to form the consciences of her members; and they as citizens are free to conform the life of the City to the demands of their consciences." The unity is not in the power of either church or state, but in "the oneness of man as Christian and as citizen." Murray continued his contribution in the collection of essays, *We Hold These Truths.* Certainly not all Catholics agree with Murray, but with the discussions on religious liberty and freedom that are occurring in the Roman Catholic Church as a whole, it is likely that his view will win wider and wider acceptance.

Protestants continue, as usual, to be fragmented. There is the hardline separation principle, represented in the Protestants and Other Americans United for the Separation of Church and State. The views of this group have distinct tinges of anti-Catholicism. There are also Protestants who feel at home with the writings of the American Jewish Committee lawyer Leo Pfeffer, who is deeply involved in cases that seek to get all traces of particular religions out of the public life. But in more recent years a more moderate "wavy line" between church and state is being drawn by others, such as John C. Bennett in his *Christians and the State* (1958). Denominations are taking positions; the United Presbyterian Church is particularly active in this regard, recommending that churches give up all special tax-free and other privileges in order fully to emancipate themselves from special status in the state. "Church and state" is one of the most crucial areas of continuing discussion, and perhaps out of many more books and pamphlets, dealing with law cases, theology, historical factors, and social conditions, a consensus will emerge in Christian ethics, Protestant and Catholic together.

The question of civil rights is currently in the foreground. On this issue there is significant consensus among writers in Christian ethics, Protestant and Catholic, arrived at by diverse theological and ethical paths—namely, that segregation is wrong, and that integration is right. A number of essays and books have helped to shape and express this consensus, such as Liston Pope's widely read *Kingdom Beyond Caste* (1957) and Kyle Haselden's *The Racial Problem in Christian Perspective* (1959). Leadership of clergy in the struggle, both the notables like Martin Luther King and many lesser lights, indicates that on this point there is enough assurance of the moral rightness of the general position to prompt men to participate actively in its actualization. There are disagreements on questions of strategy and tactics, and some of these have issues of ethics at their roots (see, e.g., Ramsey's *Christian Ethics and the Sit-in,* 1961), but pluralism of action substantiated by pluralism of theories and convictions seems to be the state of affairs that will continue.

Ethical problems of medical care have received far more extensive treatment by Roman Catholics than by Protestants. The manuals of moral theology discuss problems of sterilization, euthanasia, abortion, birth control, the "patient's right to know," prolongation of life, etc. There are also particular books on medical ethics—for example, Father John P. Kenny's *Principles of Medical Ethics* (1952; 2nd ed., 1962). Another recent Catholic study of great importance is Norman St. John-Stevas's *Life, Death and the Law* (1961). The only comparable Protestant book is Joseph Fletcher's *Morals and Medicine* (1954). Paul Ramsey has given some attention to these questions, and Richard Fagley, in *The Population Explosion and Christian Responsibility* (1960), deals with one of the big issues in which medical and vast public ethical questions come together. On questions related to both population control and issues of medical care, Catholics tend to take a firm stand against man's right to take life and prohibit it from coming into being, though the occasions for discussion of crucial marginal cases are increasing. Dr. John Rock's *The Time Has Come* (1963) and the writings of Father John A. O'Brien of Notre Dame indicate new openness particularly on the control of birth. Certainly Protestants need to do more work in relation to the host of issues involved in medical care, and in public policies in which medical action is required.

The work that has been done on sex ethics by Protestants has largely been directed to a student population. There are a number of books by Peter Bertocci, William Hamilton, and others that seek to speak to the actual problems of the younger unmarried person. There is also the literature that takes a large historical or biblical approach, such as books by William Cole, and Otto Piper's *The Biblical View of Sex and Marriage* (1960). Currently American Protestants are reading *The Ethics of Sex* (1964), by Helmut Thielicke, a German theologian and preacher. On the whole, we have far from an adequate discussion of this important area in Protestantism. Roman Catholicism continues to instruct on questions of sex in the manner of traditional manuals of moral theology, though here as elsewhere account has to be taken of new medical possibilities, of the changing cultural ethos, and other factors.

Any survey of literature on Christian ethics and moral problems that sought to be complete would require much more extensive development than has been given here. But the vastness of material is important to visualize, both because of its intrinsic importance and because it indicates the extent to which Christian ethics in America has been occupied with questions of practical morality. This has been the genius of American work, particularly in Protestantism: ethics has not been done here as exclusively in relation to dogmatics, to exegesis, and to philosophy as it has in Europe. But this preoccupation has also left large areas of fundamental importance inadequately explored.

chapter 2

Theology
and
Ethics

What then . . . is an "ethic" which by definition makes a theme
of the ethical? And what is an ethicist? We can begin more easily
by saying what, in any case, an ethic and an ethicist cannot be. An
ethic cannot be a book in which there is set out how everything in
the world actually ought to be but unfortunately is not, and an
ethicist cannot be a man who always knows better than others what
is to be done and how it is to be done. An ethic cannot be a work
of reference for moral action which is guaranteed to be unexceptionable, and the ethicist cannot be the competent critic and judge of
every human activity. An ethic cannot be a retort in which ethical
or Christian human beings are produced, and the ethicist cannot be
the embodiment or ideal type of a life which is, on principle, moral.

Dietrich Bonhoeffer[1]

This quotation from Bonhoeffer might very well be abrasive to some
of the most cherished expectations that men have from the study of
Christian ethics. When students read a book or article on Christian
ethics, they often would like to have spelled out for them how everything in the world ought to be. Unfortunately the world is in strife
between groups and nations; men ought to be at peace with one another in Christian love. Unfortunately the motives one has are often
compromised by the situation in which he must act; men ought to be
able to live with a purity of intention regardless of the consequences.

Or when one reads a book on Christian ethics, he expects to find a great deal of moral wisdom, for it is assumed that the writer of such a book ought to know better than others what to do and how to do it. The ethicist, readers expect, should be able to define the goals toward which men ought to be working, and he should be able to guide their use of proper means to achieve them. Or the book on Christian ethics ought to be a guidebook to Christian conduct, some might say. The reader faces a particular temptation, obligation, or opportunity; an ethics book ought to tell him the proper rules by which to act. It ought to say whether premarital sexual intercourse is right or wrong, whether resort to coercive power in international relations is right or wrong. And the writer of such a book ought to be able to survey the human scene and say the appropriately moral things about gambling, war, affluent society, and family life. Or one might read an ethics book in order to nourish his moral life; it ought to have the effect of cultivating his own moral wisdom. And one might hope that the author of such a book would be an exemplary man—he ought in his action to demonstrate the Christian moral life.

Fond hopes that the study of Christian ethics will lead to the resolution of all the serious moral questions that face human beings are bound to meet disappointment, and for some very good reasons. Dietrich Bonhoeffer's circumscription of an ethic and an ethicist would not be seriously challenged by most men working in the field of Christian ethics today. Many of the crucial issues over which there are differences of judgment, however, lie within the boundaries he suggests. If an ethic cannot "set out how everything ought to be but unfortunately is not," does this imply that it cannot suggest how *some* things ought to be? If "an ethicist cannot be a man who always knows better than others what is to be done and how it is to be done," does this imply that he cannot be one who *sometimes* knows better than some others do what ought to be done and how it ought to be done? If an ethics book cannot be an unexceptionable guide to moral action, does this imply that it cannot *give any direction* to human conduct? If "the ethicist cannot be the competent critic and judge of every human activity," does this imply that his learning may not make him *more competent than some others* are to judge *some* human activity? If the study of ethics does not create Christian moral men, does this imply that it is *absolutely divorced* from the actual moral existence of the Christian community?

Bifocal Character of the Study of Christian Ethics

On the one hand Bonhoeffer is saying in effect, "Do not expect the study of Christian ethics to be *immediately* applicable to all moral problems." On the other hand, what many persons expect from the study of Christian ethics is moral wisdom, moral counsel, moral rules which will resolve the tensions they feel in their personal moral responsibilities, or in the issues of the world. A distinction between *ethics* and *morals* is useful to set in order two tasks that are involved in Christian ethics. *Ethics* is often used to refer to a task of careful reflection several steps removed from the actual conduct of men. It is a theoretical task: reflection on the ways in which moral action occurs, the assumptions and presuppositions of moral life. *Morals* is often used to refer to the actual conduct of men. It is a practical task: giving direction to human behavior in the light of what one believes to be right, or good. At the level of *morals* one is asking, "What ought I do in this place of responsibility?" "Is what I am interested in *really* good?" At the level of *ethics* one is asking, "What fundamental principles are involved in determining an answer to the moral questions?" "What is the nature of obligation?" "What is the nature of the good?"[2]

In the study of Christian ethics, these two sides are always present: the clarification of the fundamental principles of the Christian life, and the interpretation of how the Christian community needs to make moral judgments and to act in the light of its faith and its religious convictions. For example, in one of the greatest American books in Christian ethics, Reinhold Niebuhr's *Nature and Destiny of Man*,[3] the student is given an interpretation of human nature, defined in relation to historical and philosophical alternatives, in relation to scripture and human experience. This is *theological ethics*. He is also given direction as to how one thinks about the moral world in the light of these theological ethical convictions. This is *Christian morals*. The meaning of being a sinner, being under God's grace, and being under the absolute law of love is not given to exhibit Reinhold Niebuhr's ethical brilliance; it is given so that men may more adequately fulfill their moral obligations to God and to the finite world of men. In Roman Catholic papal encyclicals on ethics,[4] one finds a brief exposition of the fundamental convictions of that Church pertaining to man's moral nature, the natural law, and the effects of redeeming grace—ethics. But these are given for the purpose of guiding men in their responses to issues of economic justice, of political policy, and of marriage and family relationships —*morals*. Or in Karl Barth's writings on ethics in his *Church Dogmatics*, the basic theological ethical principles derived and expounded in terms of his Christology in Volume II, Part 2 are supplemented in Volume III, Part 4 by extensive discussions of what it means to have faith in this Christ in marriage, in relation to the preservation of life (war, abortion, capital punishment, etc.), and in other areas.[5] Some writers choose to work primarily at the basic principles, and to some earnest moral men they often appear abstract and impractical. Among American writers, H. Richard Niebuhr in both *Christ and Culture* and *The Responsible Self* works primarily in the *ethics* side of the discipline.[6] Other writers are concerned to inform the moral action of the Christian community with a sense of urgency and relevance, writing tracts for the times from Christian viewpoints. To some students of theological ethics, such writings often appear to be milk rather than good red meat.

The double-sided enterprise goes on in the classroom as well. There are teachers of ethics who lead their students into the refinements and intricacies of the problem of law and gospel, or into the exegetical and theological foundations of the idea of the state, without ever addressing a problem of human conduct or indicating that moral judgments in politics require many other considerations besides Romans 13:1-7. They feel vindicated by being "theological," or by a sense of dealing with what is "really basic." There are also teachers of Christian ethics who are so concerned to be relevant that their lectures become extended social commentary, or more sociological and political than theological in the fundamental thought patterns that direct them. Neither emphasis is without its virtues, and neither without its vices. The main virtue of the first is that it clarifies the foundations in the Christian message for understanding the relation of God to the world and man in theological ethical terms; its most common vice is that it often assumes that the resolution of an exegetical or theological problem is the resolution of a moral problem—that to find a correct theological doctrine of the state is a more important contribution to the Christian community than to clarify choices between parties and candidates in an election by a discussion of the moral issues involved. The virtue of the second, more practical view, is its effort to be informed by what is actually going on in the world, and to promote the activity of the Christian community in the particular moral issues and judgments that time-bound men face. Its most common vice, however, is oversimplified thinking about the relation of theological and ethical principles to empirical data and present struggles of men.

The distinction between *ethics* and *morals* is shared by theologians with philosophers and with writers from other religions. There are philosophers who seek to avoid any realm of practical life in their discourse. R. M. Hare, for example, in *The Language of Morals,* conceives of ethics as "the logical study of the language of morals." [7] Language, not human action, is the first point of reference for analysis; and certainly Hare does not seek to prescribe human behavior. But even with his special abstract interest, the actual morals of the philosopher are not hidden. Among other examples that Hare uses in working out his abstract problems is the importance of taking a bath! Other philosophers have moved between "ethics" and "morals" more freely. Bertrand Russell and John Dewey, both talented in abstract discourse, have written tracts informed by their basic reflections on many moral topics that face men. The general field of ethics, Christian or non-Christian, seems to demand a double-sided approach—reflection on basic patterns and principles, and reflection on what men ought to do.

Three Centers of Attention in Ethical Thought

The theoretical and practical concerns of ethics become interwoven at various points; or to put the issue in Henry David Aiken's terms, men move between the levels of moral discourse. The question "Why be moral?" might be answered in such a way that a response to the question "What ought I to do?" is entailed. The major portion of this essay will delineate three substantive concerns of ethical reflection that are held in common by Christian ethics and other ethics. With each, however, the distinctive approach of Christian ethics is differentiated. The three substantive concerns are with the location and nature of the good, or value; the nature of man as a moral agent in the world; and the criteria of judgment needed for the determination of conduct.

Location and Nature of the Good

Jesus said, "Why do you call me good? No one is good but God alone" (Luke 18:19). Aristotle asks, "What then is the good of each? Surely that for whose sake everything else is done. . . . Now such thing happiness, above all else, is held to be." [8] "And God saw everything that he had made, and behold, it was very good." (Gen. 1:31). For R. B. Perry, "The highest good is doubly ideal. It is the ideal object of an ideal will. It is an ideal object in the sense that it is constructed out of the objects of the original interest which compose the integral will. . . ." [9]

These four selections all use the word *good*. It obviously has different references; Jesus was speaking about men, and then about God; the author of Genesis was speaking about the goodness of created beings; Aristotle wrote about happiness as the end, the ultimate goal and purpose, of men; Perry is involved in definitions of *ideal objects* and *ideal wills*. For Kant, the issue of goodness was located in the human will. And more references could be given. The student of ethics is compelled to assert that in one way or another every writer in the field gives some location or locations of the good and engages in some discussion of its nature. For some philosophers it is defined in very inclusive terms—being itself is good. For others, there are objective values, or essences of various forms of the good that exist as things in themselves. For G. E. Moore, the good is simple and indefinable, like the *yellow*. For hedonists, the good is pleasure; for some rigorists the human good is obedience. For H. R. Niebuhr, things are of value in relation to God and to each other. The location of the good is thus sometimes defined to be within the self—a satisfaction of some desire or interest; sometimes as objective—something real existing out there; and sometimes in relational terms. Its nature is sometimes understood as indefinable, sometimes in terms of utility, sometimes in terms of desire, sometimes in terms of *being*.

Christian ethical reflection also interprets what the nature of the good is and where it is located. Theologians turn their attention to this problem not in a speculative frame of mind, but in an effort to understand what the fundamental presuppositions of the Christian life are. Even in this search for clarification of assumptions they are not engaged in something unique; most philosophers in their definitions of goodness begin with the fact that it exists and men experience it, therefore one is provoked to reflect upon it. But when the theologian turns his attention to this problem he begins with certain convictions of the Christian community. These convictions are not merely propositions taken from scripture and treated like the premises of arguments; they are the convictions that inform his life of faith—indeed, they are the convictions of his faith. The nature and location of the ultimate good are delineated in religious, theological terms. The understanding of the manifold forms of goodness in creation and human experience is explicated in terms of the relation of these things to the goodness of God. Others may answer the question, "Why be moral?" in terms of "It is natural to be moral, i.e., to seek one's own happiness." The Christian answers it differently. He is moral because God is good, and because God has called him to responsibility for the goodness of the world in which man lives. He is moral out of gratitude to the goodness of God, made known in creation, made known in the preservation and governing of the world, made known in the face of Jesus Christ. God is good; God has created all things and seen that they are good. The theological side of Christian ethics is directed toward the interpretation and specification of the Being and Goodness of God. In relation to him, and to his goodness, all created forms of life have their appropriate value. In relation to him, man is obliged to seek the good of others, to concern himself with the care and well-being of men and nature.

Theologians interpret the nature and source of the good differently. For the Catholic tradition, which thinks in terms of natural law, God has created men with an inclination toward the good, and an inclination away from evil. Thus there is a goodness in nature which seeks to realize itself; it can be known, and this knowledge used to direct conduct. To be created by God is good; to *be* good is to act in accordance with one's true nature given in God's creation. For Lutheran interpretations, God's goodness is made known to men in his law and in his gospel. In his law it acts to keep order in the works of men and the world of nature, it gives a structure to human society so that men can live together. In his gospel, God's goodness (specified in terms of righteousness) is given for the justification of men, for the forgiveness of their sins, and for them to share in human existence. For some contemporary theologians—for example, Karl Barth and Dietrich Bonhoeffer—the center of goodness, indeed *the Reality,* is Jesus Christ. They remind us of the assertions in Colossians and Ephesians that all things are created in and through him; that he has overcome the principalities and the powers. Jesus Christ is the Reality—of the good, and all of life is to be lived in such a way that it attests to him. In "liberal" Protestant ethics, the reflections on the nature of the good have been somewhat different. God is love; love is good; the Christian life seeks to realize love in every possible situation. Jesus, both in his life and his teachings, expressed the centrality of love as the good, and thus in direction from him, and in imitation of him, men are to be inwardly loving in their intentions and motives, and to be outwardly loving to establish those relations among men that most closely approximate love.

For most Christian writers, human goodness is always and only a secondary good. It is a created good—only God is good in an ultimate sense; and it is a corrupted goodness, for men have not lived in accord with the goodness of God. Christians understand the possibility and the actuality of goodness in the world as dependent upon the prior goodness of God. Men are righteous (a word which requires much more specification than can be given here) only by virtue of God's righteousness. Goodness in creation is in every moment dependent upon God's goodness. Or, if the Christian life is defined in being directed toward an end, toward a goal, it is a goal determined by a vision of God's goodness. Or, "We love, *because he first loved us*" (1 John 4:19).

The more theoretical reflection about God, his nature and his activity, is carried on through study of the scriptures and the theological tradition. The Bible makes the message of God's goodness known to men; it is in the Bible that a people (both the people of Israel and the Christian community) has recorded its action in the light of God's goodness; its understanding of what is required of man in the knowledge of God. Within scripture there is the movement back and forth between theology, "ethics," and "morals," between convictions about the nature and activity of God and the nature and activity of man in relation to God. So also in Christian ethical reflection there is movement back and forth between an understanding of God as the one who alone is good, but created all things good, preserves all things, and acts to redeem all things on the one hand, and the interpretation of human life and its current responsibilities in the light of these basic convictions on the other.

Christians' *attitudes and basic dispositions* toward the world are governed by their acknowledgment of God as the good: they are his servants; they are dependent upon him; they tend and care for a world which is not theirs but his; they are responsible to him. The *actions* of the community are directed by the *knowledge* of God's goodness: its members seek to preserve the good that God has created; they seek to act in such fashion that love and order are enhanced in the human community; they seek to act in such fashion that good is redeemed out of evil in the world.

Philosophers and other men have convictions about the good in the light of which they act, and counsel the actions of others. Christians are not unique by virtue of having such convictions; they are distinguished by the convictions that they have. Their interpretation of what is worthy of men's interest and pursuit, of men's care and energy, is governed in large part by their religious convictions. These convictions are specified and expounded in the Bible and in the tradition of the church. God is good; created beings are good by virtue of God's goodness; men ought to seek the good in accordance with God's own good activity and in accordance with man's knowledge of God's goodness. This power and goodness of God is made known in Jesus Christ. Knowledge of goodness is given in knowledge of Jesus Christ and in the interpretation of life in relation to him.

Nature of Man

In Genesis 1:27, the famous biblical assertion about man is made: "So God created man in his own image, in the image of God he created him. . . ." Immanuel Kant wrote concerning the principle of reason in man:

> Thus nothing remained but that perhaps an incontrovertible, objective principle of causality could be found which excluded every sensuous condition from its determination, i.e., a principle in which reason does not call upon anything else as the determining ground of the causality but rather by that principle itself contains it, thus being, as pure reason, practical of itself. This principle, however, needs no search and no invention, having long been in the reason of all men and embodied in their being. It is the principle of morality.[10]

St. Paul wrote, ". . . for I have already charged that all men, both Jews and Greeks, are under the power of sin, as it is written: 'None is righteous, no, not one; no one understands, no one seeks for God. All have turned aside, together they have gone wrong; no one does good, not even one' "

(Rom. 3:9-12). He also wrote, "Therefore, if any one is in Christ, he is a new creation; the old has passed away, behold, the new has come" (2 Cor. 5:17). Erich Fromm has written, "If he faces the truth without panic he will recognize that there is no meaning to life except the meaning man gives his life by the unfolding of his powers, by living productively. . . ." [11]

Discussions of ethics always include the delineation of some view of man. Indeed, the understanding of the nature of man is one of the keystones to every ethical system. For some interpreters, man is fundamentally a rational being, capable of knowing what the good is, and capable of directing his conduct according to that proper knowledge (Kant). For others man is governed more by his self-interest than by his benevolence for others. Some picture man as a creature with conscience, capable of bringing self-love and love of others into harmony with each other (Butler). For Berdyaev, the essence of human nature is a radical freedom, so that man in effect has the capacity to create himself and his world. But those who believe that men are determined by the mores of their communities (Durkheim) or by some law of nature which requires that each creature struggle for himself, would radically disagree.

One finds a variety of portraits of man in the literature of Christian ethics, as well. For Roman Catholics, the problem of morality lies as much in knowledge of the good as it does in the will to do the good; in fact, man's will is governable by his intellect. In the Protestant tradition the human will is seen to be the locus of much of the moral problem; men are curved in upon themselves as an expression of their sin (Luther). For some Christians, man is viewed primarily under the aspect of sin: to be sure, he is justified by God's grace, but for purposes of morality it is best to remember first that he remains sinner. (R. Niebuhr in some places). For other theologians, man is viewed primarily under the aspect of grace: to be sure, he remains a sinner, but the primary fact of his existence is his justification and sanctification by God, and a view of his moral existence begins at this point (Barth, F. D. Maurice).

Christians and non-Christians alike have their theories about human nature, and these theories are important aspects of their views of moral activity. Philosophers may see man in relation to his community, or in relation to his libido, or in relation to some definition of a law of nature. Theologians see man in relation to God; the basic perspective in which he is understood is that given in the Bible and Christian tradition. When Christians engage in ethical reflection, then, they have a distinctive point of reference for their interpretation of man as the moral agent. Theological understanding of man is sometimes reduced to propositions about human nature on the basis of some of the first theological premises, but more frequently it has existential qualities to it. The intention is not to make universally applicable statements about men, so much as it is to understand the existence of human beings, made for each other, in their relationship to God. Christian interpretations are interpretations in faith; they are informed by the life of the community of men who acknowledge God as Lord, and they are informed by the knowledge of God who has brought mankind into existence.

In Christian ethical reflection, the interpretation of man's moral existence is centered in large measure on his relationship to God. He is a creature: thus he is not able to claim for himself final authority in anything that he does. He is always one who is under authority; he sees himself to be under the sovereign action of God. He is dependent; nothing is his by his own right, he is "more acted upon than acting," in the words of Luther. He is limited; God has limited him by his creaturehood and continues to limit him by the particular circle of life into which he is born and lives. He is sustained; God's own governing power sustains him, and he is sustained by others whom God has created for him—his family, his government, his church. He is restrained; God restrains him through the restraint of others who act upon him. But in all the aspects of his creaturehood he is created in the image of God: he can participate creatively in the activity of history; he can act for others as God has acted for him in Jesus Christ; he can have purposes for his existence as God has purposes for the whole of creation.

Man, in Christian ethical reflection, is understood to be under obligation to God, to be called to a life of obedient service to God. He is also understood to be part of a rebellious humanity, a disobedient humanity, which seeks to overcome the limits of its creaturehood and claim for itself the right to determine history. The interpretation of what man ought to be and to do is made in relation to what God wills man to be and to do. God has disclosed his activity in the history of the children of Israel; he continues to be the Lord who calls men to obedience to him within the events of their history and culture, their family and economy. Thus in man's moral reflection he is obligated to seek to discern what God is calling him to be and to do in his duties and opportunities in life. But he thinks and acts in repentance, for he knows that he is a creature whose ways are not God's ways, and that he has estranged himself from God in unfaithfulness and disobedience to him.

But man is not only created and ruled by the Lord God; God is also man's Redeemer. This also informs man's existence. He is called into his moral activity by God, who has acted for the redemption of the world in Jesus Christ, and who continues to act redemptively in the world. The Christian image of man is constituted in part by the knowledge that God is good—that he has revealed himself in Jesus Christ as the Redeemer of all things as well as the Creator. Thus there is a newness of life; there is ultimate assurance of the triumph of righteousness over the powers of sin, death, and evil; there is a love that overcomes the world. There is freedom, not only by man's natural capacity to initiate action, but freedom from self-justification; freedom to love, freedom to take risks. Theologians differ in their interpretation of the significance of man under the aspect of God's redemption. For some, the primary weight rests on the fact that man is free from bondage to sin because God has acted to forgive him; this is one of the stresses of the Reformation. For some, God's grace is infused into the mind and the will of man through participation in the sacraments, and thus his capacity to act is enhanced; this is a stress in traditional Roman Catholicism. For John Wesley and others, God's gift of grace in conversion really restores man's nature, so that he can overcome his sins and live a morally new life. For such a person as F. D. Maurice, whose theme was "Christ is the head of every man," it meant living in the assurance that love is more real than sin, that life is more real than death, that goodness is more real than evil.

The Christian reflects upon the significance of man's life for other men in human community. Theologians in the biblical tradition have always stressed the social character of man's existence. Men are called to sustain each other, to know each other, to restrain each other, to live for each other. God has so created life; God's love so impels men to live together. Thus the natural communities in which men live are understood in the light of their function for men under the divine activity and order. And particularly, theologians view men as called to be in the community which acknowledges God to be the Lord: the community of the church.

Convictions about man are obviously not unique to Christian moralists; they are a main ingredient in every moral view. But the Christian interpretation is differentiated by a particular point of reference: man is understood in relation to God—Father, Son, and Holy Spirit. This understanding affects men's disposition toward the world—it is God's, and only in a secondary sense their own; it is to be ordered through human action in accord with what God wills and what God is seeking to do. Man's view of himself is that of a servant of God, one who is under obligation to God. It also affects the ways in which men think about their purposes and actions in the world. Men are to be related to one another in a manner fitting God's creation and redemption; they are to fulfill the purposes and duties which they discern to be true for humanity under God's disclosure of himself. The mirror in which they understand themselves, singly and together, is Jesus Christ, the revelation of God.

Criteria of Moral Action

Just as writers of books of ethics all have something to say about the nature of the good and the nature of man, so also they reflect upon the criteria of moral judgment. Kant's propositions which state the categorical imperatives are well known. For example, he states it in the following way at one point: "Act only according to that maxim by which you can at the same time will that it should become a universal law." [12] The "double love commandment" from the sayings of Jesus is even better known: "The first is . . . 'you shall love the Lord your God with all your heart, and with all your soul, and with all your mind, and with all your strength.' The second is this, 'You shall love your neighbor as yourself' " (Mark 12:30-31). In the Decalogue, we are given a whole set of criteria for conduct: "Thou shalt not steal, Thou shalt not kill," etc. Stephen Toulmin defines the function of ethics in the following manner: "We can provisionally define it as being 'to correlate our feelings and behaviour in such a way as to make the fulfillment of everyone's aims and desires as far as possible compatible.' " [13]

Each of these selections suggests certain rather specific considerations or criteria that men ought to have in view as they determine their course of action. One ought not to do anything that he would not wish everyone else to do; one ought to love the neighbor; one ought to strive toward a harmony of self-realization of various persons. There are others that are readily recalled from the literature of ethics: seek the greatest good for the greatest number, "Do unto others as you would have others do unto you," etc. Criteria are sometimes stated as the goals to be sought in action; sometimes they are stated as laws or governing rules. In the biblical literature, "Seek ye first the kingdom of God," is a religious-ethical statement that defines a goal to be sought; "Thou shalt not commit adultery" is the statement of a governing rule. Traditional terms of differentiation between these two basic postures in relation to the moral life are *teleological ethics* and *deontological ethics*. There are writers in both Christian and non-Christian ethics who seek to hew rather closely to one general pattern or the other, but most writers move freely between them. St. Paul, for example, in a remarkable passage of moral counsel in the framework of the Christian gospel (1 Cor. 10:24-11:1) apparently sees no serious tension between statements of both types. He admonishes Christians, "Let no one seek his own good, but the good of his neighbor,"—a goal-directed statement; but he also asserts, "Be imitators of me, as I am of Christ,"—a statement of a pattern to which the Christian life is to be conformed. Perhaps it is fortunate that St. Paul was not tutored in the fine distinctions that professors of ethics have learned to make!

The ends that men believe ought to guide conduct are related to their views of the good and of the nature of man. If pleasure is the chief good, and if man is a rational animal capable of directing his actions toward such an end, obviously the criterion of action could be stated in terms of an end: "Direct your action toward the maximization of your pleasure." Or it could be stated in terms of a moral law: "So act in every situation that your pleasure is enhanced." Christians view the criteria of action, however, not with reference to man alone, but with reference to what God enables and requires men to do. Their interpretation of moral responsibility is set within the framework of God's disclosure to man that he is his Creator, his Ruler and Judge, and his Redeemer. It is also set within an understanding of man as a being called to loving obedience by God, who enables and requires man to live responsibly. Perhaps the most important differentiation of Christian reflection about moral conduct, however, is that it places the responsibility within man's relationship to God. For Christian morality, the ultimate loyalty is not to the criteria set by any human community; the court of judgment is not a system of ends or laws designed by moral philosophers. Christians *live in a sense of personal responsibility to a living God* in their actions. Thus the ultimate criteria of moral action are never derived from a book of rules, as if such were the final authority. They are never derived from a set of humanly defined goals. The Christian seeks in his moral judgments to be obedient to the living God, who is seeking to address man in each particular responsibility, and whose activity is reflected in each event. Thus the various relative criteria that Christians use are more like lights to aid them in walking in the way that God is leading, than ends to be achieved by calculated means, or laws to be obeyed at all cost.

St. Paul told the Corinthians, "All things are lawful, but not all things are helpful." The life of the Christian community is not finally judged by the legality of its behavior—with reference to moral as well as ritual laws defined by men. Rather, moral judgment requires a discernment of what things are helpful and what things are not helpful. In response to what God enables and requires, how do we discern what things "build up"? How do we discern what manner of life is worthy of the gospel of Christ? (Cf. Phil. 1:27 ff.) The Christian is not without guidance. Indeed, he finds his own moral judgments and actions directed by much that is in scripture, as well as by the counsels of the church in the tradition and the present.

Paul did not hesitate to suggest that Christians imitate him, as he imitated Christ. The Gospel narratives abound in the call to discipleship; to follow Jesus Christ. The persistence of this theme is by no means accidental in the history of the criteria for Christian action. Dietrich Bonhoeffer has written the most powerful tract in our time on this theme. In *The Cost of Discipleship* he quietly affirms that Jesus Christ calls men to perfect obedience, and to suffering.[14] The words of Jesus and the life that he lived both bring to view the cost of living out a responsible moral existence in discipleship. John Calvin is a part of a long tradition of Christian writers who interpret discipleship in the language of self-denial and cross-bearing, echoing again the call of Jesus to deny ourselves, take up our crosses, and follow him. This imperative mood is heard together with the indicative in discerning our moral responsibility in the light of Jesus Christ. God's deeds for man in him permit us to seek the good of the neighbor; to identify ourselves with the suffering, the oppressed, and the outcast. But we are also required to follow him—to have his mind. In Barth's language, "permission" and "command" are not antithetical to each other; rather they are two sides of the same thing.

The teachings of Jesus stand as our judge in our particular moral obligations, and they give direction to our consideration of the responsibilities we have in the tangled, complicated spheres of our lives. We cannot literally apply them and expect to resolve the complex political, economic, and personal issues that confront us. But we would hardly be true to our heritage in the Christian community if we thought about these complicated issues without hearing the counsel of the words of Jesus—without viewing these issues in the light of the One whose name designates our very lives.

Scripture contributes from many of its passages to our consideration of what we are to be and to do in moral life. The Old Testament gives many accounts of the life of a people who interpreted their own participation in history under the sovereignty of God. From their action, and their understanding of their action, we can better see our way on the path of obedience. St. Paul borrows freely from the Stoic wisdom of his day in filling out the meaning of not being conformed to this world, but being renewed in our minds by Jesus Christ. The Christian community is not bound to a single definition of a categorical imperative, or even to a single moral proposition drawn from scripture. It is not definable exclusively as "the people who follow the law of love." In living obedience to a living God, it seeks to discern and to act in responsibility in the light of God's revelation in scripture, with its richness in variety as well as its singleness of purpose.

But Christian *morality* is never derived from scripture alone, nor is it explicable out of dogmatic propositions alone. To be responsible to God requires that one have knowledge of the world in which he is called to live. Thus there is a pressure toward knowing as accurately as possible the human conditions in which Christian obedience is exercised. In political judgments, wisdom and knowledge in the political arena are brought to bear in the determination of conduct. In international relations, knowledge of alliances and balances of power, of the technical ways of maintaining peace, of ideologies and aspirations of men are all points of consideration in the determination of judgment and action. Knowledge of the effects upon the family of an industrialized, bureaucratized society are important in discerning the particular moral responsibilities of Christians in that area. Further, the Christian community does not simply intuit what the right moral action is by having the Bible in one hand and the newspaper in the other. A procedure of critical reflection within the community, and within each Christian man, is necessary. Perhaps there is here and there an artist, or a virtuoso of Christian morality, who seems naturally to do the right and the good—the *saint*. In the main, however, the ethicist has a function in the community to guide its reflection and aid in its consideration of what is required.

The criteria of Christian conduct are not necessarily exclusive of the criteria defined by other communities or other moralists. Many particular considerations are shared between Western humanists and Christians, between political philosophers and theologians. But not every assertion of every moralist can be absorbed into the criterion of Jesus Christ. The criteria of racist morality, whether defined by Nazi Aryan moralists or by Southern White Citizens Councils, are clearly antagonistic to the principal considerations given in the Christian gospel. The criteria of a secularist's struggle for economic justice, however, are more congenial. Christian morality is distinguished not by each particular detail but by the ultimate loyalty, and therefore the ultimate criterion, under which it brings all relative criteria. Christians have to use reason in their judgments and actions as much as other men do; they reflect upon them in such a way as to seek to discern the mind of Christ, the will of God. But Jesus Christ is not just a criterion of judgment; he is the living Lord of the community. Thus moral reflection never has the absolute importance it might have for some philosophers: Jesus Christ may enable and require actions that are imprudent according to canons of rational morality. The presence of the Spirit in the church might prompt an obedient action which is not defensible by even the best rational reflection of the wisest and most learned theologians of the church.

The Religious, Existential
Character of Christian Life

Just as philosophers reflect "ethically" on basic principles, and "morally" on conduct, so do the theologians. But the fundamental understanding of the nature of moral life is to be radically distinguished between them. The Christian life is a life of faith (both loyalty and confidence, in the terms of H. R. Niebuhr [15]) in a living God. The moral life of the Christian community is deeply conditioned by the fact that it lives in faith in God, the Father of our Lord Jesus Christ. It trusts in him—he stands over all human communities, codes of morals, and ethical thought as the object of ultimate loyalty. It lives in responsibility to him, and views all the historical particular responsibilities in the light of obligation to God. It hopes in him—moral evil and defeat never lead it to despair. The life of morality is an expression of the life of worship and devotion, just as it is of the life of theological reflection, for the consciousness of God is sustained by "religious" activities. The moral action of the community is thus understood in personal terms, as well as in institutional and rational terms. Each man is personally responsible to God for the conduct of his life. The community bears a sense of personal obligation to walk in the way that God leads. There is no easy separation between the life of faith and the life of morality; thus the nourishment of the more distinctively religious relationship also affects the more distinctively moral relationships. And man's moral actions are performed with a sense of *personal* responsibility for other men and for the world of nature and social institutions. The activity of men wherever they live and work is understood to be activity in response to God's sovereign lordship.

This existential character of the Christian life makes rationally closed and consistent "systems" of theological ethics dubious. Men have written "systems" of Christian ethics, and undoubtedly will continue to do so. There will continue to be those who believe that "love" is the single foundation upon which Christian ethics is built, to the neglect of faith and hope. There will be those who build their views around a vision of God and interpret the history of the field in the same manner, as did Bishop Kirk.[16] There will be others who stress the idea of Christian perfection, interpreting the Christian life on the basis of the efficacy of conversion to transform moral character. Others will find the keystone in man as sinner, and from this point interpret the morality of men in the world. Some will fix upon the sovereignty of God, and seek to view in all events the presence of the divine Lord. Others will fix the study of ethics upon a doctrine of natural law.

While the drive toward coherence in the interpretation of Christian ethics is good and necessary as a part of the pedagogical and academic work, it can readily be distorted into a pattern that has falsely designated the fixed points. If love becomes the fixed point, one needs to remember H. Richard Niebuhr's warning that to say "God is love" is not to say "Love is God." [17] If a doctrine of man the sinner becomes too fixed as the major premise of Christian ethics, the efficacy of God's redeeming work might be underestimated. If the teaching of Jesus, or the example of Jesus, is the center, a Tolstoyan interpretation may occur in which Christian ethics becomes merely a statement of the law of life to be set along side of other such statements. Every effort to make a closed system of Christian ethics stumbles finally on the richness and openness of the Christian life.

Theologically conceived, Christian ethics has a fixed point of reference —it is God's nature and his action, revealed in Jesus Christ, in scripture. But there are no single and simple propositions that exhaust this center. There are many indicators of it, in the story of the people of Israel and the experience of the church. There is a unique revelation of it in Jesus Christ. But the one who is revealed continues to rule and to redeem, and thus he can call men to new and surprising forms of obedience, as well as to the relatively customary actions that fulfill his purposes. The Christian life is lived in obedient response to the living God. Much can be known about his nature and activity, about what he enables and requires men to be and to do. But the human response *is not to propositions or knowledge about God*; it is the living God, active in creation, in the Son Jesus Christ, and in the Holy Spirit in the church, to whom the world and the church in the world are called to obedience. This is response not to a single portrait of Jesus Christ, etched by the imagination; rather to the living Son of the Father, who is risen Lord, teacher, example, redeemer, and sanctifier. It is response not to a moral consensus drawn out of scripture or tradition, but to the promptings of the Holy Spirit as men deliberate together to discern the mind of Christ in their moral responsibilities. An understanding of moral life as being related to the living God sits loose to the saddle of all closed rational systems of ethics—Christian or philosophical.

Circumscribed systems tend to close off the richness and openness of events in the world to which we are called to live in responsibility. No ethic, Christian or non-Christian, can prescribe on the basis of some fixed touchstone what one's response to particular persons or events ought to be. There are some limitations that might be set: for example, surely a relationship of love rules out sadistic cruelty as a moral virtue in the family. But the response of love is conditioned by the particularities of the child and the parent, the particularities of the events of this day rather than yesterday. Similarly in other spheres of man's moral existence, there is an openness which calls for readiness to hear what God is requiring of men in the new time and place. A system of Christian ethics that seeks to determine too precisely the proper form of the state from the Book of Romans or the Book of Revelation will stumble on changing historical events. "Authority," for example, is something different in a Western democratic state of the twentieth century from what it was in Europe during the period when kings claimed divine right. It is different in eastern Europe from what it is in the new nations of Mali and Indonesia. A rigid prescription of the form of the state on the basis of some prior fixed ethical statements is futile; thinking about the nature of the state in relation to the heritage of ethical reflections *and* the historical events in which states are acting and taking shape is fruitful. Moral action takes place in a continuing field and time span of activity, it initiates changes and directs events that are already occurring. Thus Christian morality must keep in view the openness of the historical and natural world in which men are called to responsibility.

The study of ethics, then, in its utility for morality, lies in the understanding, clarification, direction, setting of limits, and illumination of the way in which responsible men participate in human life. But the study of ethics can never replace the personal responsibility to act—in relation to the action of God and to the actions of other men.

chapter 3

Context Versus Principles:
A Misplaced Debate
in Christian Ethics

The field of Christian ethics has been the location of a debate over the past decades between roughly delineated parties representing an allegiance to the use of formal prescriptive principles on the one hand, and those representing the cause of the more existential response to a particular situation on the other hand. The debate has taken place in Europe and the United States, it has taken place in Catholicism and in Protestantism. In European Protestant literature Karl Barth's *Church Dogmatics,* particularly Volume II/2, Bonhoeffer's *Ethics,* and Niels Søe's *Kristelig Etik,* have represented what has been called a "contextual" approach.[1] More traditional Lutheran theologians who stress the importance of ethics under the law have a larger place for traditional ethical principles. Werner Elert and Walter Künneth would be representative of this group.[2] In Catholic literature there was a movement in the early years after World War II that came to be called "situational morality." A critic has typified it in the following terms.

> The ultimate differences between this new morality and traditional morality come down then to this: In an objective system of ethics the moral judgment is submitted to an extrinsic norm, an ontological norm founded on the principles of being. In situational ethics the moral judgment is measured only by the subjective, immanent light of the individual in question.[3]

Reprinted by permission of the *Harvard Theological Review* and Harvard University Press from *Harvard Theological Review,* Vol. 58, No. 2, April 1965 © Copyright 1965 by the President and Fellows of Harvard College.

In contrast to the situational emphasis is the whole tradition of natural law ethics and moral theology as this developed in Roman Catholicism. It should be noted that some of the recent Catholic ethics continues to be influenced by a situational approach, though not in the extreme way of earlier materials.[4]

In American Protestant ethics, a number of writers have been called "contextual," or "situational" ethicists. Among them are Paul Lehmann, Alexander Miller, Joseph Sittler, H. R. Niebuhr, Albert Rasmussen, Joseph Fletcher, Gordon Kaufman, Charles C. West, and the author.[5]

Writings have been published in criticism of the contextual viewpoint by John C. Bennett, Paul Ramsey, Alvin Pitcher, Clinton Gardiner, Robert Fitch, and Edward L. Long.[6]

The purpose of this study is to show that the debate is no longer a fruitful one. The umbrella named "contextualism" has become so large that it now covers persons whose views are as significantly different from each other as they are different from some of the defenders of "principles." The defenders of the ethics of principles make their cases on different grounds, and use moral principles in different ways. Finally, I will argue that there have been, and legitimately can be, four different base points for Christian moral discourse, and that no matter which point a writer selects to start from, he moves into considerations that are dominant in the other three if he seeks to develop a very complete Christian ethics.

Before engaging in a development of the major theses, however, it is important to notice that the debate has located the problem of Christian ethics at a particular point, namely the question, "How does the Christian community, or any of its conscientious members go about making a particular moral judgment or decision?" This question to a great extent determines the levels of discourse in the argument. Henry David Aiken, in an essay that ought to have great importance in theological ethics, has distinguished four levels of moral discourse, of which the answer to this question is only one. He has called them the "expressive-evocative" level, the "moral" level, the "ethical" level, and the "post-ethical" level. The first is almost ejaculatory in character; it is characterized by an unreflective moral comment that expresses feelings of indignation or of approval. At the moral level, the reflective question begins to emerge, for there men are asking, "What ought I to do in this situation?" "Is that which I admire so much really good?" Reasons are given for the choices that men make; rules are turned to in order to justify moral judgments. The discourse is essentially practical, in a sense that does not derogate "practicality" to expediency. The third, or ethical level, is the one on which questions are raised about the rules or considerations that justify a particular moral judgment. "Can the rules or the reasons by which I have justified a particular decision *really* be defended?" At this level men seek to give reasons for those other reasons that more immediately determine moral conduct. For example, if the answer to the question, "What ought I to do" is decided in terms "I ought to do what the Christian community has long expected men to do in comparable situations," the ethical question becomes, "On what grounds are the expectations of the Christian community accepted as normative?" The post-ethical level raises the question, "Why be moral?" At this point perhaps the offering of "good reasons" finds its limits, and an element of commitment made in freedom enters in.[7]

Aiken's pattern has been introduced here in order to indicate that the context vs. principles debate has emerged on the second level of discourse, the moral level. It has come about in an effort to clarify an essentially practical question of morality: What ought I to do? In the polarization of the discussion, some have said, "Immerse yourself in the situation in which you live, and in which God is acting, and then do what appears to be the right thing in faith." Others have said, "Look to the objective morality of the Christian and Western tradition, for there are principles of conduct that have been derived from nature and revelation that will show you what you ought to do." Obviously the discussion moves rather quickly from this "moral" level to the "ethical" level, and the defense of each side takes place in the effort to say why the contextualist or the principled approach is the right approach. Presumably, for Christian moralists, the answer to the post-ethical question is the same, namely, "one ought to be moral because it is part of one's faith in Jesus Christ to conduct one's life in a way that is good for man." Within this general answer, however, there are very different accent marks, and these in turn affect the way that discourse goes on at other levels. The concerns of this essay begin with the moral level, and move to the ethical level, although some references are necessary to the post-ethical level as well. This is so because the debate with which we are dealing itself begins with the practical moral question.[8]

The Contextualist Umbrella

Any discussion that men force into a debate inevitably polarizes opinion, partly for the sake of clarifying the fundamental issues that divide, but partially for the sake of the convenience of lecturers in survey courses. Such has occurred in the current discussion in theological ethics in the United

States. The contextualist pole has been covered by an umbrella that is so large that it begins to collapse. Men of quite different persuasions are placed under it. Men who might finally argue that assessment of the context is a matter of the first order of importance in moral decisions make that particular case for very different reasons. Writers have different contexts in view. Thus I shall show that the label itself is no longer very useful, since the differences of opinion among those so called are very great indeed.

For what reasons are men called "contextualists?" There are almost as many reasons as there are contextualists. In the area of social ethics there has been a growing concern over the past few decades for accurate analysis of what is actually taking place in the world in which Christians act so that their moral conduct can be more realistic and responsible. The realism that is sought is not at this point a critical assessment of the limitations of man's capacities to know and do the good by virtue of the limitations of his finitude and sin. It is a realism about what is actually occurring, and thus about where the pliable points, the interstices in human society, are in which Christians can act, and from which can come some of the desired effects or consequences. The responsibility that is sought at this point is in relation to spheres of activity already existing. Put simply, some contextualists are saying, if you wish to act out of moral intentions in the political sphere of life, you must know the context of politics with as much accuracy and insight as is humanly possible. This means, then, that the study of politics, and of the scientific interpreters of political activity is essential for Christian moral action. If you wish to act with moral intentions in the economic sphere of life, you must have a disciplined knowledge of the economic context of moral intentions and actions. If you wish to affect the social morality of a local community, you must know that social context, its power structure, its mores, its institutional arrangements, its population movements, and so forth. Thus this particular contextual intention leads to the use of technical social analysis in the moral decision-making of the Christian community. It sometimes leads to primary research by the ethically motivated Christian scholar, in order to understand what forces are actually shaping events in a society.

An example of contextual analysis of this sort, motivated by this particular reason for being a "contextualist" is Kenneth Underwood's *Protestant and Catholic*. In this widely known study, Underwood's intentions are basically ethical. He analyzed the staggering weakness of the Protestant moral community in Holyoke, Massachusetts, when it faced the question, "What ought we to do?" in a particular situation. The situation was an invitation extended to Margaret Sanger to lecture on planned parenthood in a dominantly Roman Catholic city in the 1940's. Underwood put detailed sociological research to the service of a moral intention. In order to understand what the Protestants did do and did not do in those circumstances he made a detailed study of the city of Holyoke and its churches. He did a comparative analysis of the authority of Protestant and Catholic religious leadership, of the beliefs of Protestants and Catholics on religious and civil questions, of the class structure of the churches, of the relation of the churches to the labor movement, to business, and to politics, and he studied the history of Protestant involvement in politics in the city, and other matters. Underwood's conclusions are in effect these: Protestants were socially ineffective partly because they failed to understand the community situation in which they lived; they were unrealistic about the social context of which they were a part. If Protestants wish to affect comparable situations in other urban centers, they ought to take the social context—its political, religious, and economic aspects—more seriously than they normally do.[9]

A similar pattern of contextualism occurs in other areas of Christian ethics. In the ethics of medical care, for example, there is a constant reference to the particular circumstances of the patient. One might bring moral generalizations to bear on the question of abortion in general, for example, but physicians will often modify the implications of such generalizations with particular reference to the situation of the pregnant woman. This became a matter of international attention in the recent Finkbine case. The possibility of malformation of the child due to the drugs that were used during the pregnancy was the most important datum used in the decision of the parents to seek abortion. Under these particular circumstances, it was argued, abortion is morally responsible. The "context" was determinative of the decision.

The importance of knowing the actual social or personal situation is obviously not the only reason for being a "contextualist." Some writers propound the point of view in the first instance for theological reasons. This is the case for Karl Barth, as every reader of the *Church Dogmatics*, II/2, knows. Christians are to be obedient to the command of God. But the command of God is not given in formal, general ethics; it is not given in traditional rules of conduct. It is given by the living God in the concrete situation. It is a particular command addressed to a particular person in a particular sphere of activity, in a particular time and place. "The command of God as it is given to us at each moment is always and only one possibility in every conceivable particularity of its inner and outer modality."

> It is always a single decision. . . . We encounter it in such a way that absolutely nothing either outward or inward, either in the relative secret of our intention or in the unambiguously observable fulfilment of our actions, is left to chance or to ourselves, or rather in such a way that even in every visible or invisible detail He wills us precisely the one thing and nothing else, and measures and judges us precisely by whether we do or do not do with the same precision the one thing that He so precisely wills. Our responsibility is a responsibility to the command as it is given us in this way.[10]

Clearly Barth is not arguing for a "contextualism" on the grounds of a social realism that exists in the case of Underwood. Behind this particular quotation there is a whole doctrine of God who is for man in Jesus Christ, who is free, who is living and present to men in faith in the world. The fact that the ethics is expounded in terms of the particularity of God's command is more the function of Barth's doctrine of God than it is the function of a theory of human moral responsibility for a particular occasion. Theological conviction is the primary criterion by which an interpretation of the moral life is to be judged for its validity. This is clear from Barth's own extended discourse on the question "What are we to do?" The answers are given primarily in theological and religious terms, not in ethical terms. "We are to respond to the existence of Jesus Christ and His people. With our action we are to render an account to this grace." [11] "We are to accept as right, and live as those who accept as right the fact that they do not belong to themselves, that they therefore do not have their life in their own hands and at their own disposal, that they are made a divine possession in Jesus Christ." [12] "We are to accept it as right that God never meets us except compassionately, except as the One who comes to the help of our misery, except apart from and against our deserts, except in such a way as to disclose that what we have deserved is death." [13] "We are to accept it as right that God is our righteousness." [14] Further discussion of the question "What ought we to do?" adds little of moral particularity to the answer. We approach God as those who are ignorant and stand in need of divine instruction and conversion. We are to have complete openness, bracketing and holding in reserve what we know about the rightness and goodness of past decisions. We are to obey the command of God joyfully. We are to accept responsibility personally.[15]

Barth's ethics is called contextual or situational because certain basic theological affirmations permit only an ethics that is open to the present and the future, that is radically concrete in its commands. God's freedom to be for man in his grace, God's lordship over all things through his creation, redemption and reconciliation of all things, God's present activity and direct speech to man, God's calling each man to responsibility to him in the particular sphere of his life: these affirmations permit no general or formal ethics, but only an ethics of obedience in the particular time and place. Among American theologians, Joseph Sittler and Paul Lehmann also come to a contextual or relational ethic out of doctrinal affirmations, rather than from independent ethical grounds.

Joseph Sittler states that the Christian moral life is the actualization of man's justification in Christ. In man's organic relationship to God's work and presence, and to other men, the will of God is met as both known and unknown. "It is known in Christ who is the incarnate concretion of God's ultimate and relentless will-to-restoration; service of this will is presented to the believer not as a general program given in advance but as an ever-changing and fluctuant obligation to the neighbor in the midst of history's life." [16] The Christian perceives the neighbor's good and acts in continuity with his life in Christ and the ever-changing and fluctuant situation of the other person. Echoing Luther, Sittler says that the Christian moral life is "faith-doing." It is not a programmatic set of ideals, or a pattern of pre-defined obligations and duties. The authorization of this point of view is biblical.

The language of Christian ethics is in accord with the language of revelation, and the language of revelation is in accord with the nature of God's relationships to men and the world. This language or speech is organic, and not propositional. Just as the Bible does not define the nature of God, or prove his existence, or elaborate his attributes in rational categories, so in the area of ethics the Bible does not give abstract counsels, duties, obligations, or ideals. Just as "God simply *is* what God manifestly *does*," so there is an "inner logic of the living, the organic, the destiny-bound," that is expressed in "time terms," which is appropriate to the Christian moral life, and thus to ethics.[17] Biblical speech about God, the church, and man is all characterized by the language of organic relatedness.

Thus the Christian is organically related to his neighbors, and to the events and occasions of his historical life. He is also organically related to Christ; at least there is a continuity between the Christian and Christ that is best depicted in relational language. Thus

> the Christian life is here understood as a re-enactment from below on the part of men of the shape of the revelatory drama of God's holy will in Jesus Christ. . . . Suffering, death, burial, resurrection, a new life—

these are actualities which plot out the arc of God's self-giving deed in Christ's descent and death and ascension; and precisely *this same shape of grace* in its recapitulation within the life of the believer and the faithful community, is the nuclear matrix which grounds and unfolds the Christian life.[18]

Out of this matrix comes faith-doing in the "ever-changing and fluctuant obligation to the neighbor in the midst of history's life."[19] Christian ethics has to be in accord with these prior theological affirmations, which in turn are consonant with the character of the relations of God to man and man to other men. Thus there is an immediacy to the commands in the Christian life that is "not communicable in the causalities of propositional speech."

Paul Lehmann is the one author who extensively uses the particular term contextual. Like Barth and Sittler, his primary intention is to delineate a position in Christian ethics that is not alien to the fundamental dogmatic statements of the Christian church. He seeks to shape an ethics that is in accord with God's revelation in Jesus Christ, particularly with an interpretation of that revelation that stresses God's freedom in his humanizing work for man. He seeks an ethics that takes the Christian community seriously as the matrix of the Christian conscience, rather than as a prescriber of Christian moral propositions. Such an ethics then is one that delineates the Christian's participation in the world as one which coincides with what God is doing for man in a very particular set of events. The Christian is to have a theonomous conscience, a conscience "immediately sensitive to the freedom of God to do in the always changing human situation what his humanizing aims and purposes require. The theonomous conscience is governed and directed by the freedom of God alone."

> Christian ethics in the tradition of the Reformation seeks to provide an analysis of the environment of decision in which the principial foundations and preceptual directives of behavior are displaced by *contextual foundations* and *parabolic directives*. In a word, the environment of decision is the context for the ethical reality of conscience.[20]

Such an ethics is grounded in the divine indicative rather than the divine imperative. "The primary question is not, 'What does God command?' The primary question is 'What does God do?'"[21] Christian ethics analyzes what God is doing as its first order of business, not what the churches have said God has ordered men to do. It is the theological discipline that reflects on the question, and its answer, "What am I, as a believer in Jesus Christ and as a member of his church, to do?"[22] The answer is that I am to do what my theonomous conscience says I should do as it is immediately sensitive to what God in his freedom is doing.

There are three contexts out of which Christian behavior comes for Lehmann. The largest and most determinative is the theological one, namely the context of what God is doing. This is known in faith in Jesus Christ. Thus he develops a Christological statement that undergirds the assertion that God is doing "political activity," or "humanizing work."

> A theology of messianism [Lehmann's characterization of his Christological theology] is theology with the accent upon the politics of God, that is, upon what God has done and is doing in the world to keep human life human. For such a theology, three christological affirmations acquire particular significance. They are the doctrines of the Trinity, of the threefold office of Christ, and of the Second Adam and the Second Advent.[23]

The second context is that of the Christian community. Jesus is really present in history among the true people of God.

> It is this reality of the *koinonia* . . . which denotes the concrete result of God's specifically purposed activity in the world in Jesus Christ. We might, therefore, say that Christian ethics is *koinonia* ethics. This means that it is from, and in, the *koinonia* that we get the answer to the question: What am I, as a believer in Jesus Christ and as a member of his church to do?[24]

The third context is the particular situation in the world in which God is acting, and in which the Christian acts. In his affirmation of the importance of the concrete place of Christian activity, Lehmann executes his sharp critique of those who would view Christian ethics in more rationalistic terms, stressing basic moral propositions from the Christian tradition, and seeking to deduce the ways in which these can be applied to particular situations. Lehmann, on his theological grounds (not on ethical grounds, that is, not on the basis of an argument about the futility of imposing rationally derived propositions on to the dynamics of human history), bypasses this more rationally reflective procedure in favor of one that perceives, apprehends, or is sensitive to what God is doing. The stress is on other aspects of the self than the purely cognitive or intellectual aspects. He finds in the koinonia a coinciding of the response of Christians to what the community knows God has done and is doing. This leads relentlessly to highly particularized responses and actions, always sensitive to the historical present, rather than to generalizations about what ought to be.

For Lehmann, as for Barth and Sittler, Christian ethics that stress the importance of the particular situation, and the immediacy of involvement and response in that situation is legitimated on theological grounds. A quarrel with these men about the issue of contextualism must properly be a theological discussion. It necessarily involves the large and important question of the relation of ethics to dogmatics, and also the more particular questions about whether these men have properly appropriated the fundamental theological affirmations of the faith. The question of independent moral responsibility, or moral realism, in itself is not an appropriate question. There is a highly concrete sense of the place of responsibility and of the character of personal responsibility in these ethics, but it is theologically authorized. Contextual ethics are sound because they are consonant with what the Christian community knows God to be saying and doing, as this is made known in scripture.

There is yet a third reason for contextualism in Christian ethics, namely an understanding of the nature of human selfhood, of existence. Ethics is contextual because persons live in a pattern of human relations which inevitably make moral responsibility a particular response to persons or events. A social theory of the self requires a relational or situational ethic. Social views of self, however, are not the only anthropology that bring contextualism into Christian ethics; a more individualistic existentialism does so as well. Ethics is contextual because men are free to shape their own existences in faith by their responsible and creative decisions in the world. A view of social selfhood is to be found in the writings of H. Richard Niebuhr; a more individual approach can be found in the ethics of Rudolf Bultmann and others. In either case the anthropology is also authorized by an interpretation of theology; it is not absolutely independent. But each has a degree of autonomy that is notable, and on this ground can be dealt with in a way different from Barth, Sittler, and Lehmann. For purposes of brevity only Niebuhr's discussion will be used to make the point.[25]

For H. Richard Niebuhr, the notion of moral responsibility is so closely related to the idea of man as the responder that each necessarily implies the other. "What is implicit in the idea of responsibility is the image of man-the-answerer, man engaged in dialogue, man acting in response to action upon him." [26] He distinguishes this view of man, and consequently of ethics, from those that used the image of man-the-maker and thus worked with basically teleological images, and man-the-citizen and thus worked basically with legal images and with a sense of duty or obligation. The case for the view of man-the-answerer is not derived in the first instance from particular Christian doctrines; it was built upon "common experience." Thus there is a phenomenology of moral experience that is common to all men that makes the relational view of ethics appropriate, whether in Christian ethics, or some other view that has a different center of loyalty. When one observes moral action, he observes persons responding to the actions of other persons, or responding to events that have effects upon him. This is to be distinguished from those views that would affirm that men live and think morally first of all with reference to rules of conduct, or to ideas of what the future state of affairs ought to be. "All action . . . is response to action upon us." [27] "In our responsibility we attempt to answer the question: 'What shall I do?' by raising as the prior question: 'What is going on?' or 'What is being done to me?' rather than 'What is my end?' or 'What is my ultimate law?' " [28]

The effect of this understanding of selfhood is the delineation of an ethics that seeks to define and do what is fitting and appropriate in the particular relationships of the self. For Christians the interpretation of the situation involves an understanding of what God is saying and doing there. "Responsibility affirms—God is acting in all actions upon you. So respond to all actions upon you as to respond to his action." [29] The Christian community acts not only in response to the natural and historical context of its life, but in the light of a particular interpretation and understanding of that very particular context, namely what God is saying and doing there. Thus Niebuhr moves with ease between a view of the nature of man's moral existence to a view of the nature of God's being and presence as an active one. The two are coherent and congenial with each other, but Niebuhr does not seek to derive his anthropology from his doctrine of God. He is perfectly willing to find it in the common human experience as this was reconstructed in quite secular thinkers such as G. H. Mead, C. H. Cooley, Josiah Royce, and others, as well as theologians such as Buber. Finally, Niebuhr would say that a contextual ethics (though he fervently disliked the adjective) is necessary because of the nature of man.[30]

The fact that Christian moralists are contextualists in tendency for quite different reasons does not in and of itself imply that there is not enough common to all of them to make the use of the umbrella term appropriate. Obviously all have a special concern that the place of moral responsibility be understood to be highly specific and concrete, and that Christian ethics attend more to acting responsibly in a given place than it has done in those times and persons that seem satisfied with broad moral generalizations. There is a kind of personalism common to all of them, though it would be interpreted differently by various of them. But the main point to be noted for purposes of this essay is that men come to contextualism from different fundamental starting or base points, and the place from which they start sets the pattern for what considerations are most important in the delineation of Christian ethics. I shall return to this in a subsequent section of this study. It needs to be noted also that within a general common ground of concern for the particularities of time and place there are differences of opinion about the place and use of moral generalizations. Lehmann, for example, eschews them with a vengeance; he keeps his elaboration of the meaning of "humanizing" to a minimum. Barth, in *Church Dogmatics,* III/4, avoids formal principles, but is willing to accept the idea that for Christians certain forms of behavior are usually appropriate. Normally Christians do not take life, for example. H. Richard Niebuhr has a large place for the principles by which human action and divine action are interpreted, though he does not stipulate a series of rules of conduct.

Finally, it needs to be noted that no serious Christian moralist who champions the place of principles avoids the issues involved in their appropriation and application within unique situations. The defenders of principles seek to move from the general to the particular in a disciplined way. These observations are the occasion for the assertion that the term contextualism has been used to cover too many theological heads, and that the debate is misplaced as it has often been specified. The defenders of principles are equally hard to lump together, and to a demonstration of this I now turn.

The Authority and Use of Principles

Three of the ablest and most influential American writers in Christian ethics have defended the significance of Christian moral principles either in a self-conscious methodological way, or simply by effective use of Christian moral norms. They are Reinhold Niebuhr, John C. Bennett, and Paul Ramsey. The inclusion of the three together immediately suggests to the reader of their works that they use principles in different ways in Christian moral discourse. Niebuhr and Bennett are concerned with the use of moral generalizations to give direction to the consequences and effects of moral action; Ramsey very deliberately stresses the use of principles for the determination of the right means of conduct. To make this differentiation is not to say that Bennett and Niebuhr are unconcerned about the proper means to be used to establish a state of affairs that approximates a Christian norm, nor that Ramsey is unacquainted with the idea that right means of conduct have to be appropriate to the right ends of conduct. But the difference of concern is notable enough to indicate that the purposes for which principles are used are different, and thus these writers can not easily be lumped together.

Reinhold Niebuhr's love-justice dialectic is widely known, and thus does not require detailed exposition. In *An Interpretation of Christian Ethics,* he derives the distinctive significance of Christian ethics largely from the teachings of Jesus, in intellectual continuity with the theology of the social gospel. The problem of the Christian practical reason is then set by the discrepancy that exists between a moral ideal that is impossible of historical realization, a law of love that cannot be easily applied on the one hand, and the condition of man the sinner and the complexity of moral dilemmas on the other hand. His polemic had a particular historical reference, namely "all those forms of naturalism, liberalism, and radicalism which generate utopian illusions and regard the love commandment as ultimately realizable because history knows no limits of its progressive approximations." [31] Niebuhr's argument was not against an ethics of impossible ideals or unrealizable laws of love, but against those who too simply believed that history could be shaped by them. Thus he developed a procedure of reflection in which some approximation of the ideals could occur through the idea of justice and its ramifications for balances of power, and greater equality in the distribution of the means of power in human social affairs. Love remained the moral ideal and the moral law; indeed "the law of love is involved in all approximations of justice, not only as the source of the norms of justice, but as an ultimate perspective by which their limitations are discovered." [32] The action which seeks to achieve moral ends in the human community is always to be guided and judged by the "impossible ethical ideal" that is given in the gospel.

This basic pattern of moral reflection continued in Niebuhr's writings, though the statement of the authority of the norm and some of the concepts and their uses were slightly altered. In *The Nature and Destiny of Man* the self-sacrifice of Jesus on the cross becomes the central point for understanding the meaning of heedless *agape,* rather than the teachings of Jesus; and the dialectic is refined and complicated by the introduction of the idea of mutuality.[33] The fact that Niebuhr had an acute "contextual awareness" needs to be noted, for in the dialectic of Christian ethical thought and life it is necessary to have an understanding of what actually is going on in the realms of politics and economics, of international relations and war. Indeed, this is one pole of the dialectic. But Christian faith in effect provides a revelation of moral norms which always judges and guides the more pragmatic responses and actions to the fluctuations of human history. The norms derived from revelation are authorized by God's deed and by scripture, but they were also supported by their basically ethical significance as well. For example, Niebuhr argues for their significance in terms of the potential perversions and distortions of justice, if justice is not judged and tempered by a higher norm of self-sacrificial love.

John C. Bennett, like Niebuhr and many persons called contextualists, seeks to avoid utopianism and the lack of realism in Christian moral reflection and action. His concern also is to be significantly related to what is actually going on in human history and society. He also shares Niebuhr's view that there are norms given in the Christian revelation that can give guidance to the involvement of Christians in social change. His procedures are also well known to students of Christian ethics, particularly in the version of them he gave in *Christian Ethics and Social Policy,* where he shares J. H. Oldham's conception of "middle axioms" that stand between the transcendence of the Christian ethic on the one hand, and the situation of human sin and "technical autonomy" on the other hand. These middle axioms are goal-oriented, and not means-oriented. "The Christian ethic guides us in determining the goals which represent the purpose of God for our time." [34] Thus the church is to provide guidelines, or provisional definitions of goals that will help Christians relate the transcendent Christian ethics to given times and places. In writings subsequent to the book of 1946, Bennett has continued to indicate the necessity for more fixed principles as anchors and compasses (the words are mine, not his) for Christian ethics. Like Niebuhr, his concern is twofold; he does not wish to compromise the absoluteness of the demand of Christian ethics for indiscriminate love by some theological argument that mitigates their starkness, and yet he accepts a Christian sense of responsibility for the moral character of what is going on in human society. It is through the statement of fundamental principles and more particular derivative directives that Bennett keeps both poles in proper tension.

Paul Ramsey's polemic is against both what he deems to be the "wastelands of relativism" that are the effect of contextualism, and against those who use moral principles more for the purpose of prediction and governing of consequences than for the determination of the proper means of conduct. "*How* we do *what* we do is as important as our goals." Ramsey, like Niebuhr and Bennett, takes love to be the central point of reference for Christian ethics, although he also suggests in various writings that he wishes to resuscitate a modified version of natural law in Protestant ethics as well. "Love posits or takes form in principles of right conduct which express the difference it discerns between permitted and prohibited action, and these are not wholly derived from reflection upon consequences." [35] Ramsey's accent on the ethics of right conduct does not mean that he ignores prudential consideration of consequences, but that he wishes to make a corrective stance against Christian ethics that seem to be exclusively governed by such calculation. He works this methodological position out with reference to the situation of the Christian community in the nuclear weapons age, largely by a contemporary formulation of the just war theory. These principles of the right conduct of war are authorized by the Christian theological and ethical tradition, as it has sought to find the "in-principled" forms of love that enable conduct to be guided during conflict, and by the Biblical revelation of love made known in the faith that Christ died for all men. They are worked out in relation to the possible use of nuclear weapons, as the writers on military strategy have considered the potential function of these weapons in an open international conflict. Ramsey's procedures, as he does this, are much more akin to the rational procedures of the moral theology tradition of the Roman Catholic Church than they are to most of the work of his fellow Protestant theologians. This makes him the most audible and visible defender of "principled ethics," as Lehmann's use of the notion of contextualism makes him the most audible and visible critic of such ethics.

In this brief analysis of these writers, it becomes clear that principles are used in different ways by different writers, and have different degrees of authority. In the case of Reinhold Niebuhr, love and justice are norms that are given a minimum of definition, and certainly are not spelled out into a series of moral propositions given for the guidance of conduct. The weight of his work is so heavily upon the assessment of what is going on in society, and the pragmatic judgments made (to be sure under the judgment and guidance of the ideas of love and justice), that he could easily be located on the contextual side of the debate. John C. Bennett's statements of middle axioms are deliberately relativized as being the creatures of ethical reflection under very specific circumstances, and thus open to revision as circumstances change. Paul Ramsey's delineation of principles of right conduct are weighted with more authority, for he has a confidence in the tradition that makes him take its distillations of the bases of judgment very seriously in their own right, apart from the contemporary occasions in which they are to be applied. If our discussion was extended to include Roman Catholic ethics, an even greater certitude about certain traditional moral propositions would be disclosed. Niebuhr and Bennett tend to use principles for the determination of a better state of affairs, or for the delineation of proper goals; Ramsey stresses right conduct and means as well as calculation of ends, and in this sense shares the ethos of Catholic moral theology. Apart from such a refinement of what is involved in the ethic of moral principles, the lumping of these writers together is a serious oversimplification.

In an earlier essay, I suggested a distinction between the prescriptive use of principles and the illuminative use of principles.[36] The distinction is introduced here to indicate some of the difficulties inherent in the polarization of the current debate. For Paul Ramsey, traditional Christian moral principles have such authority that they in effect prescribe the right conduct of Christians. Another moralist can read Ramsey's arguments, take them with great seriousness as an illustration of how a very thoughtful Christian ethicist reflects upon a current moral situation, and find the principles to illuminate his own judgment without being determined by the authority of the principles or the argument. He can find other statements of principles and other arguments equally illuminating, and equally important for his own decision. If the moralist stresses the openness of the present situation, the responsibility of the person in it to make his own decision, and the power of affections, dispositions, and perceptiveness also to give guidance to behavior, he need not necessarily ignore traditional moral principles. Rather, they are a significant part, though only a part, of what goes into his own moral reflection. Principles enable him to *interpret* what is morally wrong and morally right about a particular occasion; to interpret what direction subsequent events ought to take in order to maintain the existence of the good and preserve it from disaster; and to interpret what patterns and means of action are more appropriate morally as he participates in events. But they are not prescriptive in the sense that the principles and arguments made concerning their application are the most important or sole authority for the governing of action. Thus casuistic arguments can be read with a great deal of serious interest without being determinative of conduct. In the illuminative use of principles the center of gravity is on the newness, the openness, the freedom that is present, in which the conscientious man seeks to achieve the good and do the right. In the prescriptive use of principles the center of gravity is on the reliability of traditional moral propositions and their reasonable application in a relatively open contemporary situation.

On the basis of this distinction, it is possible for persons who appear to be contextualists actually to be very serious students of moral principles and of the science of casuistry. The function that this study has, however, is different from what it appears to have for Paul Ramsey and for traditional Catholic moral theologians. But its function can be important enough to raise a serious question about the easy identification of theological moralists into two camps. Karl Barth, for example, in *Church Dogmatics*, III/4, discusses particular instances of moral decision with some care and precision as a way for the reader to become sensitive to what God might be commanding him to be and to do in an analogous situation. Even Paul Lehmann introduces the notion that God's activity is "political" and "humanizing," terms that are susceptible to more extensive exposition than he gives them, but nevertheless function as points of illumination for the actual conduct of the Christian man.

The debate between context and principles, then, forces an unfair polarization upon a diversity of opinion that makes it both academically unjust, and increasingly morally fruitless. Persons assigned to either pole are there for very different reasons, and work under the respective umbrellas in very different ways. It also becomes clear that contextualists find some moral principles or generalizations that give guidance to existential decisions, and that the defenders of principles find some ways to proceed from generalizations to particular situations. This assertion points to the theme of the remainder of the paper, namely, that Christian ethics can and does begin from at least four base points, and no matter which one is primary for a particular theologian, he moves toward the other three as he extends his moral discourse within a Christian frame of reference.

Four Base Points for Christian Moral Discourse

The four base points have already been introduced, though one not as directly as the others. There are moralists who begin with as accurate and perceptive social analysis, or situational analysis as possible. Others begin with fundamental theological affirmations. Still others locate moral principles as the central point for discussion. In addition to these three a fourth can be discerned, namely the nature of the Christian's life in Christ and its proper expressions in moral conduct. To be related to Jesus Christ in faith is to have a certain manner or quality of life which in turn has its appropriate moral expressions in intentions and actions. I shall indicate by use of examples the way in which moral reflection beginning from each of these points moves to a consideration of the other points as it engages in moral discourse.

It is appropriate to begin with the two base points that have already received most attention, namely with moral principles and with theological affirmations. Ramsey seeks to think about the use of modern weapons within the tradition of just war principles, and particularly the principle of noncombatant immunity. Noncombatants are not to be directly and intentionally killed in warfare. This is a moral proposition that is to be applied to the conduct of war in every time and place; it is as valid for the twentieth century as it was for the fifth century. Obviously Ramsey cannot, and does not wish to remain at the level of reiteration of an honored principle. He necessarily moves toward the particular context of warfare in the twentieth century, because the conduct of warfare, and even of the testing of weapons for warfare is different by virtue of the state of technology than it was when the principle was first formulated. When a large part of the economy of a nation is marshalled for the productive effort needed to conduct modern warfare, are the producers in factories combatants or noncombatants? When the scale of destruction by weapons is so great that a precise demolition of military installations is made difficult, is it meaningful to counsel noncombatant immunity? Ramsey takes the technological situation into view when he proceeds to ask these questions that any critical person would. He indicates in a number of his writings that he has read such authors as Oskar Morgenstern, and Herman Kahn as carefully and seriously as any Christian moralist has done, writers who discuss the problems involved in the use of weapons and the potential effects of their use in terms of the contemporary international situation. The point is a simple one: Ramsey moves from a basic moral principle to the problems that exist in and for its application under very particular conditions of the technology of welfare. He is cautious to keep his argument on the moral level; what makes the conduct of war right according to the just war principles is not derived from analysis of weapons, nor merely from the potential consequences of the use of weapons now being made, but from the fact that in-principled love requires guards against indiscriminate killing. But he cannot avoid dealing with what now potentially exists in the state of contemporary technology.

Ramsey also moves from a particular principle to some theological justification for the principle. He believes that the just war principles are authorized in at least a twofold manner. When reasonable men think reasonably about the conduct of war, they will make the means used in war proportionate to the ends to be sought, and the ends to be sought will also be reasonable. In this sense there is an appeal made to human reason, or to the natural law as a ground for the principles. When Christians in the history of the church's involvement in Western history have sought to understand what their central theological and moral point of reference—love— implies for the restraint of evil within social responsibility, they have worked this out in terms of just war principles. Thus there is also an appeal to the particular touchstone of Christian ethics. Augustine, Thomas, and other theologians have put the principles into love so that they can give direction to human activity. There is congruity between the particularized principles such as noncombatant immunity, and the affirmation that Christ, in love, died for all men. Thus in moving from the moral level of discourse to the authorization of moral rules Ramsey turns to philosophical and theological affirmations.

In yet another way Ramsey moves toward theological affirmations. He opens the way for a revision of ethical principles when certain theological realities take over. The principles are to be used as a service, and not as a reliance; "these rules are opened for review and radical revision in the instant that *agape* controls." In indicating where he differentiates his work from certain Catholic moralists, he suggests that "in the view here proposed, charity enters into a fresh determination of what is right in the given concrete context, and it is not wholly in bondage to natural-law determination of permitted or prohibited means." [37] Love is not only the basis for moral principles, it is an active reality that makes the moral person open to revision of the principles derived from it, and enables him freshly to determine what is right in a particular context. God's love, then, is free to alter the rules that men normally live by, though normally they ought to live by the rules derived from knowledge of God's love. A contrast with Karl Barth's procedure is instructive. Barth seems to say, God in his freedom commands man in his situation ever anew. Since he is not capricious, he is likely to command similar things, indeed the same thing over and over again. But one is not to make a moral principle out of the consistencies of God's speech. Ramsey seems to say that Christian love usually acts within the law and lays down rules or principles. Thus we normally act according to these rules. But, since Jesus Christ is Lord, there can always be a "fresh determination of what should be done in situations not rightly covered by the law, by natural justice, or even by its [Christian love's] own former articulation in principle." [38] Thus in moving from principles to Christian love, presumably to God's active love, one finds the source not only of principles, but of the fresh determinations of what should be done. What is Barth's first declaration comes in as a qualification of Ramsey's ethical style, though as a theological moralist he necessarily takes account of it.

Ramsey says little about the freedom of the Christian in faith and love to apprehend freshly what he ought to do and to be, though perhaps such a view is implicit in his understanding of the moment that *agape* controls. If he were to be more completely systematic than he has been, it would be necessary for him to develop an understanding of the Christian man in faith, who is open to the love of God both in its form of rules and its freer form. He would answer questions pertaining to the nature and authority of the Christian conscience to determine what is morally right. Thus he would move not only from principles toward the historical situation, and the theological affirmations, as he does, but also to a view of human moral life in faith.

The theological moralist whose apparent base point is certain theological affirmations about the nature and activity of God necessarily moves toward the other base points as his reflection becomes systematic. I have indicated how Paul Lehmann, like Barth, develops a view of Christian ethics that is coherent with his understanding of God's work made known in and through Jesus Christ. It is also clear from our previous exposition that Lehmann's conception of God's activity in the events in which men participate requires an acute sensitivity to what is really going on in the particular personal and social context of behavior. [39]

Although Lehmann's view of conscience has been alluded to, it is worth further elaboration here, for the possibility of the kind of contextual ethics he expounds depends in large part on the viability of his view of the nature of the Christian moral self. Certain accents are distinctive and important. Lehmann pays more attention to the role of sensitivity, imagination, and perceptiveness than do many writers in the field of ethics. In his description of the theonomous conscience we have already seen this: it is "immediately sensitive to the freedom of God to do . . . what his humanizing aims and purposes require." Immediate sensitivity to what God is doing in his freedom apparently is not something that comes from a more rationalistic ethical discourse. It assumes a transformation of the self in faith. The church is the matrix of this transformation. "The reality of the church is an ethical reality because what God is doing in the world becomes concrete in the transformation of human motivation and the structures of human relatedness which are the stuff of human fulfillment." [40] An ethics that is as free of rational calculation as Lehmann's is logically has to have a view of the self that accomplishes what precise rational discourse does for a writer such as Paul Ramsey. The activity of God, Lehmann asserts,

> is brought directly to bear upon the life of the believer by means of a functional christological context and connection. . . . It is also a way of giving to the believer a clear understanding of the environment and direction of what he is to do and thus a firm foundation for behavior. The difference [between believers and unbelievers] is defined by imaginative and behavioral sensitivity to what God is doing in the world to make and keep human life human, to achieve the maturity of men, that is, the new humanity.[41]

Lehmann's emphasis on transformation of motivation, on a clear understanding that is relatively unaided by moral or sociological principles, on imaginative and behavioral sensitivity locates the personal nexus between God's activity and human action. Whether it stands up under various forms of criticism is not the concern of this essay. Lehmann does move to the outlines of a view of Christian moral life in faith that is consistent with the other bases of his ethics. Indeed, Christian ethics aims at a quality of life of which morality is the by-product. *"Christian ethics aims, not at morality, but at maturity. The mature life is the fruit of Christian faith. Morality is a by-product of maturity."* [42]

Lehmann eschews moral principles, and seems to assert that any use of them falls into a false abstraction, separating morality from life.[43] Consistent with this is his emphasis on the freedom of God, about which he says much more than he does about the love of God, or the ordering work of God. Yet there is a consistency to God's activity, so that Lehmann reiterates that it is a "humanizing," or "maturing" activity. He desists from extensive exposition of what these terms mean. Maturity, he says, *"is* the integrity in and through interrelatedness which makes it possible for each individual member of an organic whole to be himself in togetherness, and in togetherness each to be himself."

> For Christianity, what is fundamentally human in human nature is the gift to man of the power to be and to fulfill himself in and through a relationship of dependence and self-giving toward God and toward his fellow man. Thus, maturity is *self-acceptance through self-giving.* . . . In

the fully developed Christian sense, "maturity" and "the new humanity" are identical.[44]

In spite of the severe economy of exposition, Lehmann does have a particular content in view when he uses these key terms. The effect is that these notions become principles of illumination for sensitive Christians in discerning what God is doing. They are not to be used as the first principles in the resolution of a problem in the manner of the science of casuistry. But they provide meaningful points of reference for moral judgment. Where humanizing work is going on, God is active, and where Christians perceive this they are to act so that their behavior coincides with what God is doing.

Thus Lehmann moves from his prime base of theological affirmation to a consideration of the other three bases for Christian moral discourse. His reluctance to denote in greater detail what functions as principles of illumination and judgment is consistent with his starting point and the way in which he defines it, but clearly Christians are not to be immature, nor are they to engage in anything that is inhuman, or dehumanizing in its effects.

If the ethicist begins with disciplined social analysis, he has to move to other points in order to clarify the moral judgments that he makes about what he finds to be the case. Often there is a division of labor between the social analyst and the moralist, though it is quite typical for the moralist to make a judgment on the information he perceives to be important or adequate pertaining to a particular instance, whether this information is derived in a disciplined way or by impressions. It is also the case that social analysis is often freighted with moral judgments. If Kenneth Underwood's study is taken as a case of social analysis done for ethical intention, the need for movement between principles or bases of moral judgment and empirical analysis can be seen. If the weakness in thought and deed of the Protestant churches in Holyoke is bad, as Underwood clearly indicates he believes, it is judged bad on the basis of moral and theological convictions, not sociological evidence. One can extrapolate from the analysis he makes to indicate what some of the bases of judgment are. Presumably the churches were not acting out a theologically defined conception of their mission; they were not being responsible to the God they confessed in worship. Presumably also they lacked the ethical clarity to order the various activities in which they ought to be engaged, and thus were institutionally subject to social pressures. Underwood does not draw out these things, for he is particularly seeking to show how moral communities must understand their social contexts through a process of social analysis. He does not claim that the book has Christian ethics as its primary subject matter. But a more extensive ethical treatise would require the movement in the directions of the other bases. There is something theologically awry with the actual situation, there is something morally weak about it, and the religious leaders and laity lack some qualities of Christian existence which prohibited them from becoming more active in accord with professed convictions.

The fourth base, that of a conception of Christian existence, has not been clearly represented in our previous analysis. In the case of H. R. Niebuhr, an interpretation of moral existence is clearly a major starting point for ethical and moral reflection, but in *The Responsible Self* he is not concerned to suggest the particular qualities that the religious life in faith brings into being. Further exploration of Bultmann's ethics would be one way of making the point. Man in faith has a radical freedom to be himself, to be obedient to the command of God. The moral life is to some extent then a situational expression of that faith, that freedom, and that obedience.

The interrelation between base points, with a particular prime focus on the state of the life of faith can best be illustrated by Luther's essay, "On the Liberty of the Christian Man." In this particular work, Luther describes the Christian life in the famous aphorisms, "A Christian man is a perfectly free Lord of all, subject to none. A Christian man is a perfectly dutiful servant of all, subject to all." [45] He goes on to describe the nature of this Christian liberty and righteousness, which cannot be produced by work or by any external influence, but only by the word of God received in faith. Thus, in the very description of the righteousness of the Christian, Luther immediately turns to the theological source and foundation of it, that is God's gift of his Son which is the act of God's justification of man. The concern for which Luther is most widely known even outside the Christian community enters in here, namely that law and works are unnecessary for any man's righteousness (in the sense of the gift of God's righteousness) and salvation. God counts men righteous, and in the faith of man gives the gift of liberty and righteousness. He unites the believer with Christ as the bride is united with the bridegroom. "Therefore, faith alone is the righteousness of a Christian man and the fulfilling of all the commandments." [46] Thus Luther describes the "inward man" with immediate reference to God's work for man in Jesus Christ.

This inward man, while never perfectly spiritual and holy in this life, nevertheless gives to the "outward man" certain characteristics. The works of the outward man never justify him before God, but they do express the desire born in faith to reduce the body to subjection and to purify its evil lusts. They are directed toward the neighbor in love. The attention given to the self in faith and the idea that the external actions are expressions of that faith can be seen when Luther writes:

> These two sayings, therefore, are true: "Good works do not make a good man, but a good man does good works; evil works do not make a wicked man, but a wicked man does evil works"; so that it is always necessary that the "substance" or person itself be good before there can be any good works, and that good works follow and proceed from the good person, as Christ also says, "A corrupt tree does not bring forth good fruit, a good tree does not bring forth evil fruit." [47]

Faith, then, brings with it the gifts of righteousness and liberty, which are effectual through love. Faith "issues in works of the freest service cheerfully and lovingly done, with which a man willingly serves another without hope or reward." [48]

Luther does not digress from his primary attention to give illustrations of what the neighbor's needs are; he does not describe the kinds of personal and social contexts in which the works of love are to be effectual. But obviously he assumes that they are particular and concrete. Nor does he spell out some principles of Christian love that enter into the guidance of the action directed by love to the neighbor. He does have, however, the figure of the work of Jesus Christ in view, as that which gives something of the shape of the Christian's intentions and actions toward others. The full work of Christ presents a pattern for the relation to others.

> Just as our neighbor is in need and lacks that in which we abound, so we also have been in need before God and have lacked His mercy. Hence, as our heavenly Father has in Christ freely come to our help we also ought freely to help our neighbor through our body and its works, and each should become as it were a Christ to the other, that we may be Christs to one another and Christ may be the same in all; that is, that we may be truly Christians. [49]

The work of Christ, received by Christians in faith, both empowers and shapes the arc of their relation to the neighbor, and in this sense functions as a broad, but delineated pattern for the Christian moral life.

Thus Luther touches upon the four bases that have been indicated to be necessary for a systematic Christian ethic. His primary concern in the essay on liberty is to describe the Christian life, but he cannot do this without attending to the theological sources of that existence, and to both those persons toward whom it is expressed in love, and the shape of the life that properly expresses it.

The intention of this section has now been executed, namely to show that authors of important works in and for Christian ethics tend to focus on one base point in their exposition, and even to declare that a certain base point is the proper point for beginning Christian moral reflection, and that they necessarily move toward some consideration of the other base points. This is sometimes done with great self-consciousness so that the way in which they deal with them is consistent with their starting point, or it is only indicated in a cursory fashion that cries out for further exploration. The debate over context and principles is over-simplied if it does not take into account these base points, and the way in which they are related to the discussions of context and the use and authority of principles.

For Clarification of Discussion

The way in which the debate has attended to the moral level of discourse, without sufficiently moving to other levels is in part responsible for its being misplaced. It has tended to assume that the matter of how moral decisions are made could be separated from other considerations. I hope it is now clear that if one chooses to argue against "contextualism" one has to direct his arguments to the theological and ethical reasons given for the stress on context. Thus against Barth, Lehmann, and Sittler, one's argument ought primarily to be a theological argument. It is because these men have a certain view of God and his activity that they find contextualism congenial as an approach to ethics. None of them is fixed upon the question, "How do men decide what to do?" as if this ethical question were capable of abstraction from fundamental *theo*logical convictions in the strict sense. If one chooses to argue against H. R. Niebuhr, he would have to argue not only on theological grounds (not explicated in this essay), but on the grounds of a moral anthropology. Is man to be understood as responder and answerer, or is he better understood as maker and citizen? If one chooses to argue against the demand for refined social analysis of the context of action, the character of one's concerns might be directed to whether that context is properly understood through the means of social research, and whether such a proposal does not carry with it unexplicated ethical and theological assumptions.

Similarly, if one argues against principles, one has to be particular about certain questions. From what sources are the principles derived? From nature, or from Biblical revelation, or from the ethos of the Christian community? How are principles used? For giving direction to goals, or for the determination of right conduct? As prescriptive principles, or as analytical and illuminating principles?

If one persists in choosing sides in a misplaced debate, there are still questions that have to be dealt with. How does one move between moral principles and theological affirmations? Do certain defenses of principles assume certain views about God that are not necessarily consistent with such ethics? What is assumed about the nature of the moral self in various uses of principles? About the amenability of the social and personal world to subjection to principles, and actions governed quite exclusively by principles? How does one move between theological affirmations, moral principles and moral judgments? Through a view of sensitivity and imagination? Through rational calculation?

Further elaboration of these questions, raised by this paper is not necessary. One larger one still looms, namely is there one normative starting point, or base point, for work in Christian ethics around which other discussion ought to cohere? On this question the author has convictions, but their exposition lies outside the scope of this methodological analysis.

chapter 4

Two Approaches
to Theological Ethics

Any essay entitled "Two Approaches to . . ." alerts the reader to both the utility and the peril of typologies. As an exercise in reflection, efforts to distinguish by way of contrast necessarily require exaggeration of the positions under scrutiny. Yet, it is often through such development of contrasts that issues of importance for discussion become clear. Our concern is to examine two approaches to relating theology and ethics.

In their simplest and boldest contrasting forms, they may be stated as follows. The first approach claims that Christian faith enables men to perceive the presence of God in the human, to perceive what God is doing in the world. It is clearly discerned in this perception what men are to do as moral agents. The second approach claims that the faith of the Christian community is expressed in beliefs about God given in the biblical accounts of his deeds in the world, and in the form of propositions. On the basis of these beliefs about God, human events requiring moral action are interpreted in such a way that inferences are drawn pertaining to what God's purposes and will might be in those events. Reflection on these purposes leads to the determination of actions which are in some sense authorized by them, inferred from them, and consistent with them.

It is possible that persons who state their case in terms of the first approach are operating in the "first order of discourse," namely, that

Reprinted with permission from *Union Seminary Quarterly Review,* Vol. XXIII, No. 4, Summer 1968.

which is appropriate to the immediacy of occasions of moral discernment. On the other hand, persons who state their case in terms of the second approach may be operating in the "second order of discourse," namely, that which is appropriate to giving reasons for judgments made in a less reflective and rational manner. Thus, it is quite possible that in certain instances the two approaches are not inconsistent with each other, but are supplementary; in other instances, the two approaches might represent basically different ways of doing theological ethics.

Drawing the Epistemological Distinction

In the literature which evokes reflection on a distinction between the two approaches, there appears, in varying degrees, an affinity between the first approach and substantive theological convictions which speak about God's relation to history in terms of his activity, his presence, or his commanding in and through events. If God's activity is historical, if there is an immediacy of his presence in changing events, a more intuitive approach to knowing what he is doing and to ascertaining what man is to do in changing events seems to be required. A more dynamic understanding of God's involvement seems to require a way of knowing that involvement and knowing what man is to do which can do full justice to the highly particular, concrete situation and to openness toward the new in the future. This apparent and actual affinity, however, is not a necessary one, unless a claim is made for intuiting with absolute certitude directly and immediately what God is doing or saying and what man is to do in relation to God's doing —unless a claim is made that God reveals in absolute certitude what he is then and there doing and requiring. One may believe God is present and yet have grave difficulties in discerning what precisely he is doing. Believing that God is present and active in the human and knowing precisely what he is doing and saying in it are two different items. If one chooses to determine his action by what God is doing, he can make his judgments through the second approach as well as the first. And, for example, one might claim to perceive God's presence in an absolute fixed moral order and claim to grasp from that more static understanding what deeds are in accord with that order.

The difference between the two approaches is primarily an epistemological one. The major questions are (a) how does one know what God is doing? Or, how does one judge what God's purposes might be? And (b) how does one move from the determination of God's action or purposes to what man's proper action is to be? How does one know what man is to do? The first approach seems to rely upon a very complex form of intuition; the theologically informed and religiously sensitive perception authorizes a determination of both what God is doing and of what man is to do. The second seems to rely upon rational delineations of religious beliefs drawn from the life of the Christian community as a basis for only relatively certain judgments of what God's purposes are. In addition, it relies upon certain canons of moral reasoning for the judgment of what human moral purposes and acts are to be inferred from beliefs about God and his purposes. The first question is paramountly a concern of theology proper. But since it arises often in the context of the practical life of the religious community, it becomes a question for ethics. The second question is more properly one of ethics; its answer requires an examination of how one moves from theological statements to human moral requirements.

The two epistemological questions are not merely a matter of speculative academic interest alone. Both are involved in practical differences of opinion among conscientious Christians. Two illustrations will show why clarification of what is involved in answering these questions is important in practical morality. The first is the involvement of Christians in social revolutions. How does one decide whether he ought or ought not to align himself with a revolution? The first approach might answer the first question in this way: God is doing revolutionary activity in the world in our time. Christians are sensitive to what God is doing and ought to be doing what he is doing. Therefore, they ought to be engaged in revolutionary activities. There are two ways in which one might dispute this answer. One might assert that Christians who perceive God to be doing revolutionary activity are favorably disposed to the revolution that is going on because of moral commitments that they have, or because of certain attitudes and sensitivities they have about injustice in the world. This favorable disposition toward revolutions leads them to perceive God as doing revolutionary work. The reading of what God is doing provides a theological warrant, a justification that is important to have for religious men. It also provides a persuasive assertion to persons who take religious language seriously. Thus, the real argument is not over what God is doing but rather over the moral grounds on which a revolution is or is not justifiable. The second approach might indicate that certain moral values or purposes are consistent with beliefs in God according to the faith and life of the Christian community. This approach might well support the revolution as a practical inference, not from the perception of what God is doing but from the values and purposes that are consistent with Christian beliefs. In the second approach, differences of judgment about revolutions would occur over which values and purposes are authorized by beliefs and over which kinds of action are required or enabled by purposes and beliefs.

Theological Evaluation

The second way to dispute the answer that God is doing revolutionary activity, and consequently Christians should also be revolutionaries, would be to grant that convictions about God's action or his purposes are formative in determining the attitudes and actions of Christians and are not merely theological rationalizations. The objector might ask if God is doing only revolutionary activity. Is he doing other things as well, such as seeking to preserve order in the midst of radical change? Here the real argument is a substantive theological one; it is about what God's action is, what God's purposes are. If the disputants both take the first approach, their disagreements are those of perception of what God is doing. To settle the issue, or even to define the differences would require that each give justifications for his perceptions, which might lead into the second approach. If the second approach is accepted by the disputants, the argument would be on the evidences (biblical, theological) that would warrant a judgment of what God is doing or wills that men should do in this time.

Understanding disagreements between Christians about revolutions then, involves *how* God's actions and purposes are known, *what* is known about God's actions and purposes regardless of how it is known, *how* practical moral requirements are determined from what is known of God, and *what* practical moral requirements are proper. Do the answers to the "how" questions determine the answers to the "what" questions? In principle, no. In principle, one can follow the first approach, and be either revolutionary or counter-revolutionary. The same is true for the second approach. What the second approach does is to put more of the argument (both its "what" and its "how") into the public domain where differences of opinion can be discussed rationally, including a rational justification of a more intuitive answer to the "how" question.

The second illustration shows that the issues are present in the Bible. Some verses from the priestly code in Leviticus indicate this. "You shall do my ordinances and keep my statutes and walk in them. I am the Lord your God. You shall therefore keep my statutes and my ordinances, by doing which a man shall live; I am the Lord" (18:4-5). In the context of this passage there is no elaboration of who God is or what he is doing. Because he is the Lord, men are to obey his commandments and laws which he has made known. There is the claim to obedience which appears to be entailed in the assertion "I am the Lord." What is to be obeyed is stipulated. The hinge on which a theological assertion and moral imperatives turn is this: All the laws are to be obeyed *because* they are God's laws. But we are disposed for many reasons not to obey all the laws, though we take some of them very seriously. For example, the admonitions against incest are not disputed. "None of you shall approach any one near of kin to him to uncover nakedness. I am the Lord" (18:6). Love of neighbor is positively affirmed. "But you shall love your neighbor as yourself. I am the Lord" (19:18). But dietary laws appear to be examples of misplaced concreteness that can be neither theologically nor morally justified. "You shall not eat any flesh with blood in it" (19:26). If contemporary theologians wished to affirm that incest is wrong and love of neighbor is right, and that eating meat with blood in it is a matter of indifference, they can use either of the two approaches. For the sake of brevity, I confine myself here to the second approach. Regarding incest, a natural-law thinker might say that God has created human nature with certain inherent purposes, and that fulfillment of that nature requires conformity with those purposes and non-conformity with what is antithetical to those purposes. Incest is not in accord with nature and, therefore, is morally wrong. With regard to love of neighbor, a "biblical" theologian might say that God's fundamental nature is love, his activities are loving, and thus the love of neighbor is consistent with God's revealed presence in Christ and with his fundamental intention for the human family. Both might say that dietary laws cannot be given such justification and thus are out of order.

Theologically supported ethics, whether biblical or contemporary, turn in some way on the hinge which joins the divine and the human. "God is . . . , therefore men ought to do . . . ." Here we do not exhaust the analysis of the hinge; we merely elaborate two approaches to it.*

The First Approach: God Realizing the Human

I have stated that in principle there is no necessary connection between the "how" and the "what" questions unless a very distinct claim is made for certitude either of man's intuition of what God is doing in the moment, or of God's revelation to man of what he is doing in the moment. Yet there appears to be an affinity between the theology of God's doing and presence

---

* More sophisticated and intensive analysis of this issue is being done by Mr. John P. Reeder, Jr., of Brown University, and by others. Hopefully these contributions will soon be made public.

and the more intuitive approach to ethics. Theological ethics which ask the first question, "What is God doing?" (Paul Lehmann), or make the primary assertion "God is acting in all actions upon you" (H. R. Niebuhr), or which interpret the meaning of Incarnation in the personalistic terms of God's presence in the human (William Van der Marck, in *Toward a Christian Ethic*, for example) invite a certain inquiry. That is, how does one distinguish between personal experiences as happening and God's doing or presence in what is happening? If the moral action of Christians is to be governed not just by what is the case, by what is occurring, but by God's action or presence in what is happening (moral action requires some gap between what is and what ought to be), God's action must be discerned and must be delineated in some distinctive terms. No theological ethicist is proposing that what can be chronicled by observers is what God is doing, that by knowing social factual data I know God's presence.

It is easy, but important, to understand why this is the case. If what is actually happening (assuming the possibility of knowing this on the part of some omniscient being) is what God is doing, and if what I am to do is to be in accord with what God is doing, response or obedience to God's action would be a simple acquiescence to all events as they are being determined by powers beyond one's control. This involves one in all the problems of ethics that are entailed by rigorous determinism. Ethics based on a theology of God's action or presence vary in the degree of determinism that is involved, depending on the terms in which the perception of that action is expressed. But all assume that what is happening is subject to alteration by the responses and interventions of men, and that men are responsible for these interventions. If what God is perceived to be doing is not what is actually the state of affairs, there must be ways to distinguish the two.

The Humanization Model

The distinction in practice appears to be made on the basis of a judgment that certain qualities of life and relationships, certain purposes being actualized, mark God's presence and action. Perhaps a biblical text illustrates this point: "No man has ever seen God; if we love one another, God abides in us and his love is perfected in us" (1 John 4:12). Where there is love among men, there is the presence of God among them. In Van der Marck's terms, God is present in the human. To be human is to move toward intersubjectivity and fellowship with one another; where there is intersubjectivity and fellowship, there is God's presence. Paul Lehmann's use of humanization appears to function in a similar way: God is doing humanizing work; where life is becoming human, God is at work. H. R. Niebuhr's interpretation of God's action in historical events and human action was more complex than these other examples: God is working creatively and redemptively. He is also man's judge and stern governor. Since, *prima facie,* these aspects of God's activity are not immediately in simple harmony with each other in human experience, the perception of his action in events is a very difficult matter indeed. Whether a particular theologian makes the process complex and difficult or simple and self-evident, the perception or discernment of God's action seems to involve a movement from the presence of certain designated human qualities, values, and purposes to the perception of God's presence.

There is nothing intellectually perverse about this, since theological justifications can be given for it. If, for example, "God is for man," those relationships among men which appear to be "for man" can be indications of where God is. If, as in the case of Van der Marck, the significance of the revelation in Christ is that it makes known God's presence in the human, then where the human is, there is God. In the case of Paul Lehmann, the theological interpretation of the messianic political activity of God, based upon the New Testament witness, provides the justification for affirming that God is doing humanizing work. One cannot charge these theological ethicists with deciding in some vacuum what they like, and then asserting that because they like it, God is doing it. On the other hand, they are not affirming that whatever is, whether it is "for man" or against him, is of God's doing. (H. R. Niebuhr might be an exception to the last statement.) Since God's activity is perceived to be what is for human well-being, what is for human well-being seems to be a mark of God's presence and activity. Where the "human" is not occurring, is God absent? Where men are striving to fulfill other aims than humanizing ones, is God not present? Since divine sovereignty is not denied by these theological ethics, in principle the answers are "no." Deficiency in authentic humanity (intersubjectivity) is sin, according to Van der Marck, and man is for him, as for others, responsible for sin.

Discerning the Human

To make my general point clear, I will confine myself to the use of the "human" or "humanization" as the mark by which one perceives the presence of God's activity. The "human" in this usage is a distinctively normative or value term. It is not a descriptive term used basically to contrast man and other animals in such a way that no normative elements are included. God is doing what is normatively human. An action is right not because God is doing it; God is doing it because it is morally right. This is the hinge on which several things turn. Theology and moral sensitivities of a religious nature inform the perception of what is normatively human. But sensitive human perceptions of what human well-being really means also inform the perception of the presence of God and his action. And since it is the normatively human that God is doing, and since all that is in the human world is not fully human, what God is doing enables, informs, and requires moral actions on man's part. The assertion that God is doing the human, or is present in the human, becomes the hinge on which turn my perception of what God is doing and my perception of what I ought to be doing. And my perception of what God is doing and what I am to do (not to forget Lehmann's distinction between "am" and "ought") are theologically and religiously informed. To return to the earlier illustrations, God appears to some to be doing revolutionary activity because God does humanizing work, and revolutions aim at humanization. But also, they perceive that God is doing revolutionary work because they perceive that humanization is the aim of revolutions. Men are to be doing revolutionary work because, in faith, men are sensitive to what God is doing and are to share in his activity. If, with reference to the illustration from Leviticus, I am not to commit incest, it would be because incest is not humanizing; it would not be because "I am the Lord" and have commanded this. I can perceive that God's love is humanizing, and I ought to love my neighbor. I can discard the ordinance about eating meat with blood in it since this has no reference to humanization, thus no reference to God's doing.

How do I know what is humanizing? This is the epistemological question, the answers to which tell me both what God is doing and what I am to do (or ought to do). There are various ways in which the question can be answered: (1) The Christian is filled with the Spirit, and the Spirit in and through him discerns the absence and presence of the spirit of the human in events. (2) What is human is self-evident; every man understands for himself what is inhuman and what is human. (3) Certain general things can be said on the basis of revelation and moral sensitivity about what is humanizing; e.g., both Van der Marck and Lehmann stress in different terms that it is human to be in fellowship with others without total subordination of one's own integrity and identity. But beyond these things, there is an intuitive perception (informed by belief and sensitized by grace) of what the human is in particular instances. (4) One can move into the second approach and say that God wills the human. To be human requires that justice, love, liberty, order, trust, hope, etc., be attended to in the development of human societies and communities. What distinguishes the first approach is the degree to which the meaning of what God is doing, or wills that man should do, is not elaborated in precise terms, although some persons use more precise terms than others.

Moral Imagination

Why is this the case? Certain things are protected by this approach. In Lehmann's case, I believe he wishes to protect the freedom of God, though God will be doing always what is humanizing. Perhaps more important for our distinction between two approaches is that some claim is being made for a different capacity to discern the presence of God as a result of the acknowledged relationship to him. Van der Marck suggests that Christians recognize that their authentic humanity is a gift from God, and that in their fellowship with others they understand themselves also to be in fellowship with God. Lehmann writes about a new sensitivity and imagination, a clearer understanding that is part of the life of the Christian. The acknowledged relationship between the believer and God is said, it seems to me, both to alter one's capacity to perceive and to enable one to grasp what others do not perceive. Faith enables one to grasp better that which is human—where God is acting and where he is present.

In contrast with the second approach, this approach seems to emphasize the function of sensibilities and affections in determining both what God is doing and what man is to do. It is less rationalistic and frees the imagination to discern what one is to do. Sensibilities, affections, and imagination, however, can have a place in a theory of moral judgment-making apart from the faith context in which theological ethics works. No theologian would deny that some passionate atheists with artistic sensibilities and imagination can more finely disclose both humanity and inhumanity than can most devout men. Can one really claim that grace affects sensibility? One can claim that belief might make one understand that human fellowship does involve fellowship with God, since God is the giver of the possibility of human fellowship. But can a claim for discerning moral perceptions of the particularity of God's doing and man's doing be substantiated?

Perhaps some claims can be thus substantiated, though one would hardly be able to make predictive statements: Because X believes in Christ, he has greater moral imagination. A possible analogy for the claim would be that of a member of a family. My love for my children qualifies my understanding both of what they are and what their well-being requires. It thus affects in some way both what I seek in relation to them and how I relate to them. That the acknowledged, meaningful, lived relationship between man and God qualifies man's perceptions of the human is the claim that seems to be made. But elements of belief are also present; the positive revelation of God in scripture provides content. This living, believing relationship is one of trust, gratitude, love, hope. Perhaps obedience and other terms also would be proper.

In the introduction I made it clear that the first approach may be a first order of religious moral discourse and the second approach only a more rational justification for the first. But why are some thinkers satisfied with the first while others are unsatisfied? Many answers could be suggested. Perhaps the first is more appropriate for profoundly faithful men who deeply believe and thus clearly perceive God's presence: men of the spirit whom I have called elsewhere "moral virtuosos." Perhaps the second is necessary for the less faithful and less sensitive. The major difficulty in the first approach, however, is that it lessens the scope within which moral argumentation can take place with some objectivity both between Christians and between Christians and others. It makes more difficult the task of overcoming moral disagreements both at the level of particular practical judgments and at the level of method for making judgments. It is in the intermediate delineation of ethical terms, between theological affirmation and particular judgments, that the rational discourse so necessary to overcoming differences and to persuasion is made possible.

The Second Approach: Rational Deliberation from Beliefs

I can only hope, given limitations of space, that the reader has seen the direction in which the second approach goes. I do not suggest that the procedure outlined here is necessary before one acts, although I do believe that reflection on these matters both before and after actions might have a salutary effect in the practical realm.

The second approach, in the order of giving reasons for certain preferences in attitudes and actions, might go something like this: The living faith and historical experience of the Hebrew and Christian communities have depicted God's will and actions in narrative terms (under certain conditions men perceived God to be doing certain things) and in propositional terms (e.g., God is love). Some of these statements about God and his action include moral intentions and ends (e.g., he appears to will the preservation of human "values" that are made possible by his creation). Some are not so immediately moral in intention (e.g., he wishes men to remain in fellowship with him). Religious men—or, for those who dislike religion, faithful men—acknowledge many aspects of relationship to God: authority and obedience, father and son, giver and grateful receiver, determiner of destiny and human agency in fulfilling that determination, purposive enabler of humanization and responsive participants in that enabling, etc. These are ways of stating a relationship which requires that men attend to what they believe God to will and to have done in their own actions.

The process of moving from theological affirmations to moral imperatives is complex. It is relatively simple where God's action and will are delineated in moral terms; there, given the relationship to God in faith—articulated in terms suggested above—it is consistent for religious men to act in accord with God's will, that is, in accord with the moral purposes impacted in the stories and beliefs about God. Since these purposes are moral it is clear that human moral justification can be given for them as well as the authorization they have by being the will and deeds of God. Where terms are used to delineate God's purposes in less strictly moral terms, it is still possible to designate certain moral attitudes and intentions that are at least not inconsistent with those purposes. For example, God wills to "save" men by forgiving them and by renewing fellowship with him. Certain human attitudes and relationships with purely human ends, such as lovingness toward one another which makes possible reconciliation among men, are consistent with this purpose of God.

This process of designating attitudes, intentions, ends, and even rules of life that are inferred from and consistent with our understanding of God's relationship with men can proceed much farther. Thus, hope, trust, and love, for example, not only are possible because God is loving, trustworthy, and the object of hope, but also are requisites for the well-being of the human community and its individual members. Justice, liberty, order, and other terms can be authorized and justified in similar ways.

In the procedures of practical moral reasoning, then, these concepts of values, intentions, and attitudes operate as governing and guiding factors in the determination of what I, as a believer in God, discern to be the morally proper thing to do within the complex, changing, concrete realities of history. Perhaps what God is doing can be modestly anticipated through various kinds of reasoning: by analogy from what I believe him to have done under somewhat comparable circumstances or by inferences from certain moral attitudes and intentions which are consistent with what I believe him to be and to be doing as the sovereign power. But the claim to perceive what he is doing with clarity cannot be made. Perhaps it is lack of faith rather than lack of knowledge which prohibits this step, though it is probably both. Rather, the governing and guiding concepts function in a realm of relative—not absolute—moral objectivity, where their validity and function are subject to rational criticism, and where we can seek agreement or understand disagreement among morally conscientious men. The discernment in the context is still informed by sensibility, affections, and imagination, as well as by reason; and it may be qualified and informed by my faith and religious affections. But the extent of ethics that is in a public domain, subject to rational discourse, is enlarged.

The second approach, or second order of discourse, is of great importance both within and without the Christian community in determining what moral actions are proper in the world. It provides both a pattern of self-criticism with reference to our more intuitive judgments and actions, and a possible platform for common action without denying the importance of our particular religious sources and grounds for action.

chapter 5

God's Transcendence
and the
Value of Human Life

Throughout this chapter I shall keep in view two general areas of reference, two sources of understanding. One is human experience: of the values of human life, and of valuing. The other is Christian theology, or at least certain affirmations made in the intellectual life of faith which pertain to the valuing of human life. Any discourse which attempts to move between theology and ethics by necessity must keep these two areas and sources in view. If theological principles and affirmations pertain to human moral values, they do so in two ways. Either they are principles and affirmations which include within the divine purposes those purposes which are moral, that is, which stipulate human moral values, ends, rules, etc., or the religious community infers certain moral values, ends, rules, etc., to be consistent, coherent, harmonious, consonant with affirmations about God. If claims are made for transformation, emendation, penetration, alteration, re-orientation of human experience through religious faith, those claims are in principle subject to virtually empirical investigation. There are two pitfalls in the efforts to relate theology and ethics in general which I wish to avoid. On the one hand are the temptations to deduce too much from theological principles for ethics, a pitfall more characteristic of the religious rhetoric of some continental Protestants more than of either Roman Catholic or American Protestant theologians, e.g., the claim that what is morally right is determined by the command of

Reprinted with permission from the *Proceedings of the Catholic Theological Society of America*, Vol. 23 (1969).

God in the moment. On the other hand are the temptations to separate the ethical discourse from the theological, confining the significance of the theological to soteriology, and finding the resources for the ethical only in what (hopefully) all men can accept in common as the human and the moral.

My procedure will be to discuss three general affirmations in an exploratory way, seeking to make clear the relations between Christian belief in the transcendence of God (and the God who is transcendent) and human experience in each. The first is: Human physical life is not of absolute value, but since it is the indispensable condition for human values and valuing the burden of proof is always on those who would take it. The second is more complex. Human life has *many values*. Some of these adhere to individuals, others adhere to the relations between persons in interpersonal situations, others adhere to human collectivities, and some adhere to all three. These values are not always in harmony with each other in particular human circumstances. The third is this: Human valuing of others involves several kinds of relations, and several aspects of individual experience; it is no simple single thing either descriptively or normatively.

I. Human Physical Life Is Not of Absolute Value

Human physical life is not of absolute value. But it is the indispensable condition for human values and valuing, and for its own sake is to be valued. Thus the burden of proof is always on those who would take it. The delicacy of discerning what value is to be given to human physical life under particular circumstances when it is not valued absolutely presents one of the principal practical moral problems men have to face.

H. Richard Niebuhr, in *Radical Monotheism and Western Culture,* stated the broad outlines of the affirmation of the non-absolute value of all created things from a theological perspective. He closes his chapter, "The Idea of Radical Monotheism," with the following words: "Radical monotheism dethrones all absolutes short of the principle of being itself. At the same time it reverences every relative existent. Its two great mottoes are: 'I am the Lord thy God; thou shalt have no other gods before me' and 'Whatever is, is good.' " [1] The theme is a very familiar one in a great deal of Protestant theology. Kierkegaard wrote about the difficulties of being absolutely related to the absolute, and relatively related to the relative; Paul Tillich's idea of the "protestant principle" functioned to provide men with a point of transcendence from which all finite gods could be assessed with presumed freedom and objectivity.[2] Nothing has been exempted from the edges of this theological sword, including religion (as it is distinguished in Barth, Bonhoeffer, and many followers, from faith). The intention of many Protestant writers in this vein has been primarily religious and theological; they intended to preserve the majesty of God from confusion with lesser majesties; they intended to make the claim that God alone is worthy of absolute trust and reliance, that is, of absolute faith; they intended to drive men to faith in God by preaching the unworthiness of lesser gods. A few writers have moved on to develop some of the ethical inferences that can be drawn from the theological point; the Niebuhr brothers, for example, show in part what it means for the political community to confess that God alone is the Lord. It is not unfair, however, to charge almost all of the Protestant giants who perceived the dangers of idolatry with failing to deal with many of the hard cases in which men must judge what the proper reverence is for various relative existents.

Here we see the serious ethical limitations of affirmations of the transcendence of God if the moral inference drawn from it is vaguely the relativity of all things that are not God. A veritable host of conclusions could be drawn from this vagueness. Some of these can be easily listed. (1) Since only God is absolute, all other things are *equally* relative to him and to each other. No one, however, wishes to take this line. (2) Quite different would be this; since the importance of the doctrine of transcendence is to show the majesty and virtual mystery of God, once we see the relativity of all things in relation to him, we have exhausted the theological resources for determining the values of the relativities of life. We are on our own to explore pragmatically the great varieties of human schemes for the ordering of existents in relation to each other: reason, power, utility and other values, and many other things can be brought together in whatever combinations keep life surviving. (3) God, in his absoluteness, had the good sense to foresee the problem of the relativity of all things, and had the good judgment to designate certain persons and institutions with the authority to order the relativities in relation to each other. So men ought to obey these divinely authorized minds and powers, whether ecclesiastical or political. (4) Since man, according to scripture and his own estimate of himself, is "highest" being in the created order, all relative things are to be ordered according to his valuations. These empirically might be wrong; but if we can know what man is essentially we can know how normatively all relative things are to be ordered for man's well-being. Which conclusion one accepts will set something of the course he takes in dealing with the question of when human physical life can be taken.

When we turn from theology to human experience, we see that it is not necessary for a person to believe in the transcendence of God in order to affirm the relativity of institutions, religions, morals, physical life, and what have you. Theologians of various religious persuasions seem to take some pride in the possible historical connection between the belief in God's transcendence and the "secularization" of life, which might be restated "the relativization of all of life" in actual practice. It may make them personally happier to be with the world, but their positive attitude does not in itself resolve the problems of how to differentiate the better and the worse in the secular. Historical and cultural relativism, whatever their intellectual origins might be, are part of the conventional wisdom. And even long before there were tags to put on these notions, men had learned that circumstances of human experience often required them to alter things they professed to be of absolute value, whether these were physical life processes or institutions. "Kill or be killed," the slogan drummed into some of us during the Second World War, has a natural history, pre-dating myths of creation. One's own life is to be valued more than the life of the one who attacks, at least under most conditions—if he attacks first, if he has malicious intent, if he seeks to destroy not only one's own life but those of others, if you are under orders to kill him before he kills you in the game of war, etc. But many other things have been valued above human life; the honored legends and narratives of the things men have been willing to die for all point to the development of human convictions about things to be valued more than physical life itself—justice, liberty of conscience, exemplary witness to a belief, as well as things valued less highly by most people. It is not hard for most men to believe that physical life is not of absolute value, though in the time of assassinations, it is hard to accept the fact that others do not believe it.

How might belief in the transcendence of God qualify, alter, modify, man's understanding of, and response to, the nonabsolute human values, and particularly the value of human physical life? If there are theological grounds for accepting the finite values as nonabsolute, and if there is experiential grounds for this, in what ways might the religious belief qualify the human experience? I shall not give all the possible answers to these questions, but only some which I deem to be very important.

First, created life is accepted as a gift; it has an author and a source beyond itself, and we and all other forms of life are dependent on that author and source. Life is given to us; even if man succeeds in creating new physical life, he remains the recipient of a multitude of gifts which make this possible. Thus one could spell out a number of the characteristics of the relationship between man and God which in turn would qualify man's disposition toward the created values around him: man is a *dependent* creature, dependent upon God and upon his fellows—this he remembers in his relationships and responses; man is the recipient of good things which are not of his creation, including his own physical life—this brings a response of *gratitude* both to God and the persons and institutions which sustain the goodness of his life, etc.

Second, since only God is absolute, man must remember his finitude, not to mention his deformed existence. This, as the Protestant theological interpreters of culture remind us, requires that man always be brought under question by himself and by others, that he never absolutize his powers, his acts, his judgments. The requirement, in traditional religious terms, of *humility* constantly qualifies his tendencies to absolutize the relative.

Third, man is *accountable* to the author and source of life for his use and cultivation of life, including human physical life. He is responsible (in terms of accountable) to God for the ways in which he cares for, preserves, sustains, cultivates, and, in his limited capacity, creates life around him. His disposition is that of the free servant; not servile but acknowledging that his human vocation is under God.

Fourth, in his participation in the created order, man is *responsive to the developments and purposes which are being made possible* for him under the power and gifts of life from God. He responds not only to the immediacies of possibilities, but to the course of developments which the transcendent God is making possible and ultimately governing. This fourth brings us to a critical point, in my judgment, in Protestant theologies which most substantiate the first affirmation of this paper. That is, insofar as the transcendent God is the One beyond the Many (H. R. Niebuhr), or the unspeakable ground of being (Tillich), he is peculiarly devoid of meaningful content, and thus man is left almost no substantial theological resources in the determination of the values and purposes which ought to govern his participation in the created order, including his use of human physical life. The human ingenuity left for man to depend on in the absence of theological resources is not to be denigrated; out of reflections on human life man does develop views of the "values" which are human, and which are to be developed and sustained. But the God who is transcendent is not the totally unknown God, and thus there are more resources than man's reflections on his own existence alone.

Since the *sine qua non* of other relative values and of valuing is the existence of human physical life, it is valued and is to be valued with a high priority. To take it is to render it impossible for the other person to experience any values, and for him to contribute to the life of the community in such valued ways as it might be possible to do. Thus, while human physical life is not an absolute value, it is to be preserved unless there are substantial grounds for regarding other values to be of greater significance in the particular circumstances in which judgments are made. Human physical life is the primary gift of God on which all other gifts to man are dependent; this vacuous platitude suddenly becomes cogent when an assassin's bullets remove from the human community the values of a great man's life, not only values to himself but to the human community.

II. Human Life Has Many Values

Human life has many values. These values are not always in harmony with each other in particular circumstances. Indeed, there is no fixed timeless order of priority of the values of human life which *a priori* determines what ought to occur in all particular circumstances. Put theologically, while God's purposes for man might be summed up in some generalized unitary conception, such as "He wills man's good," man's good is a complex and not simple notion. Indeed, the religious consciousness of Christianity and Judaism has always recognized that God's purposes are multiple and not single in human life. Put in the language of human experience, men have always been aware that human life cannot exist without both freedom and order, without both love and justice, without both peace and freedom or peace and justice, and that these sometimes conflict with each other and with the value of particular human physical lives in particular circumstances.

The God who is transcendent is not a totally unknown God. People who have acknowledged him to be the Lord have historically discerned his activity in the course and purposes of events, in the lives and deeds of particular men, in the responses men have made to each other and to him. They have written accounts of human life in which they have interpreted experience in the light of the purposes of God, the values God confers upon life. They have written in propositional form some of the predicates which they have deduced from the activities of God; God is love, God is just, God is merciful, God is wrathful, God is the creator, God is the redeemer, God is the judge, God is righteous, etc. Many of these accounts and purposes are directly moral in their content; they pertain to what God wills that human life should be if it is in accord with his activities and his purposes, his will in the double sense of what he does and what he requires. To be sure, certain purposes of God are more dominant than others: his redemptive purpose triumphs over his wrath, for example, as Jonah was disappointed to find out. But in particular circumstances the significance of his redemptive purposes might well include his wrath, as religious sentimentalists often fail to see. He is loving, but the forms of his loving are at least as complex as the forms of human loving—sometimes he loves through the provision of an order, a pattern of rules for life, sometimes through spontaneity and boundless mercy, sometimes through the preservation of peace, and sometimes through the break-up of oppressive and unjust peace. Religious men, like others, long to leap to a simple unitive understanding of God's will and purpose, for if they can be true believers in such, they can provide simpler statements of what life in the human world is to be. But the impulse violates both Christian beliefs about the God who is transcendent and the complexity of the life created by him in which his purposes are to be fulfilled. God values many things in human life.

In my judgment, the most current simplification is that God wills the human, a simplification which has ecumenical auspices. The human, it turns out, is either something men are presumed to know intuitively, or it is something which must be spelled out in more rationally defensible terms—which is to open the door to complexity. It may well be that God wills the human, but the human, like the good, is not a simple notion.[3]

The things which human beings value, quite properly, are at least as many, and at least as inconsistent with each other in particular circumstances as are the purposes of God. What common human experience knows about this was depicted philosophically several decades ago by Nicolai Hartmann.[4] Not only is there a plurality of values which are abrasive to each other, but there is a plurality of virtues; indeed, Hartmann wrote about the antimony of values and of virtues. In his rigorous atheism and his rigorous assertion of the moral autonomy of men, Hartmann painted one of the most awesome pictures of human responsibility I have encountered. One might, however, learn from his phenomenological accounts of moral life without necessarily agreeing with his metaphysics and his anthropology. Human values are many, and many things which men value can be ethically and theologically justified. They do not fall into a neat pattern of priorities which smooths the abrasiveness of particular situations.[5]

Do the Christian beliefs about the God who is transcendent bear any importance upon the choices men make in the ordering of human values in the conduct of life? Or, is one left with a plurality in the transcendent matched by a plurality in the human sphere? In this brief chapter I cannot explicate my answers fully. They would, however, take the following line. Since the transcendent God is not a capricious being, man can discern the fundamental directionality of his purposes for human life. There is an orientation, an intention, which sheds its light upon which intentions and values are proper for man. And, as I indicated in the first part of this essay, man is accountable to God, whose purposes can be in part explicated, in the conduct of his affairs. One also receives his knowledge of God's purposes as a gift of light and direction in the conduct of his actions. But this directionality, which can be translated into a generally applicable ordering of human values, does not resolve the conflicts that are bound to be present in the hard cases of moral judgment. Although God is loving, and wills that men shall be loving, love is not *prima facie* consistent with the preservation of human life under all circumstances. If one chooses to say that love is consistent with man's well-being, one has only moved the problem over from one term to the other, without specifying it more carefully.

Further, the transcendence of God has personal meaning only if one has trust in the God who is transcendent, only if there is a gratitude to him, loyalty to him, a sense of obligation to him. Given this faith, then, the religious believer is obligated to seek to discern (not alone, but in the company of the people of God) what the transcendent God's purposes are for the conduct of life with its plurality of human values. But given a measure of plurality of God's purposes, there is no guarantee of man making a risk-proof moral judgment, either in God's or in men's sights. There is no prior guarantee of hitting the mark morally. Given the finitude of men, and the plurality of values discerned in human experience, there is no guarantee *a priori* of moral rectitude in all circumstances. Given man's sin (not explicated here), there is need both for guidance from the community's beliefs about God, and for the mercy which he grants to all people. The Christian beliefs about the God who is transcendent give guidance in the ordering of life with its plurality of values.

III. Human Valuing

Human valuing is complex and not simple. It involves several kinds of relations, and several aspects of individual experience. A rehearsal of the theories of human valuation is no more possible than a rehearsal of theories of value in this brief essay. To keep the topic manageable I shall confine my discussion to two principal aspects of the experience of valuing. One is valuing things and other persons for their utility for not only one's own purposes, but for purposes of the human community. The other is valuing things and persons for themselves. My interest in this distinction here is to suggest some of the different characteristics of human responses, and of personhood, which are properly involved in each of these two aspects. The first suggests a mode of life which is largely one of problem-solving, of achievement of specific purposes or ends, and tends to slip into a flat, mechanistic, view of experience. It reduces the sense of awe and wonder. The second suggests a mode of life which is spiritually profound, but tends to slip into the denigration of rationality, of the necessity for specification of ends and means. Both modes of life are advanced under religious auspices; the first is strong in the proposals of those who affirm the advances of technology and urbanization, and share the optimistic spirit that sometimes pervades successful problem solvers. (My personal conviction is that the thinness of such theologically sponsored views is becoming clear with the compounding of human failures and tragedies.) The second is strong in the proposals of radically personalistic Christians, who, in some of their rhetoric, appear to suggest that the organization of persons to be useful to achieve certain ends (particularly in the church) compromises what men are meant to be for each other. The double tendency is not new, of course; one can gain insight into it from reading the theology of Augustine, among others from the past.

It would be folly to try to argue that only a belief in the transcendence of God can justify the more personalistic vision of life, with its responses to other persons of awe, wonder, joy, reverence, and profound respect. Certain aspects of contemporary youth culture manifest this kind of valuing while at the same time rebelling against traditional religious beliefs; the relations between young people are "beautiful" in a meaningful way to them. (My son, for example, wrote recently to a friend, "The real world is beautiful, and you are part of it.") The grounds for the fresh appropriation of the Kantian principle that persons are to be treated as ends in themselves and not as means, are more a revulsion against the institutionalization of values of utility which appear to be "dehumanizing" than they are religious beliefs.

I believe it would be equally a folly to argue that no theological support can be given for the instrumental value, the utility value, of persons. If God is intent upon the preservation and cultivation of life, including as it must, men's lives in relation to each other and in relation to the rest of nature, a view of men as functionaries for the achievement of purposes consistent with those larger purposes is proper, and in order. There is an ordering activity in life, with its impositions of duties and obligations, its assignment of tasks and the requirement of their fulfillment, which is part of God's purpose for men.

The general phenomenon of valuing, then, has many aspects, and cannot be reduced to a simple notion, nor be grounded in a simple set of ultimate requirements. In "using" another person one is valuing him for his function in the social economy of life; one values his wife, even, in part for her utility—in providing for the mundane needs of the family (doing laundry, cooking meals, shopping, cleaning the house, etc.) and in fulfilling needs for affection and even sexual gratification. But relations other than utility between persons also include valuing; not all valuing of persons is reducible to utility. To respect another is to acknowledge his value, as is to reverence another, appreciate another, care for another, preserve the life of another, sustain another, love another, honor another. The valuing carried by these notions suggests in each instance an aspect of the value of the other for his own sake, an intrinsic value to the other. These notions suggest aspects of the experience of valuing, and the relationship with the other, which acknowledge the mystery, the autonomy, the value of the existence, of the other. They also suggest that the self, in such valuing, is not simply calculating in a rational way how the other fulfills one's own desires, interests, and needs, or even the interests and needs of the society. Rather they involve the affections, the emotive life of the person.

Belief in the transcendence of God is not a necessary personal condition for proper maintenance of either the utility or the intrinsic values of persons. To claim that it is a necessary condition would be to take on the obligation to prove that those who believe in the transcendence of God are better "valuers" than are those who do not believe. Christian belief in the God who is transcendent, however, does, can, should, and ought to inform and direct the valuing experiences of Christians, and the relations they have with each other and with nature.

To spell this out, I would develop two themes. One is the effect of this belief on the dispositions of the persons who believe it. To accept life as a gift, to acknowledge dependence on God for life, to acknowledge one's finitude and disobedience in humility, would all (if there is some wholeness to the person) predispose one to have respect, reverence, honor, appreciation, and love for others, and for the world. In the life of praise and adoration, of confession and repentance, which are part of the expression of this belief, of the response to the transcendence of God, the affections are nourished, and the dispositions directed toward the responses of respect, honor, appreciation, etc. The calculative rationality of valuations for utility is tempered and impregnated by the sensibilities, dispositions, and affections nourished in religious faith.

The second theme is the effect that the beliefs about the God who is transcendent would have in conditioning the ends and purposes for which the experiences of utilization of others would be directed. Since these ends and purposes can be specified in consistency with the purposes of God who is known' in Christian faith, and since ends and purposes which are inconsistent with such knowledge of God would be illicit, the utilization of other persons and of nature would be informed by the affirmations made about the God who is transcendent.

The legitimate claims of Christian thought with reference to God's transcendence and the values of human life, could be summarized in the following terms. All created things, including human physical life, are of nonabsolute value. Yet as gifts of God they are to be nourished, cared for, protected, developed, etc. The transcendent God is a known God, and the knowledge of his purposes gives direction to the ordering of life's values, but not with such clarity that man is exempted from the responsibility to judge and act in his finite condition. The relation of the believers to God in trust, gratitude, obedience, etc., places upon them the willingness and the obligation to make their orderings of values cohere with God's purposes. It also affects their personal existences, impregnating their affections and intentions, their dispositions and their purposes.

That these explorations require further precision, elaboration, and correction, goes without saying. Their fundamental warrant is this: they maintain the interaction between the positive theological affirmations of the Christian faith on the one hand, and human experience of values and of valuing, on the other.

part two

The
Moral
Virtues

chapter 6

The Moral Conditions
Necessary for
Human Community

Certain conditions must exist for any human community to maintain itself, not to mention to enrich and improve itself. Sociologists have sometimes listed these conditions as "functional requisites," or "functional prerequisites" for any society. Among the required functions they list such things as "role differentiation and role assignment," control of disruptive behavior, communications systems, adequate setting for sexual "recruitment," and many others. Behind such listings is a basic model, or an analogy being used to interpret the nature of human communities. It is the analogy of an organism; for an organism to stay alive it must necessarily be adequately fed, find a satisfactory adjustment to its environment, and the like. Sometimes the "functional requisites" that sociologists draw to our attention seem perfectly obvious, and we wonder either what is so important about naming them, or we wonder why we had not noticed them ourselves.

Perhaps what I have embarked upon in this chapter will appear to be obvious to many readers, and if it brings some fresh insight to others, they will wonder why they had not thought about it before. But I assume that our rational quest leads us to find ways of expressing more clearly what is, or at least seems to be the case. I have been asking myself, in a fashion parallel to what the "functional" interpreter of society has asked himself, "What are the necessary moral conditions for a human community to exist, to enrich itself, to flourish?" This is obviously too big a task for one chapter, since "morality" covers so many aspects of human experience, and since the realm of the analysis of those aspects of human experience is very complex. I am going to limit my considerations to answers that can fall under three terms that in the history of Western ethics have been called the "Christian virtues," namely faith, hope, and love.

What I will do with these three great terms will not please the biblical scholar, who would immediately set them in their New Testament context, and relate them to the message of that book. Nor will it please the theologian, since the Christian use of these terms ordinarily takes place within a special set of religious beliefs or affirmations. Indeed, it does not please me in my more theological or biblical moments. I will wrench these terms from their particular Christian setting, use them in such a way that some of their traditional Christian meaning continues, but set them in the context of my basic question. Thus my questions are: "Can human community exist without faith, both as trust and as faithfulness or loyalty?" "Can a human community exist without hope, both as expectation or anticipation and as the affirmation of new possibilities?" "Can a human community exist without love?" I will not turn this into another discussion of sexual morality, but into a discussion of that measure of devotion and respect that is necessary for men to live together.

One more prefatory clarification is necessary. When I am talking about human community I mean to be most inclusive. I would hope that what I say is applicable to relationships between nations and to relationships within the family, that it can refer to our life in communities ordered by civil law and in our communities ordered by custom.

I. Can Human Community Exist Without Faith?

Now "faith" is a weasel word, this we must admit. To some it means something like "the Christian faith," an historic religion. To some it means a particular religious experience, like feeling that Christ died for me. To some it means belief in certain propositions: "I believe in God the Father Almighty, Maker of Heaven and Earth, and . . ." I am not interested in exploring these aspects of "faith" in this essay. I would instead use the word in another way; "faith" refers to a kind of relationship between persons, and between groups. For the sake of explicating this kind of relationship, I will use distinctions as they were made by my late colleague, H. Richard Niebuhr. One aspect of the relationship of faith, as he stated it, is "confidence," or "trust." To say "I have faith in you" means "I trust you." The other aspect is "loyalty" or "fidelity" or "faithfulness." This suggests that a certain performance, with certain obligations, is a required part of a faithful relationship; not only do I trust the other person, but I will be "trustworthy" and "loyal" to him. Not only do I have confidence in the other person, but he can have confidence in me.

In these two uses of the word faith, it is not hard to make clear that each person and each community of persons "lives by faith." I do not mean to suggest that each person lives by faith in God, but that each person lives in the confidence that other persons and social institutions are reliable, trustworthy, and honest. We normally assume that when we ask a friend what the assignment is for a week in a history course, he will tell us the truth. His speech is reliable; he is honest, and thus trustworthy. If he does not know, we expect him to say so, and not to guess or to fabricate an assignment.

As pedestrians about to cross the street at a busy intersection, we wait for the cross traffic to stop when the light turns red, and we rely upon each driver to respond to that signal with the proper behavior. We have confidence not only in the traffic lights, relying upon their mechanical coordination, but we have confidence in human beings to share our confidence in the lights, and to perform according to the proper signals.

When we go into a restaurant that is obviously open to the public, we assume that we will be served and that what we order from the menu is available.

When the representatives of two groups involved in the negotiation of a labor contract are bargaining, in spite of their differences of opinion and judgment, and in spite of the hostility that such bargaining can induce, each side assumes that the other is "bargaining in good faith," that it is serious about its efforts, and will behave according to the agreement that is finally reached. When nation states proceed to establish a test–ban treaty for nuclear weapons, each trusts the other's intention and desire to reduce one possible provocation of war and one means of incapacitating human beings who might be injured or destroyed by further testing. When such a treaty is signed, nations assume that each is reliable, that each will act according to the word that it has pledged itself to in the treaty.

It takes little imagination to see what might happen, and does happen to the human community when "bad faith" or "broken faith" takes place. If the friend misinforms us about the history assignment our confidence is shaken; we will not rely upon him in the same way as we had previously. Either he cannot or did not get the information correctly, or his memory is not reliable, or he has deliberately deceived us. If the situation is his misinformation or bad memory, we will probably not react with such vehe-

st him. If he has deliberately deceived us, the rupture between
r, and we would find it hard to "forgive" him; what was friend-
nt become distrust, or at best mere acquaintanceship.

ivers and pedestrians could not be trusted to obey traffic signals, not
on., is life endangered, but chaos would result in the movements of
vehicles and persons, and what was tolerable order would become intolera-
ble disorder. If we enter a public accommodation, a restaurant or a resort, in
good faith that men will be served there, and are rejected because we are
Negroes or Jews, not only have we been deceived as persons, but our confidence in the reliability of institutions and men is shaken. Or confidence
in the order of society that exists, as being a "just" order in which both
we and others are respected, is rightfully challenged. We are deceived by
the system or social order that exists; the institutions and the white Protestant Christians who run them are not to be trusted. Out of such mistrust
reforms and social revolutions are legitimately born.

Agreements between unions and employers, between nation states are
themselves recognitions that the conditions under which human communities are to trust each other often need to be spelled out in great detail; the
lurking distrust and suspicion, legitimately present on the basis of past bad
experience, dictates that elaborate machinery of grievance procedures and
inspections be developed to insure that the scales are tipped in favor of
honesty in the performance of agreements rather than in favor of dishon-
esty.

My general point should be clear by now. As persons and as groups we
rely upon the reliability of the words and deeds of others; we trust in the
trustworthiness of others. If "telling the truth" is always radically relativized to the situation in which conversation is going on, if reliability is
thoroughly corrupted by the self-interest or diabolical motives of the person upon whom we rely, we not only resent being deceived, or used for
the sake of the other, but also become hostile toward those who have betrayed their trust; the unwritten moral law of human existence in societies
is itself violated, and the conditions upon which we can enjoy freedom and
peace are undermined.

Now let us look at the aspect of "fidelity" or "loyalty." Faith is not simply trust and confidence in others; this confidence itself requires performance on our part in accord with our trust in others and their trust in us.
For trust to exist between persons or groups, each must be trustworthy;
each must be faithful to the other. The necessity of being able to trust others entails the obligation to be trustworthy. The notion that a man is to be

faithful to his wife is not some curious remnant from a puritanical past that bears upon us in our time on the basis of outmoded and extrinsic authoritarian dictates of ecclesiastical institutions. By no means. The idea of fidelity in marriage, or in friendship, is a requirement for the marriage or the friendship to exist. Where one cannot trust the other to be loyal, to be reliable, the relationship of love or even of friendship breaks down.

When nations cannot be dependent upon each other to fulfill agreements made between them, when fidelity and honesty of word and deed are not practiced, it becomes prudent to hedge against the infidelity of the other nation with preparations for self-defense, for resistance to aggression, for balances of power.

I need not give more illustrations. The point should be clear. The absence of faithfulness, loyalty, fidelity, breeds distrust, suspicion, fear of being deceived, and betrayal. We can sense this by a moment of introspection. I suppose there is no more primitive moment of moral indignation in the experience of each of us than that moment when the betrayal of the trust of a friend or a community is disclosed to us, or becomes clear to us. Minority groups in a sense trusted majority groups to be faithful to the democratic creed and to the guarantees of the Constitution to insure their place in the American community; the dawning and finally dramatic recognition that the majority group is unfaithful to its creed and to the laws that all men have in common breeds resentment, bitterness, hate, and revolution.

Is not one of the most bitter moments in the personal lives of young adults that in which one finds out that the boy or the girl to whom you have committed yourself, and who you believe has been committed to you, is unfaithful to that commitment, is cheating on the loyalty you assumed to exist between you? Do we not resent most deeply those occasions when others have lied to us, when they have shown themselves to be untrustworthy in both word and deed?

Existence in the human community requires fidelity as well as confidence, trustworthiness as well as trust. Apart from these the necessary conditions of communal life itself are undermined, and personal and social life cannot flourish. No persons or groups could long flourish if they had to live in the expectation that they were being betrayed.

There lurks within persons and groups the will to betray as well as the desire to trust and be trustworthy; the tragedy of broken faith, Josiah Royce once wrote, is the greatest of human tragedies. Each of us is a promise-breaker as well as a promise-keeper; even when there is no deep intention to deceive, we still fail to keep the trust that others have in us. This fact of our common life leads to more observations about the conditions for human community. Forgiveness and reconciliation are necessary requirements of common life; this is the first observation. The second is that we need to make explicit in marriage vows, in covenants and contracts, in treaties and articles of agreement what the conditions of fidelity are so that we can be externally policed as well as internally motivated to a life of faith.

The capacity to forgive and be reconciled to others is a necessary condition for communal life. Disruptions cannot persist in human communities; the betrayals and bad faiths of the past must be overcome for the sake of the flourishing of persons and communities. We know this to be the case in the intimacy of the family; the inability to be reconciled to parents or siblings, the nourishing of bitterness, corrodes the common bonds. In the relations between the nations after a war we have seen the significance, not perhaps of forgiveness, but at least of a mercy that is not vindictive toward the defeated enemy. It was not only in the interests of the American nation, but for the welfare of the human community, that defeated Germany and Japan were brought into economic and cultural restoration with other nations of the world. But to speak of forgiveness and mercy is to speak of attitudes and deeds of love, to which we will turn later on.

Human and social relations of faith require explication in vows, covenants, articles of agreement, treaties, and contracts. Two reasons for this explication are important. One is that in more impersonal relationships it is necessary to detail the conditions to which each party is faithful, so that the terms of trust and of expectation of trustworthiness are clear to all involved. Commitments are partial and not total in business transactions, in relations between nations, and many other spheres of common life. The limits and the obligations need to be made clear, so that the letter of the law defines the terms of the relationship of faith between persons and groups. The letter of the law becomes enforceable, policeable.

But surely another reason for vows and articles of agreement is that parties involved do not always feel moved to be faithful to each other. Love for one's spouse does not always flow with superabundance so that each partner joyfully meets the needs of the other—to dry the dishes, to put children to bed, as well as to be spiritual and physical companion. Vows make clear that each is obligated to the other even when desire runs counter to obligation.

Vows and agreements give an explicit structure to the relationship of faith, they detail the forms that this faithfulness is to take. They also provide the authorization of claims upon the other, even when the other is not inclined to be trustworthy and faithful.

I hope, then, I have shown that faith, in the forms of trust and trustworthiness between persons and groups, is a necessary condition for human communities to exist and to flourish, and for persons in them to find peace and freedom for fulfillment of life.

II. Can Human Community Exist Without Hope?

What do we mean by hope? For what things do men hope? Hope, we know, can become a sentimental pollyanna attitude toward life, deceiving oneself about the realities of suffering, evil, and injustice. Hope can become a shallow optimism renewed only by shoddy slogans, like "We must be hopeful." But hope can be a genuine anticipation and expectation of a new day, a new possibility in life, a newness of life. Hope can be confidence that the future is for men, and not against men. In the Christian community from time to time this has been the case: Christians lived in the expectation of the coming of God's kingdom, in the expectancy of a newness of life coming into human experience. Hope, like faith, is not a self-enclosed thing; one hopes for something, or one lives in hope because some things are possible. Some men hope and long for death; some hope and long for a new justice and peace in the world; some men hope for the second coming of Jesus; some for the classless society. What men hope for conditions what purposes they have, what they live for, what they desire from day to day, what they are, what they say, and what they do. Hope looks to the future, not as the end, nor as a threat to what is, but as an open field of possibilities of human fulfillment and achievement.

Human communities do live by hope, as well as by faith. And as faith can be idolatrous and misplaced, closed and crippling, so hope can have objects that have demonic effects. Hitler lived by hope; Martin Luther King lived by a dream which was a hope; a fraternity student preoccupied with his sexual prowess lives in anticipation and hope, the new nations live in their sense of "rising expectations." Being faithful to the wrong person, the wrong cause, the wrong community can debilitate human communities; hoping for the wrong ends can be demonic. We need to distinguish between better and worse anticipations and expectations, between evil and good objects of hope. But the opposite of hope is hopelessness, despair. Can communities exist in perpetual despair? Without expectation of a new and better life to come in the future?

Gabriel Marcel, who like Josiah Royce has thought profoundly about the meaning of hope and fidelity, suggests that the antithesis to hope is the capitulation to fate. In the capitulation to fate, to the sense that what is has come about by an inexorable and immutable course of events over which men have no control, comes the depths of despair. Hope lives in the confidence that the future is open, that new possibilities of life exist, that present social systems and present patterns of life are not fated by the blind god Necessity, but are susceptible to alteration, to recombination of the elements of life. Hope assumes that freedom exists: freedom to become what one now is not; freedom to change not only the course of one's own life, but the course of the social history of which one is a part; freedom to alter those patterns of community that oppress human dignity and human aspirations.

Hope in the human community can be passive, or it can be active. Passive hope sits and waits, expecting other persons or other communities, or some great interruption in the historical process from some power beyond it, to fulfill man's expectations. The dispossessed, aided by apocalyptic Christianity, have often borne their hopeless despair with patience, expecting to find the fulfillment of their aspirations in the "sweet by and by." Christianity has provided a narcotizing hope which has led not to the struggle to change the conditions of life, but to a passive suffering patience with the injustice that is. Such hope may function to salve the wounds that societies create in human lives, but it finally is unrealistic, offering illusions for reality, and thus is itself very close to despair. Indeed, the resignation to fatedness with its attendant despair breeds illusory hope.

But hope that is confident not in some recompense coming in the sweet by and by, but confident in the possibilities that are present in each generation and each community is an active hope. Martin Luther King's dream does not refer to an age to come, beyond the experiences of men in American society, history, and life. It is a vision of the possible, grounded in the expectation that the vision can be realized. It is a hope that energizes the wills of American people, that moves them forward toward a social order in which all men can flourish, and none are artificially closed off from the possibilities of realizing their potentialities. It is a hope that defines moral purposes, intentions, convictions, and goals that give direction to the present actions of men. Hope both activates, and gives direction to activity.

Hope requires a performance in accord with what is hoped for. Hope becomes active hope. It is confidence that the conditions of human life can be altered, that the future can be opened up, that life is not fated.

Human communities degenerate when they lose such hope. At best they become patiently passive; but such patient passivity is hardly a realization of the human potential for activity, for growth, for the realization of the potentialities of persons. At worst life becomes desperate. Desperation in human communities leads to a flight from reality, to finding those ways in which the conditions of despair can be drugged out of consciousness, suppressed from memory, temporarily forgotten. Or desperation leads, as we so clearly know, to rebelliousness, to the outbreaks symbolized in recent American experience by the name "Watts." Despair leads to meaninglessness and to hatred; the human spirit can stand hopelessness for just so long. Without the possibilities of expectation of change, of an open future, actions expressing hostility rather than hope burst forth.

Hope is not optimism generated by slogans or self-prodding. Hope is confidence that the future offers possibilities for man, for human fulfillment and realization. A new surge of hope brings with it the performance of deeds that change the character of the human communities in which we live, bringing them more into accord with man's deepest moral and spiritual aspirations. The confidence that the future is open, that it is not a threat but a promise, that it offers opportunities without the artificial imposition of barriers, is necessary if the human community is to flourish. Without hope the human spirit withers; without hope the human communities cringe in fear, or rebel in undirected hostility.

III. Can Human Community Exist Without Love?

Surely not all the facets of love can be expounded in this brief treatment. "Love" is used in so many ways, has so many inflections that what one says briefly is subject to misinterpretation. I do not wish to address the relations of love and sexuality, although obviously societies cannot exist without sexual love. Rather I shall limit myself to aspects of love that are kindred to faith and to hope. I cannot refrain, however, from quoting at some length a moving elaboration of "love" written by H. Richard Niebuhr:

> Love is rejoicing over the existence of the beloved one; it is the desire that he be rather than not be; it is longing for his presence when he is absent, it is happiness in the thought of him; it is profound satisfaction over everything that makes him great and glorious.

Love is gratitude; it is thankfulness for the existence of the beloved; it is the happy acceptance of everything that he gives without the jealous feeling that the self ought to be able to do as much; it is gratitude that does not seek equality; it is wonder over the other's gift of himself in companionship.

\\ Love is reverence; it keeps its distance even as it draws near; it does not seek to absorb the other in the self or want to be absorbed by it; it rejoices in the otherness of the other; it desires the beloved to be what he is and does not seek to refashion him into a replica of the self or to make him a means to the self's advancement. As reverence love is and seeks knowledge of the other, not by way of curiosity nor for the sake of gaining power but in rejoicing and in wonder. In all such love there is an element of that "holy fear" which is not a form of flight but rather deep respect for the otherness of the beloved and the profound unwillingness to violate his integrity.

Love is loyalty; it is the willingness to let the self be destroyed rather than that the other cease to be; it is the commitment of the self by self-binding will to make the other great. It is loyalty too, to the other's cause—to his loyalty. As there is no patriotism where only the country is loved and not the country's cause—that for the sake of which the nation exists—so there is no love of God where God's cause is not loved, that which God loves and to which he has bound himself in sovereign freedom" (*The Purpose of the Church and Its Ministry* [New York: Harper & Bros., 1956], pp. 35-36).

Can human community exist without rejoicing in the existence of others? Without gratitude for others? Without reverence for others? Without loyalty? To be sure, these things are most easily perceived in the intimate relations of friend and friend, of man and woman. But they are not irrelevant to the less personal relations between selves in any human community, nor are they irrelevant to the relations of groups to groups. Taking our cues from Niebuhr, let us attend to these four aspects of the common life.

First, love as loyalty. This can be converted into the words: love is fidelity, is faithfulness. We have seen how fidelity is necessary for the common life. Fidelity or loyalty is a structure through which love is expressed, and which in turn sustains love. Loyalty is no mere external coerced bending to meet the needs of others, but an inner motivation, an intention nurtured in concern for others, to fulfill obligations to them.

Second, love as reverence. Fundamental respect for others—whether individual persons or groups or nations—in which their own autonomy and identity is respected, is a requisite for the well-being of the human community. Reverence or respect does not necessarily mean that there are no reciprocal influences between persons and between groups, nor does it mean that some judgments about each other cannot be made. It does mean in the end a fundamental respect for the integrity and the "otherness" of the other, the right of each person or group to exercise its powers to give shape to its destiny.

Third, love as gratitude. Persons and communities live in mutual dependence upon one another. Each of us is sustained by the activities, the affections, the functions of others; all of us are sustained and taught by those who are better than we are in their wisdom, their moral sensitivities, their knowledge. Gratitude is a proper disposition toward others and toward groups that sustain us and the common life. Like loyalty, it can become maudlin, and even demonic if it slips into subservience to paternalism, or is not checked by the elements of respect. But it is a condition that enables human communities to exist in harmony and peace.

Finally, love is rejoicing in the other. This might be converted into the notion of celebration of others, of the goodness of life, or the well-being of humanity. Rejoicing, celebration, praise, are elements of the life of the human community which add to its vitality, its moral quality and its spirit.

Many moral and spiritual conditions are necessary for the existence of community about which nothing has been said in this chapter. Nothing has been said about justice, though it is not only a requisite, but also is a characteristic that keeps fidelity from being suppressive, and love from being sentimental. Nothing has been said about courage, though it might be seen as an aggressive extension of confidence and of hope. Nor has anything been said about wisdom or prudence, or about temperance. Yet, I hope what has been said indicates that the so-called "Christian virtues" are not merely frosting added to the cake, something "super-natural" added to the natural. Rather one can find in the basic understanding of these virtues insight into the requirements of modern life.

I have made no theological argument. But my affirmations point beyond themselves. What makes for faith and hope and love in the life of men? What sustains faith and hope and love? What goodness and power sustains the human community? The Christian testimony is clear. Our relationships and deeds of faith, hope, and love, point to the goodness and power of God.

chapter 7

The
Personalist
Factor

Personalism, as a factor in contemporary Christian ethics, is not easily delineated. It refers to a number of different concerns and interests in both Catholic and Protestant thought, as well as in contemporary philosophy. Sometimes it is used to suggest the antithesis of the impersonal, or the depersonalized elements in human life. In the face of the highly segmented and functional relations of contemporary society, men have sought to recapture a sense of wholeness in human relationships. In the face of technical orientations of human activity, men have sought to grasp the meaning of human existence in terms that do not reduce individuals to their roles in society. Sometimes the impersonal is associated with external moral demands placed upon selves by authoritative institutions. Thus rationalistic casuistry based upon a nineteenth century view of natural law principles appears to violate both the complexity of human life, and the integrity of individual consciences. Accompanied by ecclesiastical authority, this casuistry reduced the agency of individual selves by requiring that they submit to, and be conformed to non-historical and depersonalized moral principles. Sometimes personalism has been associated with moral autonomy, and also with certain patterns of self-realization. Thus we have heard that indignities have been done to persons by insisting that they have obligations to others in the human community, and that they must con-

Delivered at the 1967 colloquium of the Contemporary Theology Institute held at Loyola College, Montreal, Quebec, Canada. Printed by permission of the Contemporary Theology Institute.

front limits of permissible behavior in the authority and rules of human institutions. Often associated with this is the positive moral assumption that the end of life is the fulfillment of the individual in the terms that he sees fit. Thus personalism has been part of an anti-legalism and anti-authoritarianism that is prevalent.

Theologically, personalism has been associated with the recovery of certain motifs in the Bible. The relation between God and man has been couched in terms of personal relations: speaking and hearing, responding, I-Thou fellowship, rather than in terms of the relation of Being itself to finite beings, or of First Cause to other levels of causality. The church has come to be understood in more personalistic terms: it is the people of God, thus suggesting that both its historical character and its personal character need more accenting than other "images" of the church suggest.

The analytical-descriptive task and the normative-propaedeutic task have often not been well distinguished from each other in the personalistic resurgence. That is, on its analytical side, some thinkers have sought to indicate what the nature of personal existence is, how it is related to biological nature and how it is differentiated from it, what the characteristics of community among persons are as differentiated from more mechanical or biological relationships, how aspects of the self traditionally divided between appetite, intellect, and will, need to be reconsidered in relation to the ways in which men perceive, think, and act, and the like. But this analytical task has all too often run together with a normative function: it has been part of a protest against the impersonal and the depersonalized patterns of life, part of a new style of aspiration about the human community, part of a program, often utopian and romantic, that is propounded by clergy and others.

This chapter does not attempt to clean out all of the vines and underbrush in the jungle of personalism. Its goals are more limited. I shall isolate two issues that need further clarification and development within the wide range of personalistic thinking, particularly in Christian ethics. These two issues are (1) the need to account for persistence and consistency, as well as change, choice, and action, in the existence of persons—that is, the phenomenon of "character," and (2) the need to account for the relationships between more "personal" forms of community and the more structured centers of power and order in human society.

The Phenomenon of Character

In some of its popular forms, personalism tends toward occasionalism. It values the self in its particular moments of personal response to other persons and to God. It places in a higher order of importance the particular acts of persons than it does the being of the persons who act. It determines the goodness of deeds with reference to particular circumstances (quite properly), but has little concern with good men. It celebrates the meaningful if not ecstatic moments of human experience, and often looks upon the more prosaic and routine events of life to be at worst overcome, and at best merely tolerated.

Yet, in ordinary moral life, we come to expect that certain people will fairly consistently act in certain ways. Under similar circumstances they will do similar things; their choices seem to be in part predictable, and thus there appears to be an implicit if not explicit consistency in the values to which they are loyal; their motives, insofar as one can judge them, appear not to be erratic, but to persist through different experiences and different actions. Indeed, a great deal of ordinary moral action relies upon the reliability of others; it is predicated upon some degree of predictability of the behavior of others. We assume that there are some relatively stable characteristics in our selves, and in the selfhoods of others. Indeed, we rely upon persons to have certain characters.

As an example, I cite a phase of my career that recently ended, namely being responsible, as chairman, for the conduct of the affairs of a university department, and for the development with my colleagues of its policies. Over a relatively brief period of time, I could predict with a high degree of accuracy what the responses of various members of the department would be to various proposals that were made. I was rarely surprised by the comments of particular persons, rarely surprised by the ways in which they would vote. I could anticipate the arguments that various persons would make on the issues that confronted the faculty. Each of its members was free; he could respond freely to the occasion and the issues that were under consideration at a particular time. But each also was a man of character, of personal integrity, and thus to a considerable extent his responses were predictable. They were predictable insofar as a major point of reference for them was consistency with past actions, with norms or values applied in previous instances, with visions that they had of what the department ought to become, with characteristics of imagination or caution that had been expressed on previous occasions.

This assumption of the existence of character in ordinary life poses two issues for ethics. One is how, in an analytical mode, one is to understand this phenomenon of "character"; the other, in a normative-propaedeutic mode, is what inferences are to be drawn from this understanding for the moral tasks of a community, in our case, the Christian community.

To observe that the actions and responses of free men are highly predictable is not in itself to give an account of that predictability. Indeed, various accounts have been given of that predictability. One could go to Freudian psychoanalysis for one set of generalizations that could be explanations for certain aspects of it; one could go to cultural anthropology for another set. I am not concerned here to give a genetic account; I shall not try to show under what conditions consistency of behavior arises. Rather I shall attempt to indicate some of the factors that seem to be operative in the phenomenon of character. This exploration is tentative, and subject, of course, to critical scrutiny and correction. First, some observations about experience.

One can "count on" certain persons to fulfill their obligations as a member of an academic department. These obligations would include attendance at departmental meetings, and at committee meetings, preparation of reports, rigorous examination of materials brought up for judgment, willingness to defer other interests for the sake of the needs of the department, and forthrightness of speech in participation in departmental meetings. Not only can some persons be counted on to fulfill their obligations; the manner in which they fulfill them is also predictable. Some are more willing than others to attempt new programs: some are more ready to take risks than others. Some operate consistently on the basis of a concern not to embarrass the department in the eyes of certain persons in the university whose vision of the department they accept as normative; others are insistent that in all affairs the rules be obeyed in detail. Some are more rigorous in making judgments according to high standards that they had set for themselves and for others; others are more flexible in their judgments, more willing to be governed by "extenuating" circumstances.

What affirmations or assertions help us to make sense out of these observations?

First, predictability of action is dependent in part upon the commitment or loyalty to certain standards, norms, rules, principles or values that a person has adopted, or have been authorized as requirements for his action as a person with certain roles in a particular community. Consistency of action has as one of its referents these factors that are objective to the self, that require the self's conformity to them, or that have an oughtness which is brought to bear upon particular occasions in the experiences of the self. A faculty member's judgments of a particular thesis are predictable because he makes them in the light of certain standards of scholarship which he has clearly in his mind, and which he expects a graduate student to adhere to. A Christian saint's deeds may be predictable because he brings to bear upon his actions the love commandment which is the outward precept of Christian faith and experience. The consistency of behavior is not just the expression of his desire to have present behavior in conformity with previous behavior, nor just an expression of habituated conduct; it is a function of the acceptance of certain values and rules as normative.

Second, predictability of action is dependent in part upon the subject's use of a particular frame of reference for the interpretation of what is going on, and what is required of him in the sphere of his action. By frame of reference I wish to suggest something less specific than rules and values, though it would include values and possibly rules. The function of religious beliefs in moral life can be seen in part at this point. Because one believes that God wills the redemption of life, one interprets with some consistency various situations as places in which the Christian is to act so that reconciliation takes place between persons. If one is committed to discipleship to Jesus Christ, he will interpret the various occasions for serious moral actions as those in which he witnesses to his discipleship. Jesus Christ gives a perspective to the moral life, and what he means to the disciple provides a frame of reference from which he proceeds to interpret the significance of what is taking place, and also what should take place. As in the case of values and principles, the predictability of action rests on the consistent reference to a person, or a frame of reference that has objectivity, that exists in terms susceptible to delineation.

Third, predictability of action is also dependent upon the internalization of certain values and beliefs; there are the possibilities of habituation of motivation, and of certain dispositions toward the world, the formation of certain intentions so that persons have characteristic attitudes, or bearings toward one another and toward the world. The particular moral action is governed, then, not only by reference to objective principles or beliefs which can be brought to bear upon it, but also by the formed tendencies and directions of attitudes and intentions. Persons can be described as being "loving persons"; in so doing we often mean to suggest that they seem habitually to be motivated by love for others, or that love is so much an attitude of their wills that we expect them to do the "loving" thing in changing and differing circumstances. This "lovingness" does not come into being only on particular occasions that prompt or require a loving response; it is a readiness to respond in particular places and times in a loving way. There are persons who have a marked direction in their behavior; they may, for example, seem persistently to be seeking the well-being of others; they have a characteristic intentionality. They have so internalized this characteristic intention that their actions seem spontaneously to direct them toward the needs of others rather than toward their own interests.

The word "character" can be used to point to those more persisting characteristics of selfhood, which are expressed in the particular responses and actions of persons. Actions themselves are not only expressions of subjective character. Character comes into visibility only through actions, and thus we see its effects when persons respond to other persons or to events in a manner that has some consistency with their actions under similar conditions. The observation that a person has a certain character is made by inference from conduct over a period of time; it is a generalization based upon inferences from particular occasions. Thus persons have identity as moral beings through the existence of their "character."

Obviously, one can say that certain characters are bad and others are good. The judgment is governed by our moral evaluations of the objective values and beliefs and the subjective dispositions and intentions that seem to be the loci of predictability of action. Thus we see that if we believe certain things to be true and good, it is important that we learn how certain characteristics of selfhood can be formed around these things. This points to the normative and propaedeutic tasks involved in the practical life of the Christian community.

Often when the notion of personalism is used, it refers quite inchoately to some understanding of what persons essentially are, and therefore actually ought to be. In the normative usage of the idea of the person, men seem to suggest that to be a person is to have integrity; not just any integrity, but integrity around some value or characteristic that they believe to be good. This may be love, or it may be a sense of joyous spontaneity and freedom, or it may be a sense of wholeness and well-being. My point is that character or integrity around values that are important does not just come into being spontaneously as selves act from occasion to occasion. A formation process is necessary for persons to become morally "good" characters. It is precisely this necessary formation process that is often overlooked in our celebration of personal freedom and response. To write about it seems to suggest a new form of heteronomy; that is, if one has come to a celebration of personhood as a result of one's rebellion against the imposition of extrinsic rules and norms that have been imposed upon persons by authoritarian institutions, one is not likely to welcome the reintroduction of *paideia* to form persons, precisely because this suggests a restriction of personal liberty and worse, the manipulation of persons into conformity with some pre-established mode. Concern for the formation of character of a particular type seems itself intrinsically to be a restriction of the freedom of persons, who have the right to find that mode of personal existence that is most authentic with reference to themselves.

A theoretical and a practical issue are joined here. The theoretical issue is the extent to which the bases of some consistency of action are themselves restrictions of personal freedom and authentic existence, restrictions that have to be overcome if personal integrity is to flourish. The practical issue is whether any efforts on the part of Christian communities to form character are necessarily heteronomous (or whether such heteronomy is itself intrinsically bad, as many modern men tend to believe), and thus a violation of what the gospel intends that men should be. It is the contention of this chapter, a contention not fully developed here, that apart from (a) some references to values and norms objective to the self, and (b) some internalization of values and meanings, there can be no sense of self. The sense of self, the identity of the I, depends upon the norms and values, both objective to the self and internalized by the self, that one adheres to. Thus, if the Christian community wills that those persons who are its members will respond on particular occasions to events and other persons in a manner that is worthy of the gospel of Christ, it must consider at the practical level how participation in the life of the people of God does, can, and ought to provide the characteristic marks of Christian personal existence. Indeed the more men seek the good that is being made possible on particular occasions, and rely upon their personal responses, not dictated by authoritarian rules of conduct, the more it is necessary to attend to a Christian *paideia*. If one would affirm that to be truly Christian is to be truly human, it is not self-evident that the common human reference will come into being of the self apart from some attention to the development of character. If one would affirm that to be a Christian is to be human with particular characteristics that are inferred from the scriptures and the history of God's people as being normative, it is even more necessary to consider what kind of common life, pedagogy, liturgy, experiences of moral action, etc., become the matrix for the objective and subjective norms of Christian personal existence.

Most men have characters—they can be counted upon with some predictability to act in similar ways under similar circumstances, and generalizations about them can be made upon the basis of inferences drawn from particular actions over a period of time. Since their characters are marked by the presence of certain valuations and commitments, one issue is what values and commitments are valid. Here the content of the Christian faith and tradition can be brought to bear. Since the characters men have developed through their experiences and their convictions, the church needs to be concerned with becoming the matrix in which its values and loyalties become the marks of character. Character does not happen automatically as a gift of grace received in the sacraments or in the hearing of the word; it happens as a community finds ways to form personal existence in dependence upon and in accord with the grace that it is given.

Personal Community
and Impersonal Social Order

A persisting problem in personalistic ethics is that of the relation of personal relations, in which there is a response of selves to others in love and in fullness of communion, to the impersonal social orders in which men necessarily live. One finds older sociological distinctions used to suggest the differences, for example: primary communities of face-to-face relations contrasted with secondary communities of functional relations, *Gemeinschaft* with *Gesellschaft,* community with institution. One finds newer terms being used that make roughly the same distinction, e.g., personal community contrasted with organic community. Both Catholics and Protestants are susceptible to a kind of romanticism about community; in their desire to foster and enjoy communities of love they sometimes lose sight of the necessity of social structures, institutional arrangements, and patterns of authority. This is one actual and potential difficulty in personalism in Christian ethics. Another is that the terms which seem relevant to describe and discuss the ends of "community" cannot be transferred to moral issues in the social order, with its arrangements of power, without giving a note of sentimentality and unrealism about issues in that order. One needs to admit that many Christians live a good double life—seeking intimacy of personal community on the one hand and on the other being engaged in power struggles and struggles for justice. But the two are sometimes not related to each other, or at least there is no adequate theory for understanding the ways in which they are related to each other. Another difficulty, implicit in the previous one, is that the goals or values of personal forms of community need to be related to the goals or values of impersonal community; this requires a reflective process that is sometimes cut short.

The terms used to distinguish between types of social groups refer to ideal constructs; there are probably no "personal" communities without elements of order, power, authority, obligations, roles and other things that often characterize the impersonal. There are probably no "impersonal" communities that are not the places and occasions for some personal communion, for expression of deeply felt senses of personal existence and responsibility. I believe Christian ethics could begin to overcome a persistent problem if it would acknowledge the validity of this sociological observation. Indeed, on sociological, moral, and theological grounds, it seems to me that our tendencies to make distinctions between kinds of communities into a difference, and to value the personal more than the impersonal is a mistake.

The sociological grounds have been suggested. While not all communities have a table of organization, and delineation of roles and statuses, and a constitution that defines the authority and the power of various members, all communities that persist through time (and I assume that to be a community it must persist through time) develop at least an informal structure which could be designated through various means of observation and social research. Perhaps the structure is only one of expectations: one member comes to expect another to fulfill undesignated responsibilities, to meet unstipulated obligations, to do deeds that have no formal authorization. Patterns of authority can be discerned: they may be based more on the informal acceptance of the personal qualities of one person more than others to fulfill leadership roles than on formal election procedures. Patterns of personal deference emerge. This is to rehearse the obvious, but the point of the obvious is missed often by those who seek a community of love with the assumption that loving communities are spontaneous, unordered, radically equalitarian, and without duties and obligations.

Communities have what I have designated elsewhere as "moral requisites" for their existence, no matter how personal or impersonal they seem to be to the casual observer. Indeed, what I have suggested as a sociological necessity is already a moral necessity. The well-being of the group, and of its individual members, requires that certain values be adhered to, whether one has a bureaucracy in view or whether one has a "fellowship" in view. These values sometimes operate to provide the outer limits beyond which a community cannot go without being destructive of itself and its members. For example, individual liberty provides at least a touchstone that must be recalled; while both bureaucracy and fellowship require some limitation of personal liberty (either voluntarily assumed or authoritatively coerced), neither can function well if the participants cannot respond and act with some measure of freedom, initiative, and creativity. The value of individual liberties meets the value of order, and there is no perfectly harmonious resolution of this coexistence in any community. Order is a moral requisite for the persistence of the community, as well as for the development of a measure of personal liberty within it; if one could not assume orderly relatedness and interaction, if one could not assume that others will meet their obligations, a condition for the exercise of creativity, initiative and liberty would be missing. Other such "moral requisites" could be designated for the existence of any form of community. For example, love in its spontaneous expressive forms needs to be qualified by the recognition that love has an ordered form—the commitments that it entails, the structures that it requires.

Perhaps if we could formulate some of these moral requisites, these necessary values, we could perceive that beneath both the impersonal and the personal communities there is a necessary common moral basis, and that this common basis is normative for every form of human community.

The theological grounds for excessive division of the types can be exposed in part by making an observation. Protestant ethics, particularly in its Lutheran wing, has had the unfortunate legacy of a left and right handed God, that is, a God who orders one realm of life through his law—and for this such terms as justice have pertinence; and another realm of life through love—and for this terms that refer to I-Thou relations have pertinence. The ways in which distinctions in the activity of God, e.g., his creative and preserving activity on the one hand, and his redeeming activity on the other, have been made have had serious implications for Christian ethics. They seem to give warrant for moral and social distinctions between the impersonal community and the personal community, to name only the implication that is pertinent for our discussion here.

The point can be made by stating some terse propositions about the importance of our understandings of God for our understandings of human community and for Christian ethics. Any doctrine of God that radically differentiates between his sustaining, ordering and judging work on the one hand, and his redeeming, reconciling and re-creative work on the other hand leads to a perversion of our understanding of human communities and Christian morality by excessively separating the concern for order and justice from the concern for freedom and love. In the realm of social morality, such a doctrine of God is likely to suggest that impersonal communities function for the purpose of preserving life against chaos and sin, and that personal communities function for the purpose of fulfilling life in loving fellowship. The impersonal tends to be seen as not having possibilities that are reconciling and redemptive; the personal tends to be seen as not requiring justice and order. Love becomes confined to the realm of the personal, and can be romanticized and sentimentalized by utopian expectations un-warranted by either theology or experience. Justice and order can become depersonalized, untempered by love and mercy, restricted to the preservation of the old and not opened to the creation of the new.

If we cannot theologically separate nature and grace into separate spatial spheres of world and church, law and gospel, justice and love, then there is no theological warrant for our tendencies to separate the personalistic from the impersonal in human communal experience. If theologically, there is no warrant for separating nature and grace into distinct temporal moments in life, moments of preservation and moments of renewal, moments of wrath and moments of redemption, moments of restriction and moments of spontaneity, then there is no warrant for our tendencies to expect the personalistic communities to provide moments of renewal, redemption, and spontaneity apart from moments of preservation, wrath and restriction. Also, then there is no warrant for our tendencies to expect the impersonal spheres of life to provide only the moments of duty, preservation, wrath, etc., apart from moments of joy, redemption, and renewal.

A theology that acknowledges that God can reconcile men by enabling them to find a new order, and can reorder men by enabling them to know the qualities of love and joy and freedom, cannot permit the sharp differentiations some personalists seem to make between community and institution, primary communities and secondary communities, personal communities and organic communities. Each is susceptible to corruption, and each is susceptible to fulfillment. God is sovereign love through wrath as well as through joy, through justice as well as through personal communion, through structures as well as through liberty. Indeed personal communion that is not just is as deficient as justice that is not at the same time tempered by mercy and open to redemption.

chapter 8

The Christian Style of Life: Problematics of a Good Idea

What might it mean to talk about a "style of life"? The idea has had some currency in Christian discourse in recent years, both in the United States and abroad. The word "style" has several uses that might pertain to the Christian life. One is a descriptive use; a style of life would be comparable to a style of art. There are certain common characteristics of artistic expression that enable the observer to make a roughly valid generalization pertaining to an "impressionist" style, or a "non-representational" style. To the person somewhat literate in the arts, such adjectives modifying "style" enable him to pre-judge or to classify in his mind the work he has not yet seen, or has just seen. Thus when men write about a "Christian" style of life, they may seem to refer to a descriptive generalization; there are presumably sufficient visible or audible characteristics of the behavior of Christians for one to in some measure predict what the behavior of Christians will be, or to classify behavior that is observed as belonging to a class called Christian. We shall return to this kind of usage subsequently.

A second usage is a qualitative one. In common speech we say of one performer that he has "style," or of a political figure that he has or lacks "style." What we mean is that there is a quality of excellence that defies precise description, but nonetheless exists in the manner of performance or manner of life that we observe. The judgment is qualitative, though elements of a normative description are obviously in-

Reprinted by permission of the editorial board of *Una Sancta* from *Una Sancta*, Vol. 24, No. 1, 1967.

volved. To justify a judgment that one man has "style" and another lacks it, we usually engage in comparative descriptions, and hope that in the process the grounds for the claim will become evident. Thus when used in Christian discourse, men may wish to suggest that what some Christians have and others ought to have is Christian *style,* that is, a quality of excellence in the way that they live the Christian life. The judgment about whether a Christian has style or not is probably much like the aesthetic judgment made about a work of art; there are some accepted canons for rational discrimination, but other things are also involved such as our affective capabilities, our sensibilities and sensitivities. In judging the style, we assume that not all persons will agree on the proper evaluation, though we hope for some consensus. Whereas all informed men can agree on the correct answer to a mathematical problem, informed men will not agree on what excellence is in the performance of the Christian life.

I suspect that when writers use "Christian style of life" they intend a combination of the descriptive and the evaluative uses of the word. I also suspect that in some very popular discourse the term is used more because it has evocative and persuasive power for some audiences, rather than because it has clear and precise references. For some persons the term has a glorious ambiguity in which they relish; in this chapter my intention is to show that it can be explicated more clearly without losing its suggestive richness.

Does a descriptive usage make sense? Are there common "Christian" characteristics of life that form a class of behavior or of persons? To answer this, we need to make more precise what we are looking for. If we can sort out what things we might look for, we are making some progress. Do we expect most Christians to do the same kinds of things in similar circumstances? Perhaps under certain circumstances we could expect more, and others less. In situations analogous to that of the "Good Samaritan" we might expect Christians to behave in a manner similar to his deeds. On a question of the proper zoning of an urban community, we would not expect as many Christians to have the same opinion or behave in the same way. Presumably the Christian "style" in the first instance would be deeds that meet the concrete physical and spiritual needs of a stranger or a neighbor regardless of the inconvenience to the self. We might predict that conscientious Christians would "do something like that"; when we see it done, we are likely to call it a "Christian" act. If a person goes through life very consistently living as a Good Samaritan, we might judge that his life had a style. If an identifiable religious group has such characteristic ways of acting, we might use the word "style" to describe its corporate life. Perhaps there is a Quaker Christian style for example.

More than a man's faith goes into such a style; his sensitivity to suffering and injustice may be governed more by his own experience of suffering and injustice than it is by a recollection that God made himself known in Jesus Christ through costly love. He may be brought up in a family that for various reasons has nourished a sensitivity that leads to self-sacrificial deeds. Perhaps his family has some inner historical connection with a people who have been persecuted or deprived through centuries of life: Jews, Anabaptists, Negroes. Perhaps there is a family ethos rooted in part in deeply individual response to either tenderness expressed by parents, or in reaction to having not known affection and concern that stimulates deeds of sacrificial love. One might, however, make a case that a Good Samaritan style is consistent with conscientious Christian loyalty, and that such a normative description can inform those who are disposed by other factors to behave in such a way. For some men, their Christian faith may provide more "justifying reasons" than motivating ones to life in a certain way. For others perhaps their faith motivates as well as justifies and directs their Good Samaritan style.

Would a Good Samaritan style become a test of Christian behavior? Certainly it ought not become a test of Christian *faith* in the sense of trust. But would we be willing to say that those who have the Good Samaritan style show more integrity concerning faith and action than those who do not? Probably not, since there are other styles that are consistent (maybe just as consistent) with Christian faith. Perhaps there is a militant style of Christian life which does not rest with acts of personal love, but moves into the battles between better and worse, between greater justice and gross injustice with more boldness than humility, with the armor of demonstrations on the streets provoking tension, rather than the medical service of binding the wounds of those who suffer strains and stresses caused by social struggles. Such a style also could be motivated by more or by other than loyalty to Christ. Perhaps there is a free style of Christian life; indeed, such seems to be somewhat in vogue at the present time among some Christians. The life pattern expressed in behavior is a care-lessness, a demonstration in heedless behavior and iconoclastic words and deeds to show that to be a Christian is to be unbound by conventions that oppressive social customs present to one. It is to recall that "all things are lawful" even though it may be to forget that "not all things are helpful." Again, perhaps more or other than a Christian loyalty governs such a style; it may be evoked by the dreadful boredom that conventionally responsible and respectable people seem to live by.

Descriptive usages of "Christian style of life" with reference to visible behavior need to be exercised with caution. Perhaps at best there are "Christian styles" of life on this level. There can be individual and communal patterns of behavior in the world that have consistency enough to be called styles. But what we observe may be motivated by allegiance to Christ as this allegiance directs and strengthens tendencies arising from social experiences or individual experiences. One would also have to inquire whether the consistency of behavior cannot be broken; the militant Christian freedom rider may be on another occasion the Franciscan binder of wounds, and on another the rebellious challenger of prevailing modes of Christian respectability. Or different historical events might legitimately evoke a communal style that is ephemeral; in a time of civil rights crisis a more militant style may be evoked among the churches; in another crisis another style may be visible. And finally, perhaps within the Christian community various styles can co-exist at the same time; to judge the rightness of this is to raise the normative qualitative question, a question deferred for the moment.

But "style" may refer to characteristic dispositions and attitudes of Christians, rather than to highly visible deeds, though attitude and deed are related. Is there a style of Christian disposition that can be descriptively determined? Can we talk with thousands of Christians and then formulate a generalization about the "Christian attitude" toward life, or the world? What kinds of things might we look for? As a starting point we would ask about the Christian virtues, as these might be transposed into dispositional terms. Are Christians hopeful? We might say normatively that they *ought* to be hopeful, for there is a consistency between trust in God's graciousness and a disposition of hopefulness. If we found hopeful Christians, could we assess to what extent their hopefulness was a correlate of their faith and to what extent it was the result of personal experiences with other people that assured them that the possibilities of life are more manifold and powerful than its threats? And, one would wonder whether some hopeful persons are not deluded, living in a world of unreality and sheltered from evil.

Are Christians loving? It would seem that their faith ought to engender a disposition to be loving. "For God is love." "If God so loved us, we also *ought* to love one another." "We love, because he first loved us." We could make loving more explicit by suggesting with H. R. Niebuhr that love is rejoicing in the presence of the beloved; it is gratitude, reverence and loyalty toward him. The existence of attitudes like these might be inferred from actions that demonstrate joy, gratitude, respect and fidelity. Or we might detect such dispositions in the gestures and words of men. But such dispositions may come about as much by having loving parents, as by trusting in God's love.

"Perfect love casts out fear." This could be a descriptive statement as used by the author of 1 John. If it is, we ought to find dispositions in Christians, if they are in God's love, that are free from anxieties, that give an equanimity of spirit and soul. But, again, not all peaceful souls are identified with the Christian community; some men achieve inner calm by breathing exercises and some by drugs. And not all Christians have an inner peace; many are anguished about the world, the credibility of their belief and the goodness of God, not to mention where their bread for the morrow will come from.

If a Christian style refers to a set of dispositions, or to what Paul calls the gifts of the Spirit, we might draw some profile of what some Christians are, others can become, and perhaps all ought to be. But quickly one has moved from the descriptive to the normative. And since such motivations as may come from a graced and trusting Christian belief enter in confluence with many other experiences, some measure of latitude and flexibility will always be called for if one wishes to risk generalizations about a "style" that refers to dispositions and attitudes.

One may wish to say less about achieved behavior and persisting actual dispositions, and say more about the *intentions* of Christians. The "style" may be more intentional than visibly actual. But care needs to be taken in formulating such a generalization. Are we talking about existing intentions among conscientious Christians or about intentions that Christians ought to have? All the qualifications and pluralisms that can be brought to bear on descriptive generalizations about behavior and attitudes can be brought to bear on intentions.

It becomes clear that when we are talking about a Christian style of life we are speaking qualitatively, both about a pattern of life that we could develop in normative descriptions, and about the intensity and seriousness with which that style might be manifest in the intentions, attitudes and behavior of Christians. We cannot assess the behavior of Christians, or their attitudes and intentions, and give a descriptive generalization about a style of life that *thereby* becomes normative.

When we turn to the normative, we are confronted with at least as much complexity as we are in thinking in descriptive terms. Three areas of complication deserve attention here. Where do we find the normative style? How do we talk about it in such a way as to avoid "pursuit of ideals" and other theologically problematic terms? How are "styles" as norms embodied in behavior as visible and actual?

Certainly Christians in our generation have been reluctant to talk about normative style for many reasons. One is that we do not know how to decide between styles. The inner-worldly asceticism of the Troeltsch-Weber interpretation has been an actual style that for many reasons undergoes criticism now. It referred basically to attitude, but also to intention and to acts. Now we are counselled to a worldly holiness, or to a secular style, which again may be more attitudinal than visible according to a behavioral norm. When we write about a Christian style, perhaps it is best even at the normative level to be pluralistic—Christian styles of life.* We can argue for better or worse styles being more or less appropriate to the changing times on the one hand, and the continuing faith on the other. But pluralism is necessary whether we consider the matter historically, or as a contemporary issue.

Saints and Jesus

To look at the matter historically requires a kind of study that Protestants have seldom pursued; namely, of the biographies of Christians and the history of conduct of Christian groups, those declared saints and those undeclared saints, those communities that were monastic and those communities that were inner-worldly ascetic. What can we learn from a John Wollman and a John Winthrop, a John Bunyan and a John Calvin? Is a "Quaker style" important to keep in view not only as theologically legitimate, but historically effective as a mediation of God's grace and order? Is a "Puritan style" equally important and legitimate? What is right and wrong about Russian spirituality, about Franciscan style, about Saint Birgitta of Sweden or Joan of Arc? How have styles that might contribute to a normative description been related to their historical occasions and their Christian forms of piety? No historical movement or figure would give us the pattern for today; yet there may be wisdom in looking to history for a way of thinking analogically about what style ought to be nourished in our time.

---

* See my "Types of Moral Life," *Religious Education,* LVII, (November-December, 1962), 403-10.

Protestants are more experienced at biblical than historical study. But there too is plurality. I read 1 Peter as accenting a kind of submissiveness as an appropriate attitude under certain circumstances. I read 1 John as a great testimony to God's love and man's loving possibilities. I read Galatians as a testimony to Christian liberty. Not all three can necessarily be harmonized in one man at one time; not all three may be appropriate on the same occasion. Perhaps the Christian community needs persons and groups angular enough to stress one to the neglect of others, to remind the whole body of the ministries of various of its members.

The apostolic accounts of the life and teachings of Jesus are bound to be perused for some purposes of contemporary normative usage. One need be neither a biblical literalist nor a romantic idealist to see the coherence between the faith in the love and trustworthiness of God that Jesus preached and the sayings and deeds with which the gospel writers credit him. If it is meaningful to speak about a Christian style of life at all, one must assume that a consistency is possible between trust and belief in Jesus Christ on the one hand, and man's intentions, dispositions and actions on the other. To say that the perennial attractiveness of Jesus Christ arises in part out of the consistency between his faith in God and his life is not to say that is the only significance that he has. But it is to suggest that the Christian community does have a model, a norm, in relation to which all historical styles can be evaluated, and by which all can be informed. What does imitation or discipleship of him mean? This is always a proper question to ask in forming a view of a proper pattern of Christian life. It is not easily answered, as one sees in the history of Christian morality and spirituality. For some the deeds and works become the new law, more extrinsic and literal than the Holy Spirit in the heart. For others the key is the kind of relationship between God and man and between man and man that one sees there. For others, Christians are to have attitudes that are like the attitudes toward others that are portrayed in the narratives and speeches. There is always also the problem of finding the ways to express that discipleship in the present culture, with its modern modes and morals.

But the sources of insight into norm need never be mechanically sought; clearly the imagination and sensibilities of men are important in expression of faith and life styles. As Mrs. Sallie TeSelle indicates in her book, *Literature and the Christian Life*,* the concreteness of not only the parable in the gospels, but of imaginative literature, can function to stimulate imagination and concreteness in the lives of Christians.

* New Haven: Yale University Press, 1966.

Can we talk about normative styles without falling into theological pitfalls? Lutherans have been, in this non-Lutheran writer's judgment, particularly sensitive to certain problems at this point. The main one is the temptation to confuse the shaping of life in accord with one's belief with the attainment of grace and God's righteousness. Many others have been concerned to avoid the Charles Sheldon type of idealization, in which the Christian life is both the striving to approximate ideals and the wooden unimaginative application of them to human affairs. I confine myself to an assertion. When we speak of norms in the context of the Christian life, we are assuming the richness of the divine beneficence, the empowering and guiding new life given by the Spirit, and are only concerned with a matter of high order practicality; namely, what shape ought life under the impact of human decisions and actions take so that it is more in accord with that beneficence and that new life.

The Shaping of Life

Finally, how do "styles" normatively described become embodied in words and deeds? By God's graces and guidance, yes, but not without conforming and confirming thoughts and deeds of men. Here I only suggest that we need to think more clearly about how men's lives are shaped. Artistotle tells us the obvious; namely, that men become lyre players by playing the lyre, and builders by building. Werner Jaeger makes clear that while the normative styles changed in ancient Greece, *paideia* was present in every place and time. I mean to suggest that we need to explore the significance of conscious intention to shape a life in accord with God's good will, and of the practice it takes to become a fitting living active person conforming life to God's goodness. We need to explore what forms the conscience, what centers bring life to wholeness and integrity and "style," what brings lasting dispositions into being that give order and direction to gesture, word, and deed.

We do not have the cohesiveness of earlier isolated city-states or of Christendom. We have pluralism in culture as well as vast individual differences. Such observations are commonplace. But such commonplaces make no less important the task of each Christian being shaped in all his idiosyncracies and commonalities by his confirmation of and conformation with the grace and will of God. Each Christian will have his style. Nor do such commonplaces vitiate the concern for guidance in communities. We need to see more clearly the style of Christian life that helps us conform our culture and society, our time and place to the grace and will of God.

And we need to generously acknowledge that in the sovereignty of God's grace, there are many members to Christ's body, and not all have the same function. There will be the healers and the disturbers, the aggressive and the timid, those identified with the "secular" and those concerned to preserve the integrity of the tradition, the Schweitzers, the Reinhold Niebuhrs, and countless more.

chapter 9

Christian Humanism and the Human Mind

"We are evolution." So wrote the French Jesuit, Pierre Teilhard de Chardin.[1] Making the point more poignantly, he said, "We have become aware that, in the great game that is being played, we are the players as well as being the cards and the stakes." [2] Christopher Mooney, S.J. (1966) in a faithful exposition of Teilhard's passage says, "For it is not only *in* man that the movement of evolution is now carried on, but *by* man . . . Through man evolution has not only become conscious of itself but free to dispose of itself,—it can give itself or refuse itself. Upon man therefore falls the awful responsibility for his future on earth." [3] Evolution can now be carried on *in* man *by* man. This is an awesome point. What used to be shrouded in mystery, interpreted by myths, assumed to be under the determinative powers of Providence or Fate, or the effects of random chance, is becoming known and manageable through the research of molecular biologists. With the more accurate and intricate explanations of the electrochemical system of the brain comes a heightened sense of man's freedom and power to control the minds of men. This new knowledge does not in itself determine the use that will be made of it, any more than the knowledge of nuclear physics in itself determines the uses made of it. But the growing recognition of its potential uses intensifies our sense of responsibility and obligation. The *sense* of responsibility and obliga-

Reprinted by permission of North-Holland Publishing Company, Amsterdam, The Netherlands from *The Human Mind* edited by J. Roslansky.

tion, however, is not in itself determinative of the answers to the questions: "Responsible to whom? Obligated to whom? Responsible for what? Obligated for what?" This new knowledge intensifies our awareness of human freedom in the sense that we are not as enslaved to ignorance as we have been, and in the sense that we realize that men can now direct the course of human development rather than be the more passive reactors to processes over which they have little control. Men need not be the accidental effects of generations of genetic development; their knowledge of genetics moves them toward liberation from determination by random development to the liberty and power to direct future development. Men need no longer simply adapt to their natural environments, but can culturally and technically achieve the liberty to control their environments, indeed to create environments adapted to man. Men need no longer assume that their brains are stable "givens" upon which register the impressions to which they happen to become subject; they are beginning to perceive that the brain itself is subject to development, as a result of the neuro-biological experiments and potential uses of them. Thus, while men have for ages assumed that they could develop their "minds" by training and study, they now see that they can control and develop their "brains" in such a way that their "minds" are capable of new responses and new achievements.

It is this kind of knowledge, with its accompanying senses of both liberation and responsibility, both power and obligation, that Teilhard de Chardin had in mind when he made that statement, so clear that any card player can understand it: "We have become aware that, in the great game that is being played, we are the players as well as being the cards and the stakes." The cards are more complicated: molecular biology gives us an increasingly complex deck that requires elite capacities and training to understand fully. The stakes are higher: the future of man itself. But the players in many respects are the same: morally there has been no progress to compare with scientific and technical progress among the players, whether they be theologians or scientists, humanists or technologists, politicians or investors, business managers or philosophers.

Some Basic Observations

I would like to make some simple observations about this situation and about some responses that have been made to it, before proceeding to suggest some concerns and some lines of activity I believe we ought to consider. First, the *values* of human life have not appeared more clearly because we have a more accurate account of the *facts* of life. Neuro-biologists move toward giving us more and more accurate accounts of memory, but these accounts themselves do not tell us what is *worth* remembering and what is *worth* forgetting. It is worth remembering the things I have learned in reading about the research of the molecular biologists, and it is worth remembering what I learn in this conference, but it is not worth remembering what I had for breakfast this morning, or what the name of the stewardess was on the flight that carried me to Minnesota. To introduce the word "worth" is to introduce a realm of discourse that has a considerable autonomy from the realm of scientific discourse. How would I decide what is worth remembering? This could be answered by referring to many values, not all of which are necessarily in harmony with each other, and not all of which I might consider to be praiseworthy. Let me suggest a couple of them in a random way. I might say it is worth remembering what I read about molecular biology so that I can make a favorable impression on people I talk to at parties and over lunch tables; I could impress them as being a person who seems to have some knowledge outside of his own field of specialization, and thus if they value "learned men" my memory of these things would redound to my glory. Appealing to the most commonly accepted standards of moral values, however, that would not be a very *good* reason. I might say that it is worth remembering because it will be *useful* to me in my future teaching and research in ethics. Then the next question is, "What constitutes utility?" I could answer in various ways: My students and I would be forced to deal more concretely with specific issues that are very complex, and thus we would not be able to get away with platitudes and high level abstractions in a way that we have. This is an appeal to the value of "realism," of facing honestly and directly the hard questions. Or I might say that material that suggests the potentially most important consequences for man is more useful to remember than such trivial but useful information as where in the library stacks I will find Aristotle's works and the secondary materials on them. This latter reason would appeal to the values we would affirm about the continuation and development of life itself; it is more useful to retain information about materials that will have potential effects on the life of the universal human community. This, most men would agree, would be a *better* reason for remembering than would the desire to impress people with one's erudition. Why? Because life is valued, and its continuity and development is thus worthy of more attention than any one man's vanity. But in each instance I appeal to a *value* that does not immediately emerge from biological facts themselves.

My second observation is that this gap between facts about life and the values of life moves toward some closure if certain assumptions are made. These assumptions might be stated as follows. First, to know is itself of value. Why would this be? Because man has developed into the kind of being who has insatiable curiosity about himself and the world around him, and thus in the fulfillment of this drive for knowledge there is a fulfillment, development, and extension of man's existence itself. This assumption presupposes that it is good simply to be, and that to be human is in part to be curious about life, and this curiosity is good. But it does not yet face the question of the uses of knowledge.

Second, in penetrating the molecular biology of the brain, we discern (with reference to other animals, and with reference to man's own past) a direction of development, and *that this direction is on the whole worthy of sustaining and promoting.* The latter phrase jars us a little, it seems to me, because there is a kind of leap of faith involved in it. A Teilhard de Chardin makes the leap in a double move: he extrapolates from where he ascertains the evolutionary process has come to where he thinks on the basis of speculative reason it is going, with its "hominization," "personalization," etc., moving toward an Omega point. At the same time that this extrapolation is made he is impregnating it with ideas derived from Christian faith about a "Christification" of the process, its "amorization" because God entered history and nature in the person of Jesus Christ. But Teilhard's double move is questionable, and he himself was not a blind optimist about life, as our introductory quotations suggest. We can ask on factual grounds: How much extrapolation is warranted on the basis of evidence from the past? With man's new liberty and power to give direction to evolution, can we assume continuities based on projections from the most primitive forms of life? Or do we have to be prepared for radical discontinuities as a result of the new power to interpose in the developments, and thus be more modest in our projections? We could ask, on theological grounds whether affirmations about the redemption of life by a gracious deed of God properly pertain to an impregnation of the natural evolutionary process. Molecular biologists I have read are not theologians, but they are moral men; the second move of Teilhard's would not be persuasive, but the first could at least be discussed. Is there a discernible direction in the development of the brain? That is a factual matter, and subject to verification. Is that direction *good?* The answer to that suggests that the convergence of fact and value diverges again. How it would be answered would involve at crucial points "leaps of faith" on the part of the biologists; it would involve at some point a move beyond empirical and rational support to an affirmation that: (a) the continuation of life is of value; and, (b) that the development of life in the direction it is moving and could move is of value. It is the latter that is jarring, and uncertainties about it locate the moral questions we all now face together.

My third observation is of a different order. It pertains to religious and theological responses that have been made, not to any things as particular as the work of neuro-biologists, but to the awareness of man's new freedom and power to give direction to human development. This awareness has to a considerable extent been embraced as a cultural fact of great theological significance, or at least one that has implications for theology and for religious life. Among the notions overworked and imprecisely developed in recent Christian thinking are those of "maturity" and "a world come of age." If "maturity" is used analogously to its use as a chronological and biological term with reference to the growth processes from infancy to childhood, to adolescence to adulthood, it will be as misleading as other biological analogies have been for the interpretation of historical developments. Do we move into old age and death? No one knows. If maturity is used analogously to a psychological process, suggesting that in infancy there is almost absolute dependence on support from others, and that one gradually grows to greater autonomy, there might be some warrant for its use. Man has some greater autonomy with reference to nature through his knowledge and his power, though he is still dependent on many things. If maturity suggests a growth in moral wisdom, a fulfillment of potential qualities for excellence, so that religious men now heartily and indiscriminately embrace scientific and technological developments in the culture as worthy of joyful celebration, its use is dubious indeed. I believe that popular, avant-garde, religious discourse has made some mistakes in its broadside and indiscriminate celebration of the "new age" in which we are supposed to be living, mistakes that morally conscientious scientists themselves are not making. These mistakes are several. If what is celebrated is liberation from determination by nature and ideas about nature that have in some sense crippled men spiritually and intellectually, there is some propriety to the mood. If, however, in the celebration it is assumed that this new liberty and power are somehow going to be directed by moral wisdom to the well-being of man, the joy and praise is premature. If the celebration assumes that now religious men can see that the world is good and it is for man in some simple way, whereas formerly they felt it had to be denied, they have grounds for celebrating a recovered theological belief (that

God the creator of the world is graciously good and is together with his creation good *for* men). But there are no grounds for confusing this theological affirmation with the facts of historical and scientific development. What religious men believe about God (his goodness, the goodness of creation, the Omega toward which it is moving) can rightfully tell them something about what they *intend* that scientific developments be used for. It may tell them that their attitude toward scientific developments ought to be open rather than closed. But there is no warrant for assuming that the new power and new freedom are being or will be used unambiguously for human good, or for the good even of biological development. The possibilities of new freedom and new power do not either by natural endowment or by some grace of God bring with them a quality of *moral* maturity. The hard issues are not even addressed by the celebration of science and technology; celebration is an expression of an attitude, in this case an affirmative one. It does not help either the molecular biologist, or the technician, solve the problems of the ends to which knowledge and power ought to be put, the values to be served, the means of both control and development to be instituted in the use of knowledge. If the celebrative theme is to say something to the biologists, I cannot imagine what it is. I doubt if they care one whit whether Christians have now decided to embrace what some of them formerly feared. I suspect they might appreciate more understanding and hard work on the part of people primarily concerned with the ends of human existence as these ends pertain to the wider range of choice that their research now presents to men.

My fourth observation pertains to the impact on theological thinking and religious life of our awareness that we are the players, as well as the cards and the stakes. Both man's thinking about the nature of ultimate being, and his disposition in life are being altered by the awareness that we are *participants in creativity,* rather than the tenders and caretakers of something that has been created. We are shapers rather than conformers to static established shapes. The move from thinking about things as static to thinking about them as dynamic has been in the making for many decades. Philosophers like Bergson, Whitehead, and Hartshorne, and such a religious thinker as Henry Nelson Wieman, have been pointing the way in their different patterns of thought and expression. Recently in Catholic thought as well, this notion has taken hold; not only in Teilhard de Chardin, but among others. The American Jesuit, Robert Johann in his Aquinas Lecture, *The Pragmatic Meaning of God,* makes the point in this way:

Instead of separating man from his environment, personal transcendence, as presently conceived [by which Johann means something of the new freedom and power I have been indicating], means a new intimacy and a more significant involvement with it. It marks the release of limitless possibilities and opens the door to a more truly human and genuinely *creative* participation of man in the world.[4]

God, for Johann, is the "essential condition" for this creative participation and interaction, he is the one who enables all things to come into coherence and community as they interact in experience, if I understand him correctly. This is neither the time nor the place to examine critically various doctrines of God as they correlate with our new awareness of creativity. It is proper, however, to underline a trend in theological and religious reflection; namely, that man is an actor and innovator, responding and interacting with the actions of other beings, including the activity of God himself. I would be remiss if I did not recall that biblically oriented theology has found grounds in the scriptures for more dynamic interpretations of the nature of God and his relations to men and the world. Joseph Sittler, a master of theological aphorisms, put it this way, "God simply *is* what God manifestly does." [5] Gustaf Wingren, in expounding the meaning of God's law says that "God's demand that men should continue to 'have dominion' over Creation is part of *His continuing Creation of the world*." [6] This suggests that the meaning of God the Creator is to be developed in terms of a continuous creative activity of God, and that man's scientific and technological pursuits are part of the dominion over the world that man is to have and are part of God's own creative activity in the world. H. Richard Niebuhr moves from the indicative language of God's action in the world to its consequent imperative for man in his famous sentences, "God is acting in all actions upon you. So respond to all actions upon you as to respond to his action." [7]

From all this, it can at a minimum be observed that theological thought, and religious interpretation of life are affirming not static models of being (although the dynamic ones do have order and structure as part of them), but models that conceive of both God and man in active terms. They do not make man *the* Creator, however, any more than the molecular biologist claims that he or any other man has created the neurons he examines. Rather man is seen as the creative responder and innovator in interaction with development and activity that is already there, that is going on. But creative interaction is not an end in itself; what the religious man has the audacity to suggest is that he has some insight into what the outcome of that creative interaction ought to be, the direction in which it ought to go in the course of development. He has a source to which he turns for insight into the *values* that are worthy of acceptance, sustenance, and development. I have no interest here in claiming that this source is a "revelation" of God, or how it might be considered to be a "revelation" of God. We can find in the Western cultural tradition some of these values; many of them have apparently been confirmed both by reason and by experience as worthy of appropriation, or at least consideration, in thinking about what uses the freedom and power of man ought to be put to, what ends they ought to serve. We can find in them some clues about the value and meaning of existence, man together with other men.

These observations and the commentary on them are not random in choice, but are the bases from which I shall now move to more particular considerations of the human and moral potentialities and threats that the research of molecular biologists on the brain seem to portend.

A Christian Humanistic Response

What I have said before can be restated as a way of proceeding. The question that the molecular biologists are proceeding to answer is this one: "How does the brain function?" But this is not the same question as: "What does it mean to be a person?" But the two questions are related. They are related existentially for all of us, biologists, theologians, humanists alike, because we are persons who have been exposed to the knowledge that scientists have given us. Biologists are persons, living in community with others; we nonbiologists, like them, are persons, whose understanding of life is altered by the knowledge that they give us. The relation between the questions, however, is not just an existential one. Whatever qualities or dimensions we might wish to include in our understanding of what it means to be a person are biologically dependent upon our having the intricate brains that human beings have in contrast to other animals. We could not even wonder about what it means to be a person, what the ends and values of man's life are, if we did not have the memory, the ability to reflect, the cells and fluids that biologists are now describing for us. We could not ask the question of values if we did not have the brains that have developed over the long course of evolution from other forms of life, if there were not similarities between us and the rats on which so much research is done, and about which many humanists make snide comments.

Given the brain that we are now coming to know and understand in biological terms, the Christian humanist can raise three general areas for reflection. First, how are we to be *disposed* toward this knowledge and its potential use? Second, what are the "functional requisites" for maintaining *human* (personal) life? Third, are there any principles that can be formulated that will give direction to ends and means in the use of this research for the well-being of life?

Disposition Toward Research

How are we to be disposed toward the research of the molecular biologists who explore the brain, and to the potential uses of this research? I wish to stress the notion of "disposition" here, for it has proper references and limits. It refers to our fundamental *attitudes* toward, in this case, the research and its use. In themselves, as we have noted, attitudes do not tell us what to do; something more is needed; namely, intellectual reflection and the will to act in accord with the ends that are formed by both attitude and intellect.

It would not be difficult to stack the cards of knowledge, and of man's potential use of this knowledge so that a disposition of fear could be evoked. Indeed, the evocation of fear has often been the response of both scientists and humanists to new developments in scientific research. We need recall only the response of many humanists and scientists to the unleashing of nuclear energy to see how fear is not only a rather "natural" moral disposition, but also a very proper one. I recall, for example, not only the early numbers of the *Bulletin of the Atomic Scientists,* but addresses given by Professor Harold Urey at the University of Chicago after World War II, as efforts to awaken the moral sensitivities of other intellectuals to the potential dangers of atomic warfare. There was no ringing apocalypticism in these presentations by responsible scientists; there was, however, an appeal to dread: the dread of possible unintended alteration of human life, and indeed of its destruction. Such dread is fitting, now as it was then. It is not dread of biological information but dread of man's inability to organize and use it in such a way that certain fundamental values on which almost all men agree, namely, the values of life as we now know it and its continuation, would be sustained. The appeal to dread—an attitude or disposition—was not the end in itself, fortunately. In cooperation with many others, efforts were made to protect life, and to channel the uses of nuclear research so that a measure of order has persisted, though in the eyes of many of us that order remains fragile enough to warrant continued vigilance.

With reference to brain research, there has also been some publicity that evokes dread and fear in men. Essays through the years on the work of Dr. José Delgado and others, have persistently raised the question of who controls the electronic devices that in turn control the electrodes that can be placed in certain areas of the brain so that behavior itself is in turn controlled. The dread is not so much of potential destruction as in the case of nuclear war, as it is in the possibilities of the accumulation of power that could be used to determine and control the behavior of men in ways that are not possible at the present time. The latter phrase is important. There are and always have been ways in which the minds of men have been directed—by teaching, by indoctrination, by propaganda, by control of the kinds of information and ideas that men can have. Every such effort has been to train minds to respond in particular ways (and the ways themselves have varied greatly, particularly in terms of certain moral values). Perhaps the new element of dread comes in with the possibilities of determination through drugs and electrical stimulations; these possibilities portend the diminution of the liberty of individuals without power to reject or accept the stimulations of those who have power. What is dreaded is that new knowledge, which gives potential capacities to control the brain, will fall into the power of those whose values we might not approve of.

With most knowledge that evokes new dread, there is also new hope. Whether dread or hope are evoked depends upon many things, including the sophistication of knowledge about potential uses, the availability of resources to protect against misuses and to foster "good" uses. We have already seen how some drugs can be used to still the potential violence of psychotics, how many persons whose humanity and productivity in the human community have been crippled by mental illness have been able to resume fruitful and quite normal human activities. I have not found, however, any evangelistic utopians among neuro-biologists who are sounding the coming of a new age as the result of their research—a new age in which men will find some absolute good, and persistent euphoria. Even where one might find hints of a new sense of peace and harmony emerging, this is seen to raise other questions about the meaningfulness and productivity of life under such potential conditions.

What kinds of dispositions seem proper in the light of neurobiological research? On what grounds might they be deemed to be proper? The morally ambiguous possibilities of the use of knowledge is clear; one does not need a theologian to remind men of them. Though it sounds terribly like a "middle way" a case can be made for realism without despair, for hope without illusions, for avoiding the attitudes of apocalypticism on the one hand and utopianism on the other. Some bases for this can be briefly adumbrated.

First, the moral conscientiousness of the researchers themselves gives some ground for confidence. While their scientific work proceeds without immediate justification by the social and humane values that are the more professional concerns of some of the rest of us, they are men who themselves love life, defend the conditions in life which enable them to exercise their intelligence and freedom, and envision the potential possibilities for and threats to human order and life that might be forthcoming from their work. They existentially unite the humane and the scientific, and often are more aware of the relations of one to the other than some are who embody only the humane.

Second, in free societies there is a social pluralism that gives grounds for confidence, that enables men to be realistic and hopeful at once. Social pluralism in free societies, while it creates tensions and abrasiveness that make human relations complex, keeps alive a diversity of values since various communities in the society attend to the cultivation of different values. It also keeps alive a diversity of institutionalized centers of power that prohibit any one center from absolutely dominating. The normative moral concerns of religious communities, for example, are never simply embodied by universities or business establishments or the state. There is always abrasion between the interests and values of these and other groups. But, there are also centers of loyalty and commitment that they share in common which enable them to live together not only in peace, but in some creative interaction with each other. In this interaction with each other, it is possible for each to learn from the other, each to restrain and limit the other, each to make its contribution to the general direction that the society itself takes. Very often the fear that one interest or value community in the society creates in the minds of members of another is the result of absence of interaction and communication between them. It is my judgment that we can be realistic and hopeful about the uses of the knowledge that we now are getting about the ways that the brain works as long as we have a plurality of value communities and social institutions in significant interaction with each other in free societies. If an imperative is to be drawn from this, it is twofold: to keep alive various humanistic centers for interpretation of the values of life together with the scientific centers that explore its facts, and to maintain the avenues of interaction between them and other centers, such as business and the state so that policy and the exercise of power are affected by the interaction. (More on this later.)

Third, the nature of man as a moral being is such that while he is able to be "nasty, mean, brutish and small," to quote from Hobbes, he also inclines away from the evil and toward the good, to follow St. Thomas. The "evil" and the "good" are terribly vague terms in such a statement, but can minimally be given content sufficient for our purposes here. At least inclination away from evil can be transposed into "abhorrence at the destruction of what seems to make human life worth living." Historically, for example, we have seen the persistence of men's chafing under conditions that drastically limit their freedom—to choose, to act, to believe. We have seen resuscitation again and again of human longing for a better life—free from needless suffering, searching for order and peace, enlarging of the ranges of human choice. To be sure, the contrary tendencies have emerged persistently enough to prohibit a bland optimism or a blind utopianism, but countervailing tendencies to these seem also to persist, and to become correctives to what many men would consider to be aberrations from what it means to be human. Perhaps, under possible totalitarian conditions research on the brain could be used to implement the domination of man's destructive tendencies; but on the basis of man's deep longing for life, for peace, for the good, we can have some confidence that such a possibility will be limited.

Fourth, Christians and Jews particularly have certain convictions about God, the source and power of life itself, that ought to bring confidence tempered by a realistic assessment of potential human misuses of knowledge and power. There is, to quote again from Father Robert Johann, a "bearing or import of belief in God on the qualities of our lives." [8] That import or bearing is dependent upon the nature and content of those beliefs, as well as our appropriation of their significance for dispositions and attitudes toward human development. Christian doctrine, and its significance for our bearing toward life cannot be more than pointed to here. But it is at least this: that God is worthy of our confidence, and the God who is worthy of our confidence is the one who has given and continues to give life, its development and its order, the one who makes possible the restoration of brokenness in the human community, who makes possible the restraints of man's moral evil as well as the newness of life and knowledge that he enjoys, indeed the God who is himself love and power, goodness and power. The significance for our lives of such beliefs of trusting in

God whom confessionally we know in Jesus of Nazareth, ought to be, can be, and often is one of confidence without either despair or illusion, as we face the human uses of human knowledge.

Men are prone to extremes in dispositions all too often. They flutter like birds between despair and illusion. They fear a world that will destroy all that they value, or they dream of a world that will realize all that they cherish. They forget that they participate in creativity, and that this makes possible both new good and new evil. Despair results from the absence of confidence and hope; it is a resignation to fatedness (as if things will be inexorably what they will be without human initative and activity). Confidence and hope come from "a sense of *the possible*," [9] from those certainties of experience and belief that enable men to be participative and creative interactors with the processes of life itself, knowing that mistakes will be made, but also that many of them can be corrected.

Requisites for Personal (Human) Life

What seem to be the "functional requisites" for human life, in the sense not only of biological preservation and development, but in the sense of personal meaningfulness? We can begin this exploration by looking at the lists of such requirements that have been made by others. Bronislaw Malinowski was one creative analyst of human culture who stipulated several adumbrations of such requisites. On one occasion he listed seven basic needs of man, each of which is the basis for a "cultural response," an institutionalization. Metabolism requires a "commissariat," reproduction requires a kinship system, bodily comforts require shelter, safety requires protective institutions, movement requires the organization of activities, growth requires "training," and health requires "hygiene." [10] The Princeton sociologist, Marion J. Levy, Jr., raises the question with reference to the needs for a human society to exist, and lists ten "requisites": adequate physiological relationships for biological survival, differentiation and assignment of social roles, communication, a shared "cognitive orientation," or way of knowing, a shared articulated set of goals, some regulation of the choice of means, a regulation of emotional expression, adequate procedures for education or socialization, effective control of disruptive behavior, and adequate institutionalization. [11] Such lists are subject to refinement, elaboration, and revision, but for our purposes can be accepted as pointing to minimal conditions necessary for minimal continuation of human life. They do not, without extension and revision, account for many of the things that we, as human persons, find to be most valuable and rewarding in life. Just as the question "What makes the brain function?" is not the same as the question "What does it mean to be a person?" so the question "What conditions are necessary for basic survival of man?" is not the same question as "What makes life *worth* living?" If some of the things that make life *worth* living can be indicated, we are on the way to understanding what values ought to be preserved, sustained, and developed in the uses of neurobiological research.

I shall not attempt a full delineation of all the things that men strive for and live for. Rather, I shall isolate only a few that seem to be crucial to the enhancement of the human "spirit," to use a term that has no precise neurobiological references. The first is freedom, which has been alluded to as an aspiration that is persistent enough in men to give us some confidence that men will resist uses of knowledge that destroy it, and promote uses that enhance it. The preservation and development of human liberty, within the bounds necessary for order which itself sustains liberty, comes to the fore again and again in moral responses to political developments, religious developments, and scientific developments. We see it in anticolonialism, we see it in the reform of the Catholic church, and we see it in the concerns men have about the uses of human beings for scientific experimentation. Edward Shils, in a passionate critique of some of the research of his fellow social scientists, for example, raises three ethical issues that arise from experimentation itself, not to mention the uses of knowledge derived from it. Each of the three, but primarily the first, has reference to freedom. They are "the propriety of the manipulation of adult, normal human beings, even for their own good, by other human beings; the propriety of possible injury to a human being on behalf of scientific progress and the progress of human well-being; and the depth and permanence of the effects of the experiment on the individual subject." [12] Absolutized in the abstract such concerns would seem to falsify many other concerns that we have for the worthiness of life. Human beings are influenced, if not manipulated, by other human beings all their lives; indeed, culture would not persist if this were not so. The liberty and rights of some men are limited, if not injured, for the sake of progress that has moral value over and over again (for example the limitation of the liberty of a landlord to designate to whom he will rent an apartment that is involved in the progress in civil rights). But Shils is pointing to some almost primitive moral sensitivities that crop up whenever personal liberty is threatened. Men resent being "manipulated," there seems to be a betrayal of trust and confidence in it, a diminution of one's control over his own responses. Human life seems to be worth living only if the value of personal freedom is attended to, though obviously other values of equal or almost equal importance are not always in perfect harmony with it.

Another requisite that needs to be met to keep life worth living is "trust." As such perceptive thinkers as Marcel and Royce have shown, men live to a great extent by reliance upon the trustworthiness of others, and must themselves be trustworthy in order to live in community with others. Trust becomes important only when we have the development of the human brain that enables personal liberty to be meaningful, and personal relations to be determined not simply by biological interactions and necessities but by responses and commitments consciously made. To be sure, some analogies might be drawn between the reliance of chemical agents upon the functioning of each other in the workings of the brain on the one hand, and the reliance of persons upon each other for the sustenance and meaningfulness of life on the other. But "trust" as something valued in personal interrelations or in the relations between groups and even nation states, can be withdrawn, betrayed, broken, by willful acts of men. Trust, like the assurance of a significant domain of personal freedom, is a moral requisite for human life. It involves honesty, compliance with promises and commitments, conformity to rules and procedures of life that set the boundaries and directions within which human interactions occur, as well as personal confidence that others will sustain rather than betray the self. Uses of knowledge that make life and other persons untrustworthy will denigrate personal existence; uses which enhance the phenomenon and value of trust will sustain and develop it.

Personal existence in the human community depends upon relationships of love. Love is one of the looser terms in common human discourse; it refers to sexual relations in which there is an affection of the persons for each other; it refers to utter self-sacrifice as symbolized by the cross in the Christian community; it refers to the relationship of friendship; and it refers to a profound longing for various objects as potential sources of self-fulfillment. As a moral requisite for personal life, however, we might use more restricted references. It involves joyous and thankful response for the existence of others, and for the relationship between us. It directs a relation of respect for the autonomy of others, so that in love there is neither a swallowing up of others for the sake of self-aggrandizement, nor a blind submissiveness to others for the sake of the loss of identity. There is loyalty to others, not for the sake of their utility to the self, but for their very existence as others. There is trustworthiness in love; fidelity to each other is part of the order of love.* The possibility for the fulfillment of relations of love is a requisite for human personal existence. Research that is now being done on the human brain might very well lead to developments which make such relationships more possible rather than less possible; at least insofar as such relationships are dependent upon neurobiological functions, men may be able to check some of the basically physical conditions that cripple some persons, that do not enable them to respond freely in loving relationships. Certainly, the use of new knowledge for the sake of human and personal life will have to consider the importance of maintaining and enhancing the possibilities of love as one of its touchstones. Uses that deter such possibilities will have to be guarded against.

Many other requisites, in part related to freedom, trust, and love, could be developed, such as hope, justice, order, joy, opportunity for achievement, and others. I shall limit consideration to these three, for they illustrate the kinds of "moral requisites" that are dependent upon biological survival and upon the intricacies of the human brain, but take some flight from this dependence as values or concerns to be attended to in themselves. I would not claim that these values are any more dependent upon religious beliefs about God, or upon the cultivation of the religious life than they are upon the neurological structure and function of man. I would, however, indicate that freedom, trust, love, justice, joy, and hope have been nourished by humanistic Christianity and Judaism, and that in the pluralism of the society that is to come, it will be the function of religious communities, or their secular alternatives, to nourish these needs of man, and to keep their importance alive in an increasingly technically-oriented culture. If fewer and fewer men will appropriate traditional religious beliefs out of doubts about their credibility, they will nonetheless have to recognize the importance of religious faith and life in providing and cultivating the sense of the numinous, and the qualities of life that make scientific and technical life worth pursuing. While I, no more than any other theologian, would wish to justify religious belief exclusively on the basis of its bearing and import on the "quality of life" that it can bring into being, I am prepared to assert that renewed religious life, dependent upon certain beliefs, does make a contribution to humanization by sustaining and fostering the moral requisites for personal human life. Like the uses of scientific knowledge, the uses of religion are morally ambiguous: there is no absolute certainty that traditional religion will function for humaniza-

---

* This follows loosely the more beautiful passage of Niebuhr in *The Purpose of the Church and Its Ministry*, pp. 34-36.

tion just as there is no certainty that new knowledge of the brain will. But the pangs of criticism and renewal through which religious communities are now going gives some expectation that the recognition that God is for man and his well-being will strengthen man's own ability to be for man and his well-being.

Principles for Direction

Finally, some attention needs to be given to a risky effort, namely the development in more concise form of some directives, moral and social, that can be considered with reference to the uses of our new knowledge about the brain.

1. The scientific community has responsibility to man, to life (and in theological terms) to God the giver of life, to be vigilant in its own reflection about the potential uses and misuses of knowledge. This vigilance can be exercised in interaction with humanists.

2. Religious and other communities concerned with human values have a responsibility to scientists and to all men, and to God, to participate in the interactive processes out of which institutionally and culturally the uses of new knowledge will be determined. This means clearly that humanists need at least a layman's knowledge of the crucial research and its potentialities.

3. All of us have an obligation to keep active a concern for human values in the culture as a whole, through churches, educational institutions, mass media of communications, and other agencies. If such work is not done, some of the values themselves might atrophy in the consciences of men. This requires public moral discourse, not for the sake of evoking fear, but for the sake of developing the awareness of man's own worthwhileness in the light of which knowledge can be put to the service of man. I wish to underscore this third point, for all too often our immediate responses to new developments that pose threats as well as possibilities for good is to think in terms of legal restraints and direction, with sanctions of political power. To such we will turn, but even legal directives will depend for their efficacy on that nebulous "moral ethos" that will or will not exist.

4. All of us have an obligation to maintain pluralism in and through free societies, pluralism of activities (sciences, religion, arts, etc.), pluralism in institutionalization of moral concerns, and pluralism in concentrations of power. No one group is sufficient in itself to provide "answers" to existing and potential questions. There is need of others for information, insight, restraint, support, and development.

5. New institutionalizations are necessary to make possible the significant

interaction between groups with particularized interests and knowledge that can give direction to the development of man. Some such seminars and centers are coming into being, but all too often the interaction is on a random basis. There are centers for the study of population problems and for international policy that bring together the knowledge, ideas and insights of various disciplines that bear upon such problems. Further developments of this sort are in order, whether under the auspices of states, universities, churches, business, or various combinations of them.

6. Some boards or agencies with technical competence and power are needed to set limits through law and other means to potentially destructive uses of knowledge. We face this on an issue that may be in the long run of limited significance in comparison with potential uses of knowledge developed from molecular biology; namely, in the whole business of electronics and "bugging." Ways of protecting human rights to privacy, and of enforcing such protection are much the order of the day. Something comparable may be necessary with reference to other areas.

7. The freedom to do research needs to be distinguished sufficiently from the use of research so that man's right to knowledge is preserved. This involves its own risks; new knowledge may enable a development of man into something quite different from what we know in our thin slice of history. Man is no more a static part of the process of creativity and development than are some other organisms. The right to know what is involved in human development needs to be protected.

8. Much more detailed and clearer formulation of those values to be preserved and developed in human existence needs to be made so that these might function both to indicate the direction that uses of research ought to take, and the limitations of those uses that ought to be firmly formed. Biological survival is only the beginning of such a formulation, and its form is itself subject to change. To confine myself to previous remarks made in this chapter, I would say that uses which preserve and foster freedom, trust, love, justice, joy and hope are to be supported; those that deprive men of these are to be prohibited. Intensive and continuous dialogue needs to be sustained to solve the harder questions as to what new use would have what effect on what values. Amendment of possible legal restrictions will have to be possible so that prohibitions can be revised in the light of worthy new possibilities. But law and morality have a necessary conservative function in the preservation of life and what makes it worthwhile.

"In the great game that is being played, we are the players as well as being the cards and the stakes."

chapter 10

The Conditions for Hope: Reflections on Human Experience

In this essay I have three basic intentions. First, I wish to explore hope as a phenomenon of human experience. My approach is an inductive one. To what are we referring when we speak about hope and hopefulness? What are the bases of hope? (By bases, I mean the answer we give to the question, "Why do you hope?") What are the objects of hope? (By objects, I mean the answer we give to the question, "What do you hope for?") How do the bases and objects of hope qualify it? Second, I wish to explore what seems to be involved in the movement between Christian faith and belief, indeed Christian hope, and the human experience of hope. The relations between Christian beliefs and human experiences are complex and slippery, and I shall attempt to sort out what some of them are. Finally, I wish to explore the significance for our moral action of both our hope and that for which we hope.

I shall not carry on much explicit discussion with the work of Professor Moltmann, or with other authors who have informed my own thinking about hope.[1] I have used this as an occasion to sort out and put together ideas and impressions I have had about hope for a number of years. By focusing on hope here, however, I do not want to suggest that it is *the* key, the central concept to understand Christian theology, human existence, or ethics. All of these are of such complexity that one concept or notion at best gives us a particular angle of vi-

Reprinted by permission of Herder and Herder from *Continuum*, Vol. 7, No. 4, 1970.

sion into them; to honor one notion or concept with superior sovereignty so that it governs all others provides an impressive systemization, but also, in my judgment, distorts and oversimplifies.

Hope is not something, readily isolable from other things, with discreet demarcations which render it subject to simple refined analysis, any more than it is a commodity to be packaged and marketed to those who want or need it. Nor is it something which is unqualifiedly commendable in and of itself; any moral judgment about a hope depends upon what is hoped for. It may well be a fundamental requisite for personal and common life to flourish with meaning and purpose; this becomes clear when it is compared with despair, with the absence of hope. But it can be illusory, pollyanna-like, and even demonic, depending on its basis and its object.

Perhaps some further observations about hope will be useful before moving to more analysis. Hope, we know, can be a sentimental deception of oneself and others about the realities of suffering, evil, and injustice. It can be a shallow optimism sustained by shoddy exhortations. It can be genuine anticipation and expectation of a new day, a new possibility of life. It can be confidence that the future is for man and not against him. Hope, like faith and love, can have different objects. Some men hope for death, some for newness of life; some men hope for new justice and peace in the world, some for the second coming of Jesus; some men hope for a classless society, and some for the triumph of the Aryan race. What men hope for conditions what purposes they have, what they live for, what they desire from day to day, what they are, what they say, what they do. Hope usually looks to the future not as a threat to what is, but as an open field of possibilities for human achievement and well-being.

Gabriel Marcel suggests that the antithesis to hope is the capitulation to fate. In capitulation to the sense that what is has come about by inexorable and immutable courses of events over which no human has control, comes despair. Hope lives in the confidence that new possibilities of life exist, that present social systems and patterns of life are not fated by the blind god Necessity, but are susceptible to alteration, to recombination of the elements of life. Hope assumes that freedom exists: freedom to become what one now is not, freedom to change not only the course of one's own life, but the course of the social history of which one is a part.

Hope can be passive, or it can be active. Passive hope sits and waits, expecting other persons or other groups, or some great interruptions in history from a power within or beyond it, to fulfill man's expectations. Active hope moves to perform the possible, to fulfill purposes, intentions, convictions that are shaped in part by the object of hope.

These observations about hope are rather undisciplined and fairly commonplace. Now we must explore hope with a bit more precision. It is probably prudent to follow the fashion of seeing how we use the word, to what it seems to refer. Often we use it to refer to a particular desire or wish for particular objects, such as one might say after he has purchased a lottery ticket for a new car, "I hope I win." Not much more seems to be involved here than saying, "I wish I would win," or "I want to win," unless it is a greater degree of emotion that the use of "hope" might indicate. Hope, then, sometimes refers to the strong emotion involved in some desires or wishes.

Hoping to win in a lottery is an interesting example, because the element of chance involved precludes two other references the term has in other circumstances, namely, some expectation or some confidence about what will happen. Of course, not all expectations or confidences about the future would be called hopes; one can expect the worst and be in despair; one can be confident that the future portends evil, and be in fear of it. A hope is usually an expectation with a particular quality, a beneficial quality for the self or for the community. If one has purchased one lottery ticket out of ten thousand sold, and said, "I hope to win," meaning "I expect to win," or "I believe I will win," we would assume that the speaker is joking, or that the drawing was rigged in some way. I am not playing games with words. I wish to show that if "expectation" and, even stronger, "confidence" are referred to in the use of "hope," there must be a credible basis for hope or for hopefulness. (I use basis, a loose term, which can include "grounds for," "conditions for," and "cause of.")

My major point thus far is this: if my particular hope for something, or to do something, is to be more than a wish or a desire, *it must have a plausible or believable basis.* There must be conditions which permit me to expect that thing, or to do that deed. There must be grounds for confidence that I am likely to receive it, or likely to do it.

Now, we sometimes use the basic word *hope* (it is both verb and noun) in other forms. We say, "He is a hopeful person." Or we might say, "Christians are hopeful," which may be construed to mean that if a man is not hopeful, he is not a Christian, or to mean that Christian faith necessarily causes men to be hopeful. Or we might say, "Christians ought to be hopeful," which we can construe to mean that there are conditions in

Christian faith and belief which are sufficient to make a man hopeful, and that, if his life is consistent with his faith, he will, can, should and ought to be hopeful. When we speak of a person being hopeful, we are referring to a persistent tendency he has, to a *disposition*. If we wish to make an empirical judgment ("he is hopeful"), we would look for evidence of a consistency in his attitude or outlook toward others, toward events, things, etc. In this sense, hope (as hopefulness) is a virtue term: it refers to a tendency so persistent that we expect the person in the future to be hopeful as he has been in the past, and we will be surprised if he is not. For hopefulness to persist there must be bases and objects which are sufficient for it to come into being and to continue. Now we are in a difficult arena of discourse, for the expressions of hopefulness occur in particular circumstances: they are evoked by particular events, persons, and things, in particular relationships. Hopefulness, like other virtues, has a latency about it. If it were so consistently manifest that it never altered, we might wonder what necessitates it even when the conditions for hopefulness on the part of others do not exist. Most of us are not any more consistently hopeful than we are consistently loving or courageous. My point is this: perhaps certain bases and objects of hope are so sufficient for some persons that attitudes of despair are the exception, whereas for others the occasions which give rise to hopefulness are more sporadic and episodic.

Why might this be the case? Let us follow through on *bases* and *objects*. (Subsequently we shall inquire about the relations between the two.) Let us say that the basis of my hope is the resurrection of Jesus Christ, or at least my belief in the resurrection. Let us say that the object of my hope is the kingdom of God, or at least my belief in God's future. If these are so central to my sense of identity and purpose that they cannot be assailed by doubts or by any evidences that there are reasons not to be hopeful, then I might expect to have a bearing of hopefulness toward the world under all circumstances. Why? Because nothing in human experience can count as evidence against the credibility of either the basis or the object.

Consistency in hopefulness might come about in two quite different ways as well. First, certain scientific and historical evidence might be given as a sufficient basis. One might say, for example, that while there are genetic loads which mankind bears, the processes of natural selection appear to make the survival and improvement of the human race likely. Or, while there are events, social systems, and persons in history which frustrate the ends of human fulfillment, on the whole good comes even out of evil. Second, the evidences of personal experience might be given as sufficient conditions for hope. One might say that when the future appeared to be closed to my aspirations and those I have for others, the doors somehow were opened, and thus all things work together for good for me, and for others. In both of these two ways there is some evidence given, but there is also a strong element of belief which seems to warrant generalizations about the future course of events.

If such persistent hopefulness exists, one can inquire what the sufficient conditions would be to alter it, to evoke dispositions inconsistent with hopefulness. Would failure to get into the graduate school I expected to enter? Would the continuation of the war in Vietnam, or the increase in respiratory diseases through air pollution, or the choking of city streets with garbage? Since belief seems to be so central to understanding both the bases and objects of persistent hopefulness, the evidences would have to be strong enough to alter the beliefs. In the instances of scientific or historical or personal evidences as the bases of hope, such things might affect the belief, though they might not. If, however, belief in the resurrection is the basis, and the kingdom of God is the object, both are outside the boundaries that can be reached by personal and historical evidences.

Let us look at the more episodically hopeful man; he is probably a more typical member of the human community as a whole, and also of the Christian community. The causes of his hopefulness come in smaller sizes, and the objects are achievable intentions. If *his* circumstances appear to be alterable, he feels a sense of freedom and can be hopeful. If the Negro ghetto resident perceives that he is not fated to live in a rat-infested tenement on welfare checks because of concrete evidences of other achievable possibilities, he might be hopeful. His hope requires concrete experienced causes and achievable objects. Greater hopefulness among urban people might be evoked when air pollution control is effective, when labor relations are good, when dozens of other sufficient and efficient causes are present. The generalization that a "sense of the possible" is the necessary condition for hope still holds (Lynch and others), but the possible must be near, and not remote, in time and space. Its bases must be present in experience, its object achievable. And such a man lives with episodes of despair as well as hope.

Several sets of questions can be raised by what has thus far been said. The first gets us into the philosophy of religion, where I claim no competence, but since it bears on Christian ethics I must proceed, though with caution. Are there any relations between religious bases and objects of hope on the one hand, and the experientially credible bases and achievable ends on the other hand? If there are, what are they? How are they to be understood? Some effective relationship is necessary if we are to affirm that religious faith is a ground for hope, and that a religiously based hope has some significance for ordinary moral life.

1. It might be said that there is no relation between a religious hope, immuned as it is (in certain forms) from contrary evidences of experience, and general human hopefulness. They have different bases and objects, and only a confused mind would relate them to each other. I believe there are various grounds for rejecting this position, and that these are assumed in much of the recent literature on Christian hope.

2. It might be said that the resurrection of Jesus Christ and the promise of the kingdom *demonstrate* that human and historical experience are open, alterable, filled with possibilities, and thus there is a basis for hope. God, who brought about the resurrection and who promises his kingdom, causes history and experience to be open. Perhaps this claim is sometimes made.

3. It might be said that *belief* in the resurrection and the kingdom is grounds (necessary, or sufficient, or corroborative) for *belief* in openness, alterability, and possibility, and thus is a basis for hope.

4. It might be said that the experience of openness, alterability and possibilities in history is grounds (necessary, sufficient, or corroborative) for belief in the resurrection and the kingdom. This possibility is, I believe, rejected in the literature on Christian hope. It would be to say, because there are experiential bases of hope, there is a basis for believing in the resurrection and the kingdom.

5. The following might be said: (a) Belief in the resurrection and the kingdom is grounds for believing in openness, alterability and possibility, and through this, is grounds for hope. (b) *Experience* of openness, alterability and possibility provides grounds for hope. (c) *Somehow* they corroborate each other, reinforce each other, inform each other, while maintaining their independence from each other.

Some such position as this fifth one seems to me to be most generally assumed, and can be made at least plausible. The "some-how" is the nut to be cracked. Let us say that my immediate circumstances are always "against me," and I have the powers neither to alter them nor "rise above" them. I despair. Is this evidence against my belief in the resurrection and the promise of the kingdom? No. Is it evidence against openness, alterability and possibilities in experience? I may perceive it to be such, but I ought not to generalize on my private and limited experience. Does my religious hope now make me believe in possibilities that my immediate experience contradicts? I believe most Christians assume that it can and that it should. It would not be a hope if it were fully confirmed, but it cannot be a hope if there are no credible bases for believing it to be a hope. Religious hope is grounded in faith in God, the object of hope; this faith is in principle finally immuned to contrary (and I suppose supporting) evidences in experience. But the religious hope is seen to be grounds for historical and personal hope, for which there are sometimes experiential evidences. I believe that the connection between hope based on a religious ground and hope based on experiential grounds is probably a *psychological* one; the two are joined by persons who believe that the religious has implications for the historical, though the historical evidences can never be in themselves grounds for religious hope. No matter how I try to think this through (and others are better equipped to think about such questions than I am) the relationship of religious faith and human experience seems to follow this odd pattern.

Thus, what the claim seems to be is this: belief in the resurrection and the kingdom are grounds for hopefulness even when concrete experience is to the contrary, and that same hopefulness pertains not only to the remote future, but to the present. Belief in an ultimate ground of possibilities makes possible belief in present possibilities.

I would state my personal position, however, somewhat differently from this. I would not hang the bases of hope, religious and experiential, on the single hook of the resurrection. My lay reading of the Old Testament leads me to suppose that there are religious interpretations of people's personal and historical experiences which mix (maybe confuse) the religious and historical bases. There is some confirmation of both the religious and the historical hope in experience, with significant exceptions such as Job. This seems to be part of the meaning of the Exodus. In other places also the *has* and the *will* suggest this. For example, Isaiah 60:1-2: "Arise, shine, for your light *has* come, and the glory of the Lord *has* risen upon you. For behold, darkness shall cover the earth, and thick darkness the peoples; but the Lord *will arise* upon you, and the glory *will be seen* upon you."

The memory of past events, interpreted in part as performances of God as well as men, which has been a basis of hope, continues to provide present bases of hope. Belief in possibilities in the future is based both on historical evidences and upon faith by a process of extrapolation. For me, and perhaps for many others, a religious basis for hope which is immuned from all possibilities of either support or of negative evidences drawn from experience lacks the credibility that is required for hopefulness to be engendered and to persist. Those of us in this predicament can be charged with lack of faith; we might be able to make other charges against those not in this predicament. I believe, however, that history and experience corroborate religious hope, and vice versa.

The second set of questions is this: What, with regard to the hopeful and hoping self, is the relation between a general disposition to be hopeful and particular instances of hoping and not hoping? Is a general tendency to be hopeful evoked by a more generalized basis and directed toward a more generalized object? Are specific hopings or despairings related to more particular objects? Thus can one be generally disposed to be hopeful, and specifically in certain instances be not only highly realistic about the limitations of possibilities, but even despairing?

The answer to the question of realism is assumed to be affirmative in the Christian literature on hope, and I believe that it is a correct answer. The fact that F. D. Maurice could write: "I may bid [each peasant and beggar] in the land rejoice, and give thanks, and sing merry songs to God who made him, because there is nothing created which his Lord and Master has not redeemed, of which He is not the King . . ." [2] did not prohibit him from being realistic about particular evils. It did not keep him from being involved in efforts of social reform.

This is possible for several reasons. First, the fundamental disposition of hope, in contrast to its antithesis, despair, is *based* on a general conviction which is believed to be true about God, and therefore (because of God's relations to men and events) permits or even causes hope. The theological conviction is stated in various ways: one is that evil has been overcome in Jesus Christ, and therefore while its remaining manifestations require realistic responses, there is a basis of ultimate confidence and hope which provides the most pervasive disposition. Second, there is an orientation toward a future which is not tomorrow, or the next century, but an always approaching future. Orientation toward that horizon, and toward what is said about it (it is God's future, or God's kingdom), means that nothing which happens tomorrow or in the next century can count against that future. Yet, at the same time, orientation toward that horizon affects attitudes and dispositions toward the events of tomorrow and the next decade, so that even in the presence of moral evil one sees and lives beyond its moment.

Third, it seems to be possible (though I do not have the concepts to interpret, not to mention explain this) for persons to have fundamental dispositions and orientations which affect but do not fully determine particular responses to particular objects. There are, no doubt, psychological and even biochemical factors involved in this possibility in the human organism. (Anyone who has undergone successful drug therapy during severe depression knows that chemicals can do what Christian hope cannot.) Whether the grounds for hopefulness are theological or historical is a matter of indifference; particular realistic or despairing responses do not necessarily vitiate a more general disposition of hope, any more than, if the more general disposition is one of despair, occasional hopeful responses vitiate it.

The claims of theologians that human effects or consequences of hopefulness can be based on theological belief and oriented toward an ever future object are plausible. Indeed, there might even be some persons in the world who, if asked why they have hope, would reply, "Because of the resurrection of Christ, and because of God's promises of his kingdom, his future." They might also be valiant resisters against historical and social evils, and activistic participants in the formation of a new historical order as well.

A third set of questions must be raised. How are the objects of hope and the bases of hope related? How is the answer to the question, "Why do you hope?" related to the answer to the question, "What do you hope for?"

The bases of hope and the objects of hope are often very different. For example, we might ask a civil rights leader who is hopeful why he is hopeful. He would give us many reasons: favorable court decisions, new laws, awakening consciences among some whites, growing militancy among blacks, etc. We could ask what he hopes for. The answer could be given in highly generalized terms: for freedom and for justice. Or it might be given in more specific terms: for more and better jobs for Negroes, for better housing, for black power, for the end of discrimination in athletics, for ghetto neighborhood control of schools, etc. In this example the bases of hope seem to be available instruments for the achievement of objects of hope which are independent of the bases.

It appears that when we talk about Christian hope, however, the same independence between basis and object is not the case. The answer to the question, "Why are you hopeful?" might be: because of the resurrection of Jesus Christ, or, because Israel's history shows that God wills man's well-being. These reasons for hope are backward looking; they indicate that hope is motivated by beliefs about past events. But the answer is more complete if it is this: because God promises us the future, the kingdom. I suppose that even here the cause or ground is a promise given in the past, but its immediate reference is to the object of hope, i.e., the kingdom. Here, then, the object, through the mediation of a past promise, becomes the basis for hope. The credibility of the basis is at least partially dependent upon the credibility of the object. This, it seems to me, is what a thoroughgoing eschatological theology finally demands as the condition for human hope.

An alternative to the circle around an esoteric object of hope which is its own esoteric basis would be a clear affirmation that the theological or religious affirmations *somehow* (again, somehow) give us insight into personal and historical life, and have their own credibility subject to the tests of human experience. Thus we are back at an issue which I previously noted. If the basis of hope is that even in adversity and evil in either one man's life or in the corporate life of a people there are possibilities for newness and human well-being, and if this is (in a sense) guaranteed by the religious faith that God makes sure it is the case, a premise of an argument is clearly inclusive enough to permit human hopefulness. We might shorten the discussion in the following way.

1. There is no experience of adversity which absolutely precludes the possibility of something beneficial coming out of it.

2. This is true because God has created, ordered, and redeemed life.

3. Since it is God (sovereign by definition) who creates, orders, and redeems life, we can believe that the future will be at least as open and beneficial as the past.

4. Thus there are human and divine grounds of hope, and human and divine objects of hope.

To state it this way is to render the basis and the object open to contrary evidences. That is, if one's experience is such as to render the first statement doubtful, the others are rendered doubtful. One might still believe in a god, but it would not be the God who guarantees the sense of the possible. Or, if experience is contrary to the sense of the possible, one's hope would be less an expectation of immediate possibilities, and more a projected confidence in distant and ultimate possibilities guaranteed by faith. To return to my illustration of the hopeful civil rights worker, as a Christian he might say that the reasons given for being hopeful have a more ultimate ground, namely God, and the objects given have a more ultimate object, namely God. The difference between him and the civil rights worker who is not a Christian *might* be that the latter is more subject to despair. In the one case, immediate bases and objects are related to a more ultimate basis and object; in the other they stand on their own.

A fourth set of questions comes to mind. How does the basis of hope affect human action? How does the object of hope affect human action? I have indicated that *hopefulness* is a disposition, a propensity; it might be said also that it is an attitude. But as an attitude in itself it can be based on different grounds—the dominance of the white race, for one morally rotten example. And its object, which can also become a basis, can be different—the possibility that the future will secure the interests of the white race. *What* one's hope is based upon, and *what* one hopes for will affect what one does if hope motivates action. Any moral judgment about a particular hope must be made in the light of its basis (its motivating force) and its object (its purpose or intention). Hope is itself morally neutral.

To recognize this is to shift the discussion from (a) whether hope is something to be commended in itself, to (b) whether the reasons for hoping and the object of hope are to be commended. An attitude of hopefulness affects action as action is guided by motives and intentions. Again we must face the question of the generality of basis and object. If the basis is a conviction that there are possibilities in experience and history, and the object is orientation toward openness, something of important but limited significance is being claimed. It is that against fatalism there is freedom, against hard determinism and necessity there is possibility and alterability. This is an important claim. Its limit is clear. Which possibilities are to be pursued? A *sense* of the possible does not answer hard moral questions.

If the object of hope has a more precise delineation, it can have a greater normative importance in governing action. This can be illustrated from the Christian ethics of the past. The social gospel writers had hope in the possibilities of change, but this hope was in a kingdom which they dared to define in terms of non-theological moral inferences drawn (rightly or wrongly) from the New Testament message about the kingdom of God. They inferred, for example, that democratization and socialization of institutions and power was an achievable objective consistent with the kingdom of Love. They inferred that certain social and political policies, e.g., support of labor unions and national ownership of natural resources, were consistent with democratization.

I shall not here expand this more; I wish to make a general point. Only when the object of hope is delineated with enough specificity to make possible the inference of certain achievable moral intentions can it give relatively clear direction to moral action. A general attitude of hope, with its big theological basis and big theological object, is of limited significance; in fact, it is vacuous when particular moral decisions and actions are required.

Finally, a few short comments on the theme, "The Future of Theology." Theological ethics has a future when its thinkers are willing to, and learn how to, make careful and clear moral inferences from theological affirmations. This essay is an effort to show the necessity of that. It is not as precise as is required when more limited topics are under consideration. In the absence of this process, with all the slipperiness and logical difficulties involved, we have only two other choices:

1. Theological affirmations have no relation to moral action.

2. Theological affirmations give a basis for certain dispositions and attitudes, but give no normative ethical direction to action.

And I believe both of these are inadequate and unnecessary.

Notes

Introduction

1. Reflection on the relation between practical moral activities and academic ethical reflection constitutes something of a leitmotif in Gustafson's writings, as several of these essays bear witness. Explicit attention is paid to this issue in several occasional pieces, e.g., James M. Gustafson, "Faith, Unbelief and Moral Life," *The Presence and Absence of God,* ed. by Christopher F. Mooney, S.J. (New York: Fordham University Press, 1969), pp. 19-30; James M. Gustafson, "Ethical Theory and Moral Practice," *The Christian Century,* Vol. LXXXVI, No. 51 (December 17, 1969), pp. 1613-17; James M. Gustafson, "The Burden of the Ethical: Reflections on Disinterestedness and Involvement," *The Foundation,* Vol. LXVI, No. 4 (Winter 1970), pp. 8-15.

2. Gustafson has considered various aspects of each of these problems in separate articles. The third selection in this book, of course, is his fullest treatment of the methodological procedures of ethical reflection. His most complete analysis of the role of the Bible in theological ethics is, James M. Gustafson, "The Place of Scripture in Christian Ethics," *Interpretation,* Vol. XXIV, No. 4 (October 1970), pp. 430-55. Among his various considerations of the nature of man, I have found his reflections on various images of man that have emerged in the social sciences to be suggestive; James M. Gustafson, "Man—in Light of Social Science and Christian Faith," *Conflicting Images of Man,* ed. by William Nicholls (New York: Seabury Press, 1966), pp. 51-70.

3. As Gustafson is aware, portions of this essay could be expanded in a number of directions, e.g., it omits a discussion of psychology and law as cognate disciplines of theological ethics, and it does not consider the literature concerning "revolution" or the Marxist-Christian dialogue, etc.

4. James M. Gustafson, *Christ and the Moral Life* (New York: Harper & Row, 1968), p. 9.

5. Cf. Gustafson's comments on H. Richard Niebuhr's use of the Bible; James M. Gustafson, "Introduction," *The Responsible Self: An Essay in Christian Moral Philosophy* (New York: Harper & Row, 1963), p. 21 f.

217

6. An article which may be viewed as a complement to Gustafson's comments about this "second approach" to theological ethics is the following: James M. Gustafson, "Moral Discernment in the Christian Life," *Norm and Context in Christian Ethics,* ed. by Gene H. Outka and Paul Ramsey (New York: Charles Scribner's Sons, 1968), pp. 17-36.

7. Some of the comments that follow are dependent on an unpublished paper written by Gustafson, "Is There a Christian Ethics?"

8. It could also be argued, of course, that no justification, religious or moral, affects the morality of an act. Thus, whether one gives money to the poor on the principle that the greatest good should be done for the greatest number, or whether one gives money to the poor in the belief that he confronts Christ as his neighbor in each poor man he meets, in no way influences the morality or immorality of the act itself.

9. James M. Gustafson, "Education for Moral Responsibility," *Moral Education* (Cambridge: Harvard University Press, 1970), pp. 11-27.

10. James M. Gustafson, *Christ and the Moral Life,* esp. p. 102 f., and p. 248 f.

11. The recurring charge of legalism, including an analysis of its moral and religious motivations, is discussed in relation to the distinction between an ethics of disposition and an ethics of cultural values in James M. Gustafson, "What is the Contemporary Problematic of Ethics in Christianity?" *Judaism and Ethics,* ed. by Daniel Jeremy Silver (New York: Ktav Publishing House, 1970), pp. 49-67.

12. James M. Gustafson, "Patterns of Christian Social Action," *Theology Today,* Vol. XVIII, No. 2 (July 1961), p. 171; see *The Church as Moral Decision-maker* (Philadelphia: Pilgrim Press, 1970), p. 46.

Chapter 2
Theology and Ethics

1. N. H. Smith (trans.), *Ethics* (New York: Macmillan, 1955), p. 236, Copyright © 1955 by The Macmillan Company; German edition, *Ethik,* ed. E. Bethge (Munchen: C. Kaiser, 1949).

2. For an unusually clarifying essay on this matter, see H. D. Aiken, *Reason and Conduct* (New York: Knopf, 1962), pp. 65-87. Aiken distinguishes four levels of moral discourse: the expressive ("That's good!"), the moral (approximately as above), the ethical (approximately as above), and the post-ethical ("Why should I be moral?").

3. Two vols. (New York: Charles Scribner's Sons, 1941, 1943).

4. See, for example, *The Church Speaks to the Modern World: The Social Teachings of Leo XIII,* ed. E. Gilson (New York: Doubleday Image Books, 1954), and *The Church and the Reconstruction of the Modern World,* ed. T. P. McLaughlin (New York: Doubleday Image Books, 1957).

5. G. W. Bromiley and T. F. Torrance, eds., Vol. II, Part 2 and Vol. III, Part 4 (New York: Charles Scribner's Sons, 1957, 1961).

6. New York: Harper & Bros., 1951; New York: Harper & Row, 1963.

7. Oxford: Clarendon Press, 1952, p. v.

8. W. D. Ross (trans.), *Nichomachean Ethics*, Bk. 1, ch. 7, in *The Basic Works of Aristotle*, R. McKeon, ed. (New York: Random House, 1941), p. 941.

9. *General Theory of Value* (New York: Longmans, Green & Co., 1926), p. 687.

10. "Critique of Practical Reason," in Immanuel Kant, *Critique of Practical Reason and Other Writings in Moral Philosophy*, ed. and trans. L. W. Beck (Chicago: University of Chicago Press, 1949), p. 210. Used by permission of Liberal Arts Press, a division of the Bobbs-Merrill Co., Inc.

11. *Man for Himself* (New York: Rinehart & Co., 1947), p. 45.

12. "Foundations of Morals" in Kant, *Critique of Practical Reason anl Other Writings in Moral Philosophy*, p. 80.

13. *Examination of the Place of Reason in Ethics* (Cambridge, Eng.: The University Press, 1950, paperback, 1960), p. 137.

14. R. H. Fuller, trans. (ed., rev. ed.; New York: Macmillan, 1960).

15. See *Radical Monotheism and Western Culture* (New York: Harper & Bros., 1960), pp. 16-23.

16. K. E. Kirk, *The Vision of God* (New York: Longmans, Green & Co., 1947).

17. See *Christ and Culture* (New York: Harper & Bros., 1951), p. 17.

Chapter 3
Context Versus Principles:
A Misplaced Debate in Christian Ethics

1. See Karl Barth, *Church Dogmatics* (Eng. ed.; Edinburgh: T. & T. Clark, 1957), II/2, esp. 631-701; see also *Against the Stream* (London: SCM Press, 1954), esp. pp. 53-124, and *How to Serve God in a Marxist Land* (New York: Association Press, 1959), pp. 45-80. Dietrich Bonhoeffer, *Ethics* (London: SCM Press, 1955), esp. pp. 17-25, 55-72, 194-222. Niels Søe, *Kristelig Etik* (5th ed.; Copenhagen: C. E. C. Gads Forlag, 1962), pp. 11-234, esp. pp. 108-70 (the 2d edition of this book was translated into German, *Christliche Ethik* [Munich: Chr. Kaiser Verlag, 1949], pp. 4-187, esp. pp. 83-132). The Christian ethics of Bultmann also belong in this general camp; for a discussion see Thomas Oden, *Radical Obedience: The Ethics of R. Bultmann* (Philadelphia: Westminster Press, 1964). Currently the most significant ethics text that has come from the more radical Christian existentialist group is Knud Løgstrup, *Den Etiske Fordring* (4th ed.; Copenhagen: Scandinavian University Books, 1958; English ed., *The Ethical Demand* [Philadelphia: Fortress Press, 1971]). Obviously there are severe differences of opinion among these theologians, which point already to the mistake of trying to include too many writers under one rubric as is required in a debate formula.

2. See Werner Elert, *The Christian Ethos* (Philadelphia: Muhlenberg Press, 1957; this is generally regarded to be a poor translation), and Walter Künneth, *Politik zwischen Dämon und Gott* (Berlin: Lutherisches Verlagshaus, 1954).

3. Robert Gleason, S.J., "Situational Morality," *Thought,* 32 (1957), 555. The general movement was condemned by Pope Pius XII in 1952. For a readily available example of this point of view, see Walter Dirks, "How Can I Know God's Will for Me?" *Cross Currents,* 5 (1955), 77-92. For other discussions, see Karl Rahner, *Nature and Grace* (London: Sheed & Ward, 1963), pp. 84-111; Josef Fuchs, *Situation und Entscheidung* (Frankfurt: Verlag Josef Knecht, 1952); and John C. Ford and Gerald Kelly, *Contemporary Moral Theology* (Westminster, Md.: Newman Press, 1958), I, 42-140.

4. See, for example, Bernard Häring, *The Law of Christ* (Westminster, Md: Newman Press, 1961), I, esp. 35 ff., copyright © 1961 by The Newman Press, and Josef Pieper, "Prudence," *The Four Cardinal Virtues,* copyright 1954, © 1955, 1959 by Pantheon Books, Inc., © 1965 Harcourt Brace Jovanovich, Inc.

5. See Paul Lehmann, "The Foundation and Pattern of Christian Behavior," *Christian Faith and Social Action,* ed. John A. Hutchison (New York: Charles Scribner's Sons, 1953), pp. 93-116, and *Ethics in a Christian Context* (New York: Harper & Row, 1963). Alexander Miller, *The Renewal of Man* (New York: Doubleday, 1955). Joseph Sittler, *The Structure of Christian Ethics* (Baton Rouge: Louisiana State University Press, 1958). H. R. Niebuhr, *The Responsible Self* (New York: Harper & Row, 1963). Albert Rasmussen, *Christian Social Ethics* (Englewood Cliffs, N. J.: Prentice-Hall, 1956). Joseph Fletcher, "A New Look in Christian Ethics," *Harvard Divinity School Bulletin,* 24 (1959), 7-18. Gordon Kaufman, *The Context of Decision* (Nashville: Abingdon Press, 1961). Charles C. West, *Communism and the Theologians* (Philadelphia: Westminster Press, 1958). James Gustafson, "Christian Ethics and Social Policy," *Faith and Ethics,* ed. Paul Ramsey (New York: Harper & Bros., 1957), pp. 119-39.

6. For a discussion of an unpublished paper by Bennett, see Lehmann, *Ethics in a Christian Context,* pp. 148-54. Paul Ramsey, *War and the Christian Conscience* (Durham, N. C.: Duke University Press, 1961), pp. 3-14, and various occasional writings. Alvin Pitcher, "A New Era in Protestant Social Ethics?" *Chicago Theological Seminary Register,* 48 (1958), 8-14. Clinton Gardiner, "The Role of Law and Moral Principles in Christian Ethics," *Religion in Life,* 28 (1959), 236-47. A running discussion of the issues can be found in the following references to *Christianity and Crisis:* Robert Fitch, "The Obsolescence of Ethics," November 16, 1959; Alexander Miller, "Unprincipled Living: The Ethics of Obligation," March 21, 1960; Paul Ramsey, "Faith Effective Through In-principled Love," May 30, 1960. See also Edward L. Long, *Conscience and Compromise* (Philadelphia: Westminster Press, 1954). Attention should be called to Fr. Edward Duff's discussion in *The Social Thought of the World Council of Churches* (New York: Association Press, 1956), pp. 93 ff.

7. H. D. Aiken, "Levels of Moral Discourse," *Reason and Conduct* (New York: Knopf, 1962), pp. 65-87. The essay was previously published in *Ethics,* 62 (1952), 235-46.

8. The movement from one level to another in theological ethics has been very confused. Indeed, the logic of theological ethical discourse has not been very clear precisely at this point, sometimes as a matter of conscious commitment. A great deal of work could be done in the analysis of written materials on the nest of issues opened up by Aiken's essay.

9. Kenneth Underwood, *Protestant and Catholic* (Boston: Beacon Press, 1957). A more recent study partially in this mode of contextualism is Denis Munby, *God and the Rich Society* (London: Oxford University Press, 1961). Other examples could be cited as well.

10. Barth, *Church Dogmatics*, II/2, 663-64.

11. Ibid., p. 576.

12. Ibid., p. 580.

13. Ibid., p. 581.

14. Ibid., p. 582.

15. Ibid., pp. 654-61.

16. Sittler, *The Structure of Christian Ethics*, p. 73.

17. Ibid., ch. 1, "The Confusion in Contemporary Ethical Speech."

18. Ibid., p. 36.

19. I read Sittler's book as a contemporary statement of the basic character of Luther's ethics under the gospel. Christ is the shaper of the Christian life in the participation of the believer in faith in him. Christ is also the shaper of the Christian life that is active in love to the neighbor in his particular need. In this manner Sittler is close to the theme of the best known of Luther's writings in Christian ethics, "On the Liberty of the Christian Man." See discussion of this document below.

20. Lehmann, *Ethics in a Christian Context*, pp. 358-59, 347.

21. Lehmann, "The Foundation and Pattern of Christian Behavior," p. 100.

22. Lehmann, *Ethics in a Christian Context*, p. 25. Note that the particular question of Christian ethics is on the "moral" level of discourse. Note also that Lehmann asks it in terms of "what *am* I to do," and not "what *ought* I to do." In this way he very self-consciously reduces the imperative tone in favor of a more indicative one.

23. Ibid., p. 105.

24. Ibid., p. 47.

25. For a discussion of Bultmann's ethics, see Oden, *Radical Obedience*. Barth also has an anthropology that stresses the immediacy of responsibility given to the particular person, and softens any lines of continuity between the person and his community, or the person and his ethics. I shall not discuss Barth here, though it would be fruitful to do so.

26. Niebuhr, *The Responsible Self*, p. 56.

27. Ibid., p. 61.

28. Ibid., p. 63.

29. Ibid., p. 126.

30. A similar view of man is penetrating Roman Catholic philosophy and ethics. See, for example, Albert Dondeyne, *Faith and the World* (Pittsburgh: Duquesne University Press, 1963), pp. 145 ff., and Häring, *The Law of Christ*, I, 35 ff.

31. *An Interpretation of Christian Ethics* (New York: Harper & Bros., 1935), p. 117.

32. Ibid., p. 140.

33. *The Nature and Destiny of Man* (New York: Charles Scribner's Sons, 1943), II, esp. chs. 9 and 10.

34. John Bennett, *Christian Ethics and Social Policy* (New York: Charles Scribner's Sons, 1946), p. 76. Oldham's suggestions are found in Visser 't Hooft and Oldham, *The Church and Its Function in Society* (London: G. Allen & Unwin, 1937), pp. 209 ff.

35. From Paul Ramsey, *War and the Christian Conscience,* pp. 6, 4. Reprinted by permission of the Publisher. Copyright 1961, Duke University Press, Durham, North Carolina.

36. "Christian Ethics and Social Policy" (1957), pp. 126-29.

37. Ramsey, *War and the Christian Conscience,* p. 179.

38. Ibid., p. 190.

39. See, for example, his discussion of sexuality in *Ethics in a Christian Context,* pp. 133-40.

40. Ibid., p. 72.

41. Ibid., pp. 116-17.

42. Ibid., p. 54.

43. Ibid., pp. 148 ff., and particularly p. 152. "For a *koinonia* ethic the clarification of ethical principles and their application to concrete situations is ethically unreal because such clarification is a logical enterprise and there is no way in logic of closing the gap between the abstract and the concrete." I regard this assertion to be the slaying of a straw man, for no serious moralist has believed that logic alone closed that gap. Roman Catholic moral theology, which is most susceptible to the criticism, never assumes that logic alone is the path from principle to concrete action, and always has a place for the person, with his natural and theological virtues, who acts responsibly. See, for example, Josef Pieper's "Prudence," which admittedly makes the most of the person who is the juncture between principles and actions.

44. Ibid., pp. 55, 16-17.

45. Citations here are to the edition *Three Treatises* (Philadelphia: Fortress Press, 1943), p. 251.

46. Ibid., p. 262.

47. Ibid., p. 271.

48. Ibid., p. 276.

49. Ibid., p. 279.

Chapter 5
God's Transcendence
and the Value of Human Life

1. H. Richard Niebuhr, *Radical Monotheism and Western Culture* (New York: Harper & Bros., 1960), p. 37.

2. Søren Kierkegaard, *Concluding Unscientific Postscript* (Princeton: Princeton University Press, 1944), pp. 358-68. Paul Tillich, *The Protestant Era* (Chicago: University of Chicago Press, 1948), pp. 161-81.

3. See the previous chapter and "New Directions in Moral Theology," *Commonweal*, 87 (February 23, 1968), 617-23.

4. Nicolai Hartmann, *Ethics*, Vol. II, *Moral Values* (London: G. Allen & Unwin, 1932), esp. pp. 407-43.

5. See J. M. Gustafson, "A Christian Approach to the Ethics of Abortion," *Dublin Review*, No. 514, pp. 346-64, for the way in which this affirmation of plurality affects a particular moral decision and how it is made. Reprinted in *The Morality of Abortion*, ed. John T. Noonan, Jr. (Cambridge, Mass.: Harvard University Press, 1970), pp. 101-22.

Chapter 9
Christian Humanism
and the Human Mind

1. Pierre Teilhard de Chardin, *The Phenomenon of Man* (New York: Harper & Row Torchbook, 1961), p. 231.

2. Ibid., p. 229.

3. Christopher Mooney, S.J., *Teilhard de Chardin and the Mystery of Christ* (New York: Harper & Row, 1966), p. 50.

4. Robert Johann, S.J., *The Pragmatic Meaning of God* (Milwaukee: Marquette University Press, 1966), p. 6.

5. Joseph Sittler, *The Structure of Christian Ethics* (Baton Rouge: Louisiana State University Press, 1958), p. 4.

6. Gustaf Wingren, *Creation and Law* (Philadelphia: Fortress Press, 1961), p. 150; italics added.

7. H. Richard Niebuhr, *The Responsible Self* (New York: Harper & Row, 1963), p. 126.

8. Johann, *The Pragmatic Meaning of God*, p. 1.

9. William Lynch, S.J., *Images of Hope: Imagination as Healer of the Hopeless* (Baltimore: Helicon Press, 1965), p. 32.

10. Bronislaw Malinowski, *A Scientific Theory of Culture and Other Essays* (Chapel Hill: University of North Carolina Press, 1944), pp. 91 ff.

11. Marion J. Levy, Jr., *The Structure of Society* (Princeton: Princeton University Press, 1952), pp. 141 ff.

12. Edward Shils, "Social Inquiry and the Autonomy of the Individual," *The Human Meaning of the Social Sciences,* ed. Daniel Lerner (New York: Meridian Books, 1959), p. 141.

Chapter 10
The Conditions for Hope: Reflections on Human Experience

1. My general debt is large to William Lynch, S.J., *Images of Hope: Imagination as Healer of the Hopeless* (Baltimore: Helicon Press, 1965). Two other works are important: Gabriel Marcel, "Sketch of a Phenomenology and Metaphysic of Hope," *Homo Viator* (Chicago: Henry Regnery Co.; New York: Harper & Row Torchbook, 1962) and Josiah Royce, *The Problem of Christianity,* 2 vols. (Chicago: Henry Regnery Co., Gateway Books, 1968; University of Chicago Press, 1968).

2. F. D. Maurice, *Theological Essays* (London: James Clarke, 1957), p. 123.